FEMINIZED JUSTICE

Law and Society Series
W. Wesley Pue, General Editor

The Law and Society Series explores law as a socially embedded phenomenon. It is premised on the understanding that the conventional division of law from society creates false dichotomies in thinking, scholarship, educational practice, and social life. Books in the series treat law and society as mutually constitutive and seek to bridge scholarship emerging from interdisciplinary engagement of law with disciplines such as politics, social theory, history, political economy, and gender studies.

A list of the titles in this series appears at the end of this book.

Amanda Glasbeek

FEMINIZED

The Toronto Women's Court, 1913-34

JUSTICE

UBCPress · Vancouver · Toronto

20 19 18 17 16 15 14 13 12 11 10 09   5 4 3 2 1

Printed in Canada on ancient-forest-free paper (100% post-consumer recycled) that is processed chlorine- and acid-free.

Library and Archives Canada Cataloguing in Publication

Glasbeek, Amanda, 1967
    Feminized justice: the Toronto Women's Court, 1913-34 / Amanda Glasbeek.

(Law and society series, ISSN 1496-4953)
Includes bibliographical references and index.
ISBN 978-0-7748-1711-0

    1. Female offenders – Ontario – Toronto – History. 2. Toronto Women's Police Court – History. 3. Criminal justice, Administration of – Ontario – Toronto – History. 4. Women – Legal status, laws, etc. – Ontario – Toronto – History. 5. Toronto Local Council of Women. 6. Feminism – Ontario – Toronto – History. 7. Feminism – Moral and ethical aspects – Ontario – Toronto. I. Title. II. Series: Law and society series (Vancouver, B.C.)

KEO176.G53 2009   364.3'7409713541   C2009-905206-7
KF345.G53 2009

Canadä

UBC Press gratefully acknowledges the financial support for our publishing program of the Government of Canada through the Book Publishing Industry Development Program (BPIDP), and of the Canada Council for the Arts, and the British Columbia Arts Council.

This book has been published with the help of a grant from the Canadian Federation for the Humanities and Social Sciences, through the Aid to Scholarly Publications Programme, using funds provided by the Social Sciences and Humanities Research Council of Canada.

Printed and bound in Canada by Friesens
Set in Trajan Pro, Minion, and Meta by Artegraphica Design Co. Ltd.
Copy editor: Lesley Erickson
Proofreader: Jean Wilson
Indexer: Dianne Tiefensee

UBC Press
The University of British Columbia
2029 West Mall
Vancouver, BC V6T 1Z2
604-822-5959 / Fax: 604-822-6083
www.ubcpress.ca

Contents

Tables

Acknowledgments

Writing a book is a long process, made possible because of the people you meet along the way. A number of people in particular deserve special acknowledgment for travelling this long road with me, and for putting up signposts or taking down roadblocks as I stumbled along.

Many individuals have read chapters and drafts and offered both trenchant and encouraging critiques. My thanks go to Constance Backhouse, Bettina Bradbury, Elise Chenier, Karen Flynn, Shelley Gavigan, Mary MacDonald, Sheila McManus, and Kathryn McPherson. Friends have also shared their good humour and excellent company, for which I am deeply grateful. They include Rob Heynen, Fred Ho, Gail Kellough, James Muir, Mary-Jo Nadeau, Anna Pratt, Kasia Rukszto, Joan Sangster, Mark Thomas, Steven Tufts, Michelle Webber, and Cynthia Wright. And, of course, my love and appreciation go to my family – Denise, Harry, and Sandra Glasbeek, Marie Tralka, and Daryl Taylor – for their unconditional support.

I am indebted to the knowledgable and generous staff at the Ontario Archives, as well as to Sally Gibson and Lawrence Lee of the City of Toronto Archives, who (twice) found the photograph that is on the front cover of this book. I am also fortunate to have worked with UBC Press and I thank Randy Schmidt for his nearly endless patience, as well as Holly Keller and the editing staff at UBC for their help in making this a cleaner and better work. Two anonymous reviewers provided insightful and gracious comments and this is a much better book for their contributions. Any errors or flaws, of course, remain my own.

Finally, and with much love, I want to thank Phil Maurais, without whom I might never have embarked on this journey. And to Sasha, with whom we embark on a new journey: may your world be a more just and feminist place.

FEMINIZED JUSTICE

Introduction

> In reviewing past history, we will always think of the Women's Court
> as one of our great achievements.
> — Toronto Local Council of Women, *Annual Report*, 1925

In 1911 Dr. Margaret Norris Patterson, prominent member of the Toronto Local Council of Women (TLCW), began going to City Hall to attend the sessions of the Toronto police courts, although it "wasn't ... a proceeding that she enjoyed."[1] Her distaste for these visits is not surprising. In the 1910s, police court sessions were jostling, noisy, and often malodorous affairs. "Day by day steady streams of unfortunates pass[ed] through the police court";[2] the corridors and hallways were abuzz with "a hundred voices, in subdued tones and a half-dozen languages"; and "puffs of hot, foul, trouble-laden air, which come through the closely guarded door, might easily suggest deeds of evil within."[3] Police court justice was also a form of free, popular entertainment and gossip that attracted a wide variety of Torontonians to its public galleries.[4] Wading into this boisterous din "morning after morning," Patterson and her group of hand-picked women volunteers sat in court, armed with paper, pens, and a steely determination to assess the criminal justice system from a woman's point of view.[5]

What these reform-minded women saw in court both confirmed their suspicions about criminal trial processes and fuelled their imaginations about what else might be possible. Their observations proved to them that, for women, the criminal justice system was criminogenic. The criminal categories that brought women into the courts, the policing system that enforced those crime categories, the process of judicial interpretation of guilt and innocence, and the fact that anybody off the streets could, and did, enjoy the spectacle of police court justice were themselves causal factors in women's criminality. Something had to be done.

The most immediate problem was the audience. Women who were accused of a crime suffered the humiliation of an open court in which "foot-loose men ... liked to come into the court room because it was a warm place to sit, and because their tastes were so perverted that they could find much amusement in the court proceedings." Patterson explained the consequences of the (male) public spectacle of justice: "We noticed that in the open court men often marked down the names of the women who appeared there, also the length of their sentence, and different girls told us of being met when they came out of jail by these men, who, taking advantage of their lonely, often friendless, and penniless condition, induced them to go into immorality." Rather than the solution, police courts were the breeding ground of vice. On the basis of their collected evidence, the TLCW began to agitate for a separate court, "to which men would not be admitted unless they could show just cause for being there."

But documented evidence of induced immorality was not the only requirement that the TLCW had to meet to win approval for a separate court for women. When they first suggested their idea to Senior Police Court Magistrate Colonel George Taylor Denison, he replied that "it was not in accordance with British justice to have a closed court." This, replied the feminist lobbyists, was not what they were asking for. Instead, they proposed, "they would see that there would always be present one woman who was an outsider, to fulfil the requirements of an open court." Margaret Patterson then took it upon herself to prove that the women's community to which she belonged was up to this challenge. She visited every women's social service and religious organization in the city and drew up a calendar "with each woman's name signed over the date or dates when she promised to attend." Through this demonstration that the organized women's community could provide the substantial backing necessary for both their own proposal for women's justice and the dictates of "British justice," the Toronto Women's Police Court, the first court for women in Canada, was formally approved by the Board of Police Commissioners on 5 February 1913.[6] Magistrate Denison, one of the members of this three-person police board, appointed himself to the bench. Five days later, on 10 February, the Toronto Women's Police Court heard its first cases.

This book examines the Toronto Women's Court from its inception in 1913 to its political demise in 1934. This twenty-one year period captures the tenures of two different magistrates. Colonel Denison presided over the court from 1913 until his retirement in 1921. Thanks to the lobbying efforts of Toronto's organized women's community, Denison was replaced by none other than Dr. Margaret Patterson, who would serve as the court's first, and only, female magistrate until she was forced off the bench in 1934. Although the next chapter offers an overview of the institutional setting and significance of the Women's Court, as well as the important changes that were undertaken by Patterson while she was magistrate, this book is not an institutional history of the court. The Toronto Women's Court had no single significance and was marked, instead, by contradiction. This is a core theme of this exploration. Specifically, the Toronto Women's Court was, simultaneously, a site for a feminized adaptation of criminal justice and a criminal court empowered to punish the women who appeared before it. Women's relationships to the court were fundamentally shaped by the very nature of their encounter with it.

These multiple tendencies of the court were never far from the surface. Indeed, only two days after the Toronto Women's Court was established, a *(Toronto) Star* reporter offered the following introduction to this new institution: "Anyone in search of convincing halftones for a column on the way of transgressors had better drop in at the new Women's Court ... Colonel Denison has a brand new red-carpeted platform to preside on, and the erst-while committee room, with its chaste frescoes and soft carpet, has settled down into a real court, where the law rattles through the commonplaceness of discharge, remand, and commitment."[7] This characterization of the court offers some interesting juxtapositions. On the one hand, the court's novelty is stressed through the use of terms like *chaste* that simultaneously evoke images of the young women imagined as the central beneficiaries of the Women's Court project. On the other hand, the judgments that will emanate from the yet-to-be-tarnished courtroom are commonplaces that are not simply familiar, but time-worn and old hat. Chastity, softness, and an eager sincerity mark the design of the Women's Court, its location, and its overall appearance, but beneath this exterior one finds a "real" court that "rattles" on through its usual and humdrum business. The reporter invoked biblical injunctions and sacred sins by beginning her column with references to transgressors whose stories offered parables of virtue and vice. She concluded that the process for adjudicating these cases was less divine and more the profane determination of discharge, remand, and commitment. Overall, the reporter seemed puzzled by the questions raised by the court, questions that she seemed hesitant to answer: Was the Women's Court special, unique, and distinct, or was it simply another court, like any other, yet one more part of the machinery of grinding local justice? Did overlaying a police court with the ideas of women's special qualities change that court, or did the fact that it was a court overdetermine, and undermine, the hoped-for outcome of feminized justice?

The *Star* reporter's perplexed take on the court is justified. The Toronto Women's Court employed coercive mechanisms to promote womanhood and to protect women. Feminists had problematized the law as being inherently detrimental to women and argued that a separate court for women was necessary; however, in separating women's cases out of the "ordinary" process, the Women's Court simultaneously legitimated and authorized a moral code that penalized women more than men for offences against morality. The court was justified through the deployment of familial metaphors that stressed a unity of purpose through gender-specific bonds, while maintaining adversarial processes and disciplinary practices to punish some women more than others. How can we best make sense of these dualities? Was the court's principal function to regulate sexual conduct and impose on women a rigid, bourgeois standard of femininity and morality, or was it a feminist intervention into women's legal experiences aimed at adapting criminal justice mechanisms to be more inclusive of, and sensitive to, urban women's needs? Or, if both, was one aspect of the court a by-product of the other? That is, did the rhetoric of salvation, reclamation, and protection that Toronto's female reform community used to justify the court simply mask its true nature as an exercise in coercion, or was coercion an unanticipated and unfortunate side effect of their efforts to reform the law and an inevitable paradox of maternal feminist politics?

These questions are at the heart of this book. As a product of local feminist activism, the Toronto Women's Court bore the stamp of its founders' particular political views. The TLCW engaged in a broad platform of urban reform aimed at "assist[ing] one another in all good movements for the benefit of humanity, especially those having for their first object the bettering of the conditions of women and children,"[8] of which the Toronto Women's Court was only a part.[9] But although the court shared a common logic with the multiple initiatives of the TLCW, it was also unique. It stands out among the TLCW's accomplishments not only because the members themselves declared it as one of their "great achievements" but also because it was not an institution that was used on a voluntary basis. Rather, women were brought to court because police officers had charged them with an offence. Importantly, the powers brought to bear on those women appearing in the court were not simply those of the TLCW. A criminal court, even a low-level police court such as the Women's Court, represents the exclusive power of the state to engage in punishment, often over unwilling subjects. As one contemporary police court observer put it: "respect for the law must be supported by fear, and fear may only be impressed by dramatic proofs of power."[10] The Toronto Women's Court was, thus, an ongoing experiment in balancing its police court origins, through which it exercised power over women in conflict with the law, with its specifically feminist design as an effort to save women from the criminal law itself.

Given these multiple dimensions, I analyze the Toronto Women's Court not through a single narrative but as a window on the differing relations that Toronto women had to the criminal justice system. To the organized women's community, the court was a feminist intervention into the workings of the criminal law, one that would better reflect women's specific needs as women. From this perspective, the Toronto Women's Court offers a history of white, middle-class women's politicization of the criminal justice system. At the same time, as a criminal court that routinely punished mostly poor and marginalized women for a range of disorderly conducts, the Toronto Women's Court was a police court and, for many, an institution through which they were disciplined for exercising their own agency or autonomy in ways that were troubling to the members of the TLCW. Thus, an analysis of the Toronto Women's Court also offers a window into criminalized women's experiences of the city and their often complex entanglements with the law. Just as importantly, the Toronto Women's Court was a place where these very different groups of women met and was a site through which they struggled, as women from very different social locations, with the law.

Police Court Justice

Placing a police court at the centre of an analysis of women's struggles over the meanings of justice means paying attention to the more quotidian aspects of the law, that is, to a historicization of the law as early twentieth-century Toron- tonians encountered it. Although officially a court of first resort, the police court was, for most people, *the* justice system: over 90 percent of all criminal cases began and ended at the police court level.[11] Although Toronto women stood accused of a wide variety of criminal offences – from murder and infanticide, bigamy, and assault with a weapon to conspiracy to procure an abortion – the overwhelming majority of criminal offences that brought women to the courts were summary conviction offences. This was a definition imposed by the *Criminal Code*, which specified a maximum penalty, usually a set fine or imprisonment up to six months, and the classification meant that the proceedings could be held in the magistrates' courts. In more serious cases – criminal charges of an indictable nature – the police court might be the site of a preliminary hearing. The magistrate heard the Crown's evidence and decided whether it was sufficient to warrant a trial at the General Sessions (jury trial), the County Court Judges' Criminal Courts (trial by judge without a jury), or the Assizes (quarter sessions).[12] But in addition, police court magistrates, with the consent of the accused, were empowered to try most cases of an indictable nature summarily (serious offences such as murder, rape, or treason were excluded from this option). This power gave the police courts a central function in the justice system. For example, during his forty-four year tenure as a Toronto Police Court magistrate, Colonel Denison heard over 650,000 cases, including 83 percent of all indictable cases in Toronto.[13] As one contemporary police court watcher observed, "[I]t must be apparent to everyone that the peace of the community depends more on the police court than any other institution."[14]

Despite the centrality of police court justice, few legal histories examine these lower courts, especially for what they can teach us about crime, gender, and criminal justice. Most histories of female crime focus attention on indictable offences heard at the higher court levels. There are good reasons to do so. Although they constituted only a minority of court cases, criminal cases heard at the higher courts have the advantage of leaving a paper trail and, as a result, can be scrutinized for what they can tell us about the legal ordering of social conflicts.[15] The richness of these data is decidedly lacking in police court files; in fact, so massive was the volume of this court system that records have been systematically purged from provincial holdings. But record keeping is not the only reason for the relative neglect of police court justice. As mechanisms of low law, police courts have not enjoyed the same scholarly attention that the higher courts have.[16] As Douglas Hay points out, there is an important distinction between high and the more commonly experienced low law.[17] High justice is "the word," or that version of the law that celebrates the values of fairness to individual claims against injustice. It is this version of the law with which we become acquainted through the press, drama, storytelling, reputation, and other means of public representation, which may be extended to include historical analyses. Low justice, meanwhile, is more coercive, less well scrutinized, and more violent: it is the silence of the word. This is largely a class-based distinction: "In a market, there must be expensive justice and cheap justice and, historically, this has, in large measure, translated into high justice and low justice."[18] In other words it is not in the wood-panelled chambers of high justice, in which the finer points of judicial procedure and due process are debated, but in the overheated, overcrowded, and stuffy courtrooms of low justice that the vast majority of the population meets the law. As Judith Fingard has observed, to bypass these courts is "to neglect the more prosaic common offences [that] kept the criminal courts and the prisons in business."[19] Returning those women charged with such prosaic offences to the history of female crime expands and reshapes our knowledge of women's relationship to criminal justice. In these various ways, an exploration of the Toronto Women's Court renders visible a series of tensions, conflicts, and mediated interactions between and among women of decidedly different social powers.

Opening Day in Court

And what were those tensions? Who was tried in the Toronto Women's Court, and what difference, if any, did a segregated police court make to their lives and their criminality? What were the effects of a separate criminal court, for the white, middle-class women who invented it and for the criminalized women who involuntarily experienced it? And what can the Women's Court teach us about the relationships, real and imagined, among women in early twentieth-century Toronto? Remarkably, many of the answers to these questions are suggested by the opening day of the court. The first three cases tried in the Toronto Women's Police Court on 10 February 1913 collectively contained all the main features that would characterize the court for the next two decades and foreshadowed both the achievement and the complications of this early experiment in feminized justice.

It is possible that the first day in court was deliberately staged, for it closely followed an easily accessible plotline and featured ideal-type characters.[20]

But even if the cases were not pre-selected, an all female press corps actively interested in the "vision made real"[21] was able to transform three minor charges into telling parables on morality, gender, and crime in the city.[22] The continuum between good and bad, between reclamation and damnation, between protection and punishment, and between endangered womanhood and dangerous women was made abundantly clear to those Torontonians who were no longer allowed to witness women's trials and whose acquaintance with the Women's Court had to come from the press. This continuum would also be central to the ongoing existence, legitimation, and limitations of the Women's Court for the next twenty-one years.

Ida J., described by the *Star* as "a mentally underaverage, ill-dressed colored girl," was the first woman to be tried in the Women's Court.[23] Ida was charged with vagrancy, a *Criminal Code* offence that targeted a broad range of disorderly behaviours, including, but not limited to, soliciting for the purposes of prostitution.[24] The charge against Ida did refer to solicitation. She entered a plea of not guilty, but "[q]uickly ... a male witness [gave] the damning evidence that the girl had solicited five men, and Magistrate Denison order[ed] her away with the words, 'Remanded till the 13th on your own bail of $100.'"[25] Like many of the women who would come after her, Ida did not have the money to secure her release, and she was sent to the local jail cells for three days, until her trial. She was found guilty and sentenced to jail for thirty days.

"It is a story of foulness that comes next. No quivering of face or voice here – just the assurance of a woman whose womanhood was long ago forgotten. She is Bridget D."[26] Bridget, along with Frank M., "an Italian whose face shows what he is," was charged with keeping a house of ill-fame.[27] Three male eye-witnesses, visitors to the impugned house, gave evidence against the pair, and both were found guilty, although Frank was given a longer (six-month) prison sentence than was Bridget, who was sent to jail for thirty days. Magistrate Denison reasoned that "[h]e deserve[d] it more than the woman – living on her earnings."[28] In contrast to Ida's characterization in the press as passive and somewhat incapable, Bridget, who already had several previous convictions on similar charges, took an active, and defiant, part in her proceedings: "[S]he denied everything, upbraided the judge, questioned the witnesses, and when she was led away by the matron, muttered vindictively her opinion of the law that would send folks to jail for nothing."[29] But she did not get the last word: Margaret Patterson, in court to witness history in the making, did. Patterson called Bridget a human vulture and explained to the reporters: "That is the kind of woman for whom there should be an institution. What good will 60 days do for her? She is a public menace and ought to be sent down indefinitely. What's the use of allowing her out in two months to go on corrupting the city?"[30]

Ida, Frank, and Bridget did not capture the publicly proclaimed raison d'être of the Women's Court. Although theirs were "typical cases,"[31] a prostitute, a pimp, and a madam were not the "girls" invoked by Patterson as those most likely to suffer from notoriety. To the contrary, each of these cases personified larger social problems that were widely publicized by reform groups such as the TLCW as being in need of public attention and action. By describing Ida as "mentally underaverage," news reports were drawing on the reform concept of the feeble-minded, a turn-of-the-century eugenic term that fused race, class, heredity, and sexuality together to describe "degenerate" or "unfit" persons who constituted a threat to the healthy reproduction of the Canadian nation.[32] Ida – black, poor, and sexually active – literally embodied the presumed dangers posed by the feeble-minded as well as the urgent need for institutional care of such "defectives" – for their own good. Frank's appearance in the courtroom offered an entry for another reform trope. His presence was possible because the mandate of the Toronto Women's Court was to hear not only women's but also "morals" (i.e., prostitution) cases in which men were accused with women. Frank and Bridget's case signalled the importance to Toronto reform circles of taking houses of prostitution seriously, as well as the wider and decidedly more punitive role that the court was to undertake.[33]

As a result, none of these cases was treated with the sympathy one might expect on this historic day in women's justice. The cavalier contempt in which Ida was held, the active denial of her claims to innocence, and the treatment of male testimony as more credible than her own were all at odds with the claim that the Toronto Women's Court would, and could, intervene in women's criminal justice experiences and create a more woman-friendly environment to help women redeem themselves from "immorality." Meanwhile, the active hostility directed toward Bridget belied any sense of a commonality among women. Constructed by the press and, more tellingly, by Patterson herself as an enemy of "good," Bridget represented that which had to be coercively suppressed. But Bridget's open defiance in the courtroom – indeed, her active hostility to both the law and those who embraced it – also belied the notion of women's victimization that underscored the foundations of a separate criminal court for women. These cases make it clear that the Toronto Women's Court was not simply about protecting women victimized by men. As a police court, the Women's Court's function was also to exercise its coercive powers to discipline women who violated the moral standards – and the laws – of the community.

Only one reporter remarked on the dissonance between the ideals that underlay the court and the ugly nature of its first two cases: "'Surely these women don't need to be shielded from publicity. Surely they–' begins a spectator, when a sudden call rings through the room. There probably isn't one of the women in the court who does not feel a throb of mingled pity and sympathy with the little pitiful figure who came forward. One says under her breath: 'Thank God for this court for such as she is.'"[34] The cautious doubt about the viability of a separate court for women such as Ida and Bridget was set aside by the arrival of the "pitiful figure" whose case, another reporter would claim, was "the stuff for which the court has been instituted."[35] This was "the girl," a young teenager who had quarrelled with her mother and run away from home. Discovered by a police officer, "wandering the streets, without any visible means of subsistence, and unable to give a satisfactory account of herself," she was arrested for vagrancy, although a different kind of vagrancy than that for which Ida had been arrested. "The girl" was never named. In part this was deliberate and of a piece with the aims of the Women's Court itself: the girl was to be shielded from the publicity that might lead to her ruination. But not naming her also served a symbolic function: "the girl" represented every girl in Toronto that the TLCW hoped to protect and redeem through the Toronto Women's Court.

Accounts of the girl's case appeared in three different newspapers and were remarkably similar in emphasis and theme. Most notably, these accounts are replete with familial metaphors and reach the common conclusion that the Toronto Women's Court had arrived on the scene not a moment too soon. Thus, reported the *Daily News*, "the frightened young girl ... had never been near a court room before [and] would have been branded for life if she had been obliged to appear in the ordinary court."[36] Her case was a modern day parable about the dangers of the city for young women and the redemption to be found in institutionalized motherly guidance.

Mothers are everywhere in the girl's story. When the girl first appeared in the courtroom, "a Salvation Army woman [stood] protectingly beside her." But there was "a deeper stir when the constable [said]: 'Her mother is here.'"[37] Magistrate Denison, "tempering the justice of the law with the insight of a man used to such domestic tragedies," asked the mother – a widow – to come forward to speak about the case.[38] The mother "piteously" told the magistrate twice that her daughter "ain't never done otherwise before."[39] Denison asked the girl if she knew what "the wrong road means." The young woman, bowing her head, whispered back, "But, I've made up my mind to the right road."[40] Satisfied by her awareness of the dangers she faced and by her physical display of contrition, the magistrate pronounced on the object lesson to be learned: "You hunt all around and you'll never get any better friend than your mother. Keep friends with your mother."[41] The girl was then remanded into her mother's care.

The purpose of the Women's Court could not have been made clearer. True to its avowed aims, the court, in the relative seclusion provided by the select audience, had facilitated an urban rescue mission and restored familial security to a young woman guilty of a momentary lapse in judgment. The women reformers in the court capitalized on this case to prove the value of their efforts. Margaret Patterson remarked to the newspaper reporters: "The case of that young girl shows the necessity for a court like this. In the other court a dozen men would have been watching her, would have taken down her name, and have followed her to drag her down to Heaven knows what inferno."[42] Noted feminist Flora MacDonald Denison (no relation to the colonel) also called the girl's case the "justification of our court ... She shouldn't be subjected to notoriety. She isn't a criminal. She's just an untaught little girl."[43]

In so saying, Flora Denison (unwittingly) captured the central problem that this book explores. The Toronto Women's Court was "justified" through its delivery of specialized justice to women in distress. Unlike other police courts, the Women's Court was meant to provide maternal guidance, a woman-friendly environment, and a protective (i.e., relatively man-free) ethic of caring for those who were *not* criminals. But if this was the case, how could it also justify its treatment of those women who *were* criminals, a treatment that looked very similar to that received in the regular police courts? How could the Women's Court achieve a balance between the "reclamation of the daughters of Eve"[44] and the punishment of the "human vultures" like Bridget D.? What relationships did the TLCW imagine women had to men, to the law, to crime, and to the courts that enabled them to extend their reach over both "the girls" and the Bridgets and Idas of the city with a legal authority hitherto unknown to white, middle-class women reformers? And what relationship did their imaginings of the causes of, and solutions to, the problems of women's criminality have to do with the actual incidence of female crime in early twentieth-century Toronto? The first day in the first court for women in Canada raises all of these questions. This book examines the next twenty-one years in the Toronto Women's Court with a view to answering them.

The Toronto Women's Court as a "Great Achievement"

As opening day indicates, and as this book takes as its central point, the Toronto Women's Court had multiple functions and significances that cannot be
reduced to a single formulation. For street women such as Ida J., and for
brothel-keepers such as Bridget and Frank, the court may not have looked much
different than what they would have encountered had they appeared for trial a
day earlier: Colonel Denison presided over a court that was still populated by
many men (clerks, police officers, and witnesses), and it was one in which
women's breaches of public morals were met with legal censure and punishment. For young women such as "the girl," however, the Toronto Women's Court
might have come close to matching its promise as a site of redemption and
gender-based empathy for legal entanglements. Yet even the lenient treatment
that the girl received tells a story – or, more precisely, a cautionary tale – in
which the power not only of mothers but also of the specific politics of maternal care is the moral of the story.[45]

As an institution, the Toronto Women's Police Court was a concrete reform
achievement of the TLCW. The TLCW was an amalgam lobby group made up
of the city's autonomous women's organizations, which worked in a variety of
social service causes. Although the member groups included some working-class
and non-Anglo or non-Protestant organizations, the Executive Committee of
the TLCW was astonishingly homogenous throughout the twenty-one-year
period under study. These relatively affluent, well-educated, white, Anglophone
women activists were also involved in many other social service organizations,
including the Young Women's Christian Association, the Ontario Welfare
Council, the Toronto Women's Hospital, and so on. In addition, as members of
the Local Council, they were part of the National Council of Women of Canada,
which itself was a member group of the International Council of Women. In
1923 the intermediary Provincial Council of Women was also formed. Thus,
local Toronto women activists were connected to like-minded women across
the city, the province, the country, and the world.

The movement for a separate court for women, then, was more than a local
initiative, and it was inspired by more than Patterson's visits to the police court
sessions. By observing police court justice, Patterson was fitting herself into a
new tradition in women's activism. Transforming the machinery of adversarial
and androcentric crime control was a movement that swept Canada and the

United States in the early decades of the twentieth century.[46] Jurisdictions in the United States offered an important source of inspiration. Chicago was a leader in Progressive court change, having established a Court of Domestic Relations in 1911 and a specialized morals court, designed to hear prostitution cases exclusively, in 1913.[47] That same year Los Angeles established a women's court, which was presided over by a female judge (Georgia Bullock).[48] And New York City (Manhattan and the Bronx) set up separate night courts for women in 1910 that became day courts in 1918.[49] Women's courts also existed in other US cities, such as Detroit, Cincinnati, Philadelphia, and Boston.[50] Three years after Toronto's Women's Court opened, Edmonton established a women's court and Emily Murphy was appointed as the first female magistrate in the British Empire.[51] Thus, although Toronto's Women's Court was one of the earliest women's courts in North America, and the first of its kind in Canada, it was also a local reform within a larger movement for woman-specific legal justice.

Histories of similarly inspired maternal justice projects undertaken throughout Canada and the United States during the Progressive period struggle to make sense of the multiple dimensions that characterized these courts.[52] Overwhelmingly, histories of what Estelle Freedman calls feminist institution building in women's criminal justice tend to come to the common conclusion that these projects were, at best, paradoxical.[53] Indeed, the historical evidence is damning: by highlighting women's specific moral and legal vulnerability and then intervening to create more moral, or "just," courts and institutions, the effect of feminist activism in the criminal terrain was an increased moralization, and criminalization, of women's behaviour. The evident contradictions of projects such as the Toronto Women's Court raise the question: was the court a failure? That is, were the claims of alternative, gender-based justice simply unrealizable? Was the price of this justice too narrowly conceived? And were the more punitive aspects of the court indicative of a lack of appreciation of the consequences of British justice?

A central contention of this book is that, contradictions and all, the Toronto Women's Court was neither a failure nor, even, a paradox. To the contrary, I argue that the Toronto Women's Court was an ideal reflection of the politics of the middle-class, white feminists of the TLCW. I take as my starting point the fact that the members of the TLCW themselves declared the Toronto Women's Court to be one of their great achievements. Using this declaration as an invitation to investigate, I ask not, did the court fail? but rather, what was successful about it? The answer, I argue, lies in paying more detailed attention to the maternal feminist reformers' politics of coercion. Rather than an unanticipated side effect or a paradoxical outcome, the disciplinary powers that were a part of the court's functions were actively sought out and welcomed by its feminist proponents. They were, in fact, precisely what made the court appear to be a feminist achievement.

Some historians take a more kindly view of the paradoxical outcome of these projects and attribute the limitations of these efforts to naïveté, misplaced optimism, or unfulfilled intentions. This conclusion is based on a particular understanding of maternalism as an important strategic resource for women in their efforts to pressure state projects to become more responsive to the needs of women. Linda Gordon, for example, has argued that "[w]hat makes maternalism more than just a women's paternalism ... is its rootedness in the subordination of women. Maternalism showed its standpoint – its view from underneath – and from there built a strategy for using the space inside a male-dominated society for an activism that partially subverted male power."[54] To the extent that these women paved the way for others by breaking into a masculine world of legal adjudication, and to the extent that they were able to use their influence to make demands upon the state to provide services specific to the needs of women, their activities have been assessed as successful feminist endeavours, albeit endeavours that reflected a conservative form of feminism. In this vein, the limitations of feminist gains are attributable to the enormity of their projects and the structural complications arising from their efforts to make wholesale change. John McLaren, for example, writes that maternal reformers "displayed considerable naivety in supposing that the law would be enforced in the spirit in which they intended."[55] Instead, the feminist goals of protecting vulnerable women were co-opted and reshaped into a masculinist order by male law enforcement agents. Importantly, this gap between goals and enforcement was narrowed the most when women were the presiding magistrates. Beverly Cook comes to a similar conclusion about the limited nature of the authority of Georgia Bullock, appointed in 1913 as judge in the Los Angeles Women's Court. Cook argues that through her identification with a woman-specific ethic of care, Bullock "trapped herself in a small public space" and was unable to translate her maternalist practices into the larger criminal justice network.[56] These analyses grant maternalist reformers the benefit of the doubt and argue that it was the limited number of courts, the limited authority of female professionals, and/or the limited nature of their feminist vision that resulted in the paradoxical outcome of the over-policing of women for sexual and other moral transgressions.

Other historians are more critical of maternal justice efforts. Freda Solomon argues that it was the project of women's courts themselves – not their limited number and authority or specific personnel – that led to their, at best, contradictory outcomes.[57] According to Solomon, while the Women's Night Court in New York City "broke new ground for women in public life by providing a place in the judiciary," the court itself was an anomaly that "set in motion a legal quagmire about women, sex, and crime."[58] Dorothy Chunn uses a similar evaluative framework in her analysis of Margaret Patterson's tenure on the Toronto Women's Court bench.[59] Using Patterson's magistracy as a lens into the "two-sided character of reform" and as a test case on the efficacy of legal reform as a route to women's equality, Chunn concludes that the rise and fall of Patterson offers contradictory lessons, that is, lessons "with both positive and negative effects."[60] On the one hand, Patterson's magistracy "improved the substantive position of women vis-à-vis men in the public sphere"; on the other hand, it was accompanied by "little setbacks" and did not catapult women into similar positions of authority, as hoped.[61] Part of the setbacks that these critical scholars point to is that a core feature of maternal justice was the elevation of some women to power, including the "coercive power over working-class and immigrant families."[62]

Critical historians also emphasize the normative bourgeois and white standard that underpinned the political significance of motherhood in maternalist projects. Certainly, for the white, middle-class women who used maternalism as the basis for their activism, motherhood not only signified a politics of gender, it was also linked intimately to the concept of nation-building. This politics of motherhood was far from egalitarian. As Mariana Valverde writes, these women "produced a profoundly racist form of feminism in which women of the 'lower' races were excluded from the specifically Anglo-Saxon work of building a better world through the freeing of 'the mother of the race.'"[63] The prescriptively white mother of the race was also embedded in a bourgeois normative model of family and motherhood. As Diana Pederson has argued, in positioning themselves as social or political mothers, middle-class women by definition conceptualized the working-class and poor women they sought to help as their metaphorical daughters.[64] Carolyn Strange similarly argues that middle-class women who acted in urban reform movements that carved out a specific place for female benefactors and beneficiaries drew unquestioningly on a model of *in loco parentis*, thus infantalizing women defined as in need of their help.[65] Through these mobilizations, middle-class women acted to constitute themselves not only as white women but also as members of a class.

The vested authority relations implicated in maternalism are perhaps nowhere in better evidence than in the development of female juvenile courts. John McLaren concludes that Emily Murphy's tenure as magistrate of the Edmonton women's and children's courts (1916-32) was characterized by "her personal frame of reference [as an] intelligent, successful maternal figure who, through her familial role, strength of character, and moral insight, could lead the less fortunate to a recognition of the error of their ways and personal reformation, and society to a new and more moral tomorrow."[66] Estelle Freedman's biography of Miriam Van Waters,[67] a long-time maternal feminist activist in the US juvenile justice system, similarly argues that Van Waters "assumed [in the Los Angeles female juvenile court] the role of a wise, compassionate, yet professional mother," a persona that was key to her career as "a successful, public, maternal authority."[68]

Mary Odem's analysis of the Los Angeles female juvenile courts offers an in-depth example of these women's politics of maternal justice.[69] Odem follows the US women's social reform movement's politics of "protecting and policing adolescent female sexuality" through two phases. The first phase, in the nineteenth century, centred on their battles to raise the age of consent laws. The second phase, in the twentieth century, was marked by their entry into the justice system as legal adjudicators, as they increasingly recognized the limitations of passing laws that depended on men for their enactment. She writes, "In calling for state regulation of female sexuality, women reformers specifically envisioned a maternal state."[70] Once ensconced in the legal system, however, these professional women, who acted in surrogate maternal roles, ultimately came into conflict with parents whose authority over their daughters' behaviour was being contested in the courtroom. Although these maternal courts sometimes helped to boost the parental authority of those who sought the state's help to control their "delinquent daughters," they just as often superseded this authority in the name of "protecting" young women from what they saw as the disreputable characteristics of single mothers, non-white mothers, working mothers, or poor mothers.[71] Thus, concludes Odem, one result of maternal justice was that it delegitimated some women's mothering roles in the name of providing maternal protection to young women.

These experiments in creating a maternal justice system for young women highlight its seemingly paradoxical outcomes: the success, and failure, of maternal justice was its creation of gender-specific notions of deviance and rehabilitation, which (some) women were able to implement and enforce, but which were also used to limit (other) women's possibilities to those that fit within the schemata of mother-daughter relations. Histories of juvenile justice reform also make it clear that an abiding characteristic of maternalism was authority, vested in, and out of, particular constellations of gender, race, and class relations: maternalism was as much about transforming middle-class, white women into legitimate rulers as it was about transforming the socio-political landscape that they found so unfriendly to their concerns. In a juvenile court, these relations are easily understood as maternalist because of the age differences and corresponding relationships between the principal actors. Matronly justice officials enjoyed power over young, daughterly subjects. These projects are aptly named maternal justice.

But what happens when these same kinds of authority relations are exercised over adult women, as was the case in the Toronto Women's Court? As later chapters will show, a large number of women who appeared in the women's police court were themselves mature matrons. The daughterly deference required by maternal justice was not always easily translatable in adult court. In part for this reason, many scholars prefer to treat maternalism not as a politics in its own right but as a discourse that is rendered significant when combined with other governing strategies.[72] Kelly Hannah-Moffat argues that the benefit of treating maternalism as a discourse is that it allows us to see both the internal logic of the politics and the way that discourse shaped and produced knowledge about the ostensible targets of maternal reform.[73] Similarly, Nicole Hahn Rafter challenges the presentation of the maternalists as unwitting victims of their own optimism and characterizes them, instead, as active agents in the exercise of power over vulnerable women.[74] Rafter turns the logic of maternalism around, arguing that middle-class maternal reformers deliberately infantilized criminal women to make it appear that they needed the intervention of middle-class women, when, in fact, middle-class women needed criminalized women to appear to be children so they could exercise authority over them.

Examining an adult court rather than a juvenile one forces a consideration of maternalism both as a rationalizing discourse for the governance of young women's "precocious sexuality"[75] and as a disciplinary force through which hierarchical class and race relations were rendered natural through references to familial relationships.In other words, the maternalism that organized and helped legitimate the court was not about families per se; rather, it was about the authority of some women and the subordination of others. That this more authoritarian and, indeed, punitive aspect of maternalism was at least as important as its ostensibly protective and, even, subversive values was made clear in a speech by Margaret Patterson. Speaking as a magistrate, Patterson could, in a single breath, claim that "[c]rime is only a symptom of too much leisure, and it can't be cured simply by punishment" *and* declare, with some evident exasperation, "[s]ome women make homes unhappy and do not show any remorse ... It is all I can do to restrain myself from slapping these girls."[76] Maternal power in its fullest sense is revealed here. The existence of the Toronto Women's Court suggests, in itself, that *as* self-appointed social mothers providing the right kind of friendship and moral guidance to their social daughters, white, middle-class women required, and actively sought out, some disciplinary backup for their task.

I refer to the combination of maternalism, feminism, moral redemption, and coercion that was encapsulated within the Toronto Women's Court as feminized justice. As Chapter 2 explores in detail, it is because these pillars of the TLCW's broader reform campaigns coalesced in, and as, the Women's Court that this relatively unexplored reform achievement appeared, to them, to be one of their greatest. Importantly, the women reformers for whom the Women's Court was "our Court" did not perceive its contradictions as paradoxes at all. To the contrary, for them, the coercion, the authority, the moral policing, and the increased surveillance offered to them as a result of the court's existence *were* the "great achievement." Following their lead, I treat the Toronto Women's Court not only as an extra court in the network of police courts in Toronto, and not only as a site through which the moral capacities of Toronto womanhood were measured up (and often found wanting), thereby leading to the increased moral surveillance over women in the city and a more punitive policing of women's public personae, but also as a living experiment in feminist ideals. The Toronto Women's Court was a concrete manifestation of the feminists' complex but comprehensive platform for legal, moral, and sexual equality for women. This approach opens up the court as a significant site for exploration.

Women, Crime, and Archival Gaps

To say that the court was feminism in action, however, is not to be inattentive to the criminalized women who bore the brunt of feminized justice. To the contrary, as I shall show, the young women envisioned as the chief beneficiaries of the court were a minority of cases, and a great deal of imaginative work was necessary to maintain the court as a legitimate intervention into Toronto police court justice. Ironically, it required endless effort to insist that the court merely reflected a natural division between women's and men's legal needs. Looking beyond these efforts, I demonstrate that many women were deliberately silenced or ignored in the official narratives of the Women's Court, precisely because their presence threatened to undercut the very claim of the court being a "great achievement" in the first place. Since this analysis is concerned with relationships among women as they are visible through the Toronto Women's Court, these differing expressions of power, agency, resistance, and control are important ones. They are also complex issues involving, simultaneously, careful considerations of theory and method.

The viewpoints, agency, and power of the members of the TLCW are not difficult to assess. The very fact that their vision could be made real testifies to their power, their influence, and their organizational capacities to translate their politics into action. Indeed, by anchoring this exploration of the Toronto Women's Court in the claims of the TLCW, this book not only acknowledges these women's accomplishments but also argues that their agency with respect to the criminal law is an undertheorized aspect of their feminism that is deserving of exploration. Moreover, the fact that they were well-educated, influential, white, affluent, well-organized, and, as a result, prolific women means that it is largely through their records, their speeches, their case reports, and their writings that the Toronto Women's Court comes into view. However, despite a theoretical approach that takes seriously what they were attempting to achieve, along with an abundance of sources through which to document it, I also argue that their political activism was largely ideologically informed. Their views on women, crime, and justice were at least as influenced by what they did not – or did not want to – see as by what they did see. In this way, the Toronto Women's Court was an invention that, simultaneously, allowed the TLCW to position its members as the best arbiters of female justice. This power often came at the direct expense of other women in the city.

For this reason this book also contrasts the ideas of the TLCW with the experiences of those women charged with a criminal offence. This is both a difficult and contentious task, as the concept of experience, as an epistemological foundation of social history, has come under heavy critique. Joan Scott, for example, has challenged essentialist concepts of experience, arguing that there is no such thing as unmediated experience that stands outside discourse and that can be counterpoised as "real" to the social construction of that experience as a political process.[77] Instead of treating experience as "the lived realities of social life,"[78] and subjects as having "a pre-existing identity"[79] through which events, like a trial, are experienced, Scott argues that social historians must attend to the discursive processes that produce subjectivity and create the meanings by which these experiences gain currency. Thus, rather than attempting to arrive at the truth about the experiences of a group of women known as criminals, poststructuralist historians argue that "trying to distinguish falsehood from veracity is not only fruitless but meaningless."[80] Instead, it is suggested that we focus on the various, sometimes complementary, sometimes competing, truth-seeking discourses that act as "strategic attempts to order disturbing events into credible narratives."[81]

Although this approach to social history allows for a rich deconstruction of the narratives about crime and justice told by groups such as the TLCW – and, thus, it is employed here – it is only of limited use in an examination of an institution like the Toronto Women's Court. In large part this is a methodological issue. Even if it could be said that all experience is mediated by discursive processes,[82] for the archival researcher, it is also the case that all the evidence of these processes is not readily available for analysis. That is, if the members of the TLCW spoke – and spoke often – about their ideas for feminized justice, women charged with a criminal offence speak seldom, if at all. By and large, they were poor, sometimes homeless, often illiterate, and relatively powerless women. They have left few records of their own that speak to, or of, their interpretations of gender, crime, morality, or a specialized court established on their behalf. Their actual existence is noted only in the records of what others – the TLCW, prison and reformatory officials, the press, and so on – had to say about them. And not surprisingly, what others had to say about them is often not very flattering, and the comments are always made in the context of concerns that tell us more about the group speaking than the women being spoken about. Perhaps even more importantly, many women who did appear in the Women's Court were never spoken of at all.

Part of what the Women's Court accomplished was the denial of agency to women charged with a criminal offence, likely so as not to upset the ordered narratives that gave rise to, and legitimated, the Women's Court and that granted authority to its proponents to speak about "criminal women" in the first place. Thus, although the reformers' narratives reveal a great deal about them, confining our studies to these ordering discourses ultimately only leads us to discoveries about the power of the powerful. Furthermore, I agree with Steven Maynard, who argues that it is also necessary to "historicize discourse itself ... Recognizing that discursive forms have a history, that is, analysing the material context of their emergence, is one interpretive move that makes the sharp differentiation between discourse and the material begin to fade from view."[83] Women charged with a criminal offence were an important part of the material context of the Women's Court: it was, after all, their object existence, if not their subjective interpretations, that gave rise to the need to "solve" the "problem" of women's crime. Their presence in the court must, therefore, be recounted.

For empirical data on charges and dispositions, I have used the city jail registers.[84] These are giant ledger books into which clerks entered the details and particulars of each person committed to the city jail for at least one night; consequently, they provide a wealth of empirical information on criminalized women. For each individual held in custody, the jail clerk was obligated to enter information under the following headings: date of entry, age, name, place of birth (if not Canadian-born, the number of years in Canada), city of residence, occupation, religion, educational status (illiterate, elementary, or superior), social conditions and habits (marital status and temperate or intemperate), offence, date of committal, date of sentence, when the sentence expired (at the city jail), sentence and period of same, by what authority committed, by what court tried, where discharged after leaving the city jail (another prison, bailed, released, etc.), the number of days in municipal custody, and, finally, how maintained in jail (municipal or provincial jurisdiction). Another set of city jail documents records the known addresses of persons committed to the local cells.[85] Together, these sources help to flesh out the identities and circumstances of women in conflict with the law. I have examined these jail records in three-year intervals, beginning in 1913, and collected information about 4,781 charges against women and 645 charges against men, for a total of 5,426 cases. These records do not speak to the "real" experiences of the women who faced a Women's Court magistrate between 1913 and 1934, but they do testify to a group of criminal women whose lives are deserving of examination.[86]

Nonetheless, these sources only capture a partial view of women in court: those who were not jailed prior to, or because of, a court appearance are, obviously, not recorded. Therefore, I have also turned to other quantitative and qualitative sources to round out the picture of who appeared in the Women's Court. These include official crime statistics, which were collected by the police and the provincial authorities responsible for jails, prisons, and reformatories. Newspaper reports of police court cases provide another glimpse into the daily operations of the Women's Court, although these semi-regular columns need to be treated with some caution.[87] Early-twentieth-century newspaper reports were glib, formulaic, and tended to be highly selective in what they chose to cover and how they chose to cover it.[88] The cases reported in the press tended to be those that most closely fit with, and most strongly supported, the ideals of the Women's Court in the first place.[89] Harry Wodson, veteran police court reporter for the *Telegram,* evinced a particular, if parochial, antipathy for the "fluttering lady scribes" in the Women's Court, whom he accused of writing pathetic, maudlin, sentimental, and misleading reports to elicit reader sympathy for "the diseased figure of a fallen angel."[90] But even if Wodson was correct, newspaper police court columns in combination with jail records can be used to advantage. Although jail registers tended to give information about those women least likely to be positively affected by a separate court for women, newspaper stories tended to report on those cases that demonstrated the court's power for uplift. The names and cases in these two types of sources are rarely the same. Thus, the jail register might note that eight women were committed to jail on any one day in the Women's Court, while the newspaper might focus on the one woman who was dismissed from the court with a warning and who promised to take the right road. Vagrancy and theft charges were more commonly reported than those for drunkenness, and older repeat offenders were less likely to qualify as good copy than young women arrested for the first time. The police court columns, then, offer a view of the Women's Court not seen in the jail registers and vice versa.

Finally, I have followed those women who were sentenced from the Women's Court to the Andrew Mercer Ontario Reformatory for Females, which tended to keep careful case files on many of the women in its custody. After 1914 most of the women sentenced to the Mercer were given what were known as indeterminate sentences, which allowed magistrates to sentence offenders to custodial institutions for unspecified periods up to two years, less a day.[91] Importantly, indeterminate sentences also made provincially sentenced prisoners eligible for parole. Together, the indeterminate sentence and parole eligibility meant that Mercer officials took studious notes of inmates' behaviour, conduct, associations, work habits, and other relevant factors to produce a recommendation about early release to the Parole Board. To the extent that they could, they also kept track of women after their release; often, it was the Mercer staff who were designated as responsible for the women on parole. Parole Board files supplement the reformatory case files. Mercer staff, parole officials, and the courts had an active, triangular relationship with one another. Magistrates were required to submit their recommendation for parole along with their sentencing decisions. This court file was sent to the Mercer, along with the warrant of commitment stating the offence and the sentence, and was entered into the inmate's reformatory case file. Mercer staff then added their own case notes to the file, which was then submitted to the Parole Board for its deliberations. In addition, parole officers acted as intermediaries between the convicting magistrate and the reformatory. This included instances when there was a lack of clarity about the intention of the sentence or about the subjective interpretations of the candidacy for parole of any given inmate.[92] Thus, for those women sentenced to the Mercer, some detailed files – including background histories, prior records, notes on behaviours and demeanours, and, sometimes, letters from incarcerated women themselves – are available to document the variety of experiences of criminalized women.

These multiple sources can still only tell us a fraction of the story of women's criminality and of the practices of the Women's Court. Nonetheless, the glimpses of women offenders provided through these sources serve as a counterpoint to the interpretations of their existence put forward by the TLCW. Together, these quantitative and qualitative sources reveal a picture of criminal women in Toronto that is very different to that imagined by the maternal feminists. This crucial juxtaposition is, I argue, sufficient to treat the statements about criminalized women not as revelatory discourses but as self-interested claims, to which criminal women's experiences are necessarily counterposed. In this way I seek, whenever possible, to return agency to those women whose entry and exit from the Women's Court was often so disorderly to the TLCW that they attempted to ignore them altogether.[93]

Organization of the Book

The first part of this book locates the Toronto Women's Court within its feminist origins and its functions as a police court. Chapter 1 offers an overview of the Toronto Women's Court as an institution, tracking its development and changes over two decades and paying particular attention to the changes instituted by Margaret Patterson after 1922. The chapter also locates the Toronto Women's Court within the wider North American movement for more specialized courts in which white, middle-class, professionalizing women could exercise their authority over other women's legal dilemmas. Chapter 2 elaborates on the Toronto Women's Court as paradigmatic of feminized justice and continues the exploration of the court as a specific achievement of the TLCW. I demonstrate that the maternal feminists had a comprehensive political agenda with respect to criminal law and that this aspect of their feminism has been undertheorized. Locating the Toronto Women's Court within a broader platform of criminal justice reform undertaken by a TLCW committee named the Committee for an Equal Moral Standard clarifies why the TLCW called the Toronto Women's Court a great achievement. The chapter concludes, however, with the argument that because the members of the TLCW had a limited and, in many ways, self-interested view of crime and sexual justice, a broader view of the significance of the Toronto Women's Court and the meanings of justice for women in Toronto is necessary.

Chapter 3 provides an overview of women's crime rates as they are rendered visible through the extant records of the Toronto Women's Court. The statistics available in the local jail records paint a picture of female crime that is markedly different from that produced by either contemporary reform groups such as the TLCW or historians of female crime, both of whom tend to focus on young, single women who were charged mostly with vagrancy and sentenced to the Mercer Reformatory. Instead, the chapter draws attention to the significance of repeat offenders who were arrested principally for drunkenness. The repeat offenders tended to be over the age of thirty, Roman Catholic, and extremely poor and itinerant. When sentenced in the Women's Court, they were most likely to be sent to the Concord Industrial Farm for Women, where short-term detention, rather than reform, was the goal. I argue that the very existence of this group of older, unreformable, drunken women challenges the legitimacy of the Toronto Women's Court and forces a closer examination of its practices and claims.

Chapters 4 and 5 break down women's routes into and out of the Toronto Women's Court by the five most common offences leading to their arrest: drunkenness (23 percent), vagrancy (19 percent), theft (12 percent), bawdy house offences (20 percent), and breaches of liquor laws (8 percent). Chapter 4 examines vagrancy and theft charges, as these two offences tended to bring in those women who most closely resembled the women envisioned as being in need of a feminized justice venue. Vagrancy has been studied closely by historians and criminologists, and the records from the Toronto Women's Court support claims that vagrancy was used to police sexual and racial boundaries based on hegemonic notions of white femininity. By contrast, theft has been largely unexplored in the history of women's crime. Yet, because theft occurred in a variety of places – on the streets, in department stores, and in domestic service employment relations – theft charges offer a glimpse into women's daily routines in the early decades of twentieth-century Toronto. In addition, theft, like vagrancy, offers a window into prevailing gender ideologies at the turn of the century because different gendered meanings were inscribed onto different kinds of thievery. By placing these offences together in this chapter, I show how many women – especially young, white women or women with claims to "decent" family belonging – could navigate a criminal charge by presenting themselves as "good" women. Women who rejected such self-presentations, however, tended to experience the brunt of the law, which was often justified as for their own protection. In these ways vagrancy and theft charges tested, and outlined the contours of, the legitimacy of the Women's Court itself.

Yet, if some women charged with theft and vagrancy failed to comport themselves in ways the Toronto Women's Court could understand, drunk women and women found in bawdy houses threatened to undermine the court's special status altogether. Chapter 5 examines these charges for what they can tell us about the limits of feminized justice. Women who drank and women who ran illegal liquor shops (after passage of the *Ontario Temperance Act* in 1916 and its replacement, the *Liquor Control Act*, in 1927) were a far cry from the reformable young woman who had temporarily lost her moral compass. Drunk women, in particular, offer special insight into the Women's Court as a project, because these women were most likely to be the repeat offenders whose revolving door relationship to the criminal justice system belied the promise of the court as a site of redemption. Moreover, these same women were also those most likely to work in, or to run, the city's disorderly houses. Indeed, the records of the drunks and the prostitutes show them living, working, carousing, and getting arrested together, indicating a kind of women's community not contemplated by the TLCW. Their presence in the courtroom also signals a form of female knowledge of criminal justice mechanisms that rivalled the claims of middle-class women reformers. I argue that it is for these reasons that the TLCW almost never spoke of these women in the entire twenty-one-year period under review. It is a silence that is often replicated in histories of female crime and one that this chapter seeks to confront.

Chapter 6 places women charged with a criminal offence and maternal feminists in court together through a close examination of the tenure of Dr. Margaret Norris Patterson. Specifically, the chapter explores the tenuous authority exercised by Patterson as a woman magistrate, as she attempted to bridge the twin aims of protection and punishment in the court. Her controversial dealings with two women in her court – both of whom, in different ways, challenged her legitimacy and opened up broader debates about the role of women in legal authority – reveal the complexities of this experiment in feminized justice for legal professionals, women reformers, and criminalized women. The Conclusion takes up these questions once more. Through a re-examination of the apparently contradictory trends evident in the twenty-one-year political history of the Toronto Women's Court, the concluding chapter reflects on what may be learned from this history of different women's struggles with the criminal law and the meaning of justice. Ultimately, the final word on the Toronto Women's Court – as a feminist project, a police court, an experiment in woman-centred criminological reform, an institution, and an invention – cannot be made. As the following chapters will show, the Toronto Women's Court offered vastly different meanings to the very different women who encountered it. It is precisely this that makes its place in women's legal history so compelling.

1

The Toronto Women's Police Court as an Institution

Between 1913 and 1934, the Toronto Women's Court was a site through which the organized women's community in Toronto could act as arbiters of local justice, at least insofar as criminal charges against or involving women were concerned. In this endeavour the Toronto Local Council of Women (TLCW) was inspired by a variety of political movements and developments occurring across North America that helped to convince its members that a separate court was possible and, when necessary, defendable. One of these developments was the *Canadian Juvenile Delinquents Act* of 1908 and the subsequent opening of juvenile courts in Ottawa and Toronto in 1910 and in Montreal in 1912.[1] Juvenile courts, especially those established specifically to hear cases involving girls, were sites for the elaboration of maternal justice through which predominantly white, newly professionalized, middle-class feminist reformers drew on their "expert" knowledge as matronly subjects to successfully critique, and enter into, the criminal justice system to attend to the specific needs of young girls and women.[2] At the same time, there existed a parallel development in socio-legal structures, namely, the emergence of increasingly specialized courts that focused on socialized (as opposed to adversarial) justice for specific types of offences, including, importantly, domestic mediations courts (which would evolve into family courts) and women's and morals courts.[3] Like juvenile courts, these courts, and the women who advocated for them, were intimately linked· to the Progressive-era movement of urban reform, a movement based on a belief in science, efficiency, and technocracies that drew upon its members' increasing authority as university-trained experts and their political acumen and support for a welfarist regime that would actively and rationally care for the citizenry. These contemporaneous and complementary developments were characterized by their focus on crime as a social, rather than a narrowly legal, problem.[4] Both of these court reform initiatives were also clearly important factors that helped to shape the Toronto Women's Court.

But as much as it was inspired by these similar socio-legal developments, the Toronto Women's Court does not map neatly onto either the juvenile or socialized justice models. In particular, the maternalism that is associated with juvenile justice was much more difficult to articulate and justify when the subjects did not embody, literally, let alone metaphorically, delinquent daughters.[5] Nor was the Women's Court quite like a domestic mediation court, despite the fact that Margaret Patterson established an informal domestic mediation court during her tenure as magistrate, an accomplishment that anticipated successful arguments for family courts and was consistent with the desire on the part of TLCW reformers to soften the hard edges of adversarial justice where women were concerned. It is more accurate, then, to say that the Toronto Women's Court was an important bridge between these two well-studied moments in the development of modern court architecture; it incorporated elements of both, but it was not fully one or the other.

This chapter sketches an overview of the institutional location and political project of the Toronto Women's Police Court. The court's history can be neatly divided into two parts: from 1913 to 1921, it was presided over by Colonel Denison, a male magistrate; in January 1922 Margaret Patterson was appointed as magistrate, and the character of the court changed accordingly. Patterson was unceremoniously removed from the bench in 1934, and a legally trained magistrate, Thomas O'Connor, KC, was appointed to the Women's Court bench. By then, however, the political force of the women's movement, and the Women's Court, was spent. This chapter traces the ebb and flow of the court and lays out the broad strokes of its significance, to the women's movement, in the court system, and to the broader project of legal reform in Toronto.

"The manly thing to do"

Not surprisingly, the members of the TLCW were delighted with the opening of the Toronto Women's Court and declared themselves appreciative of "the outcome of many years of struggle for its establishment and very grateful to Dr. Margaret Patterson and her splendid, self-sacrificing committee."[6] But they were not the only ones to welcome this reform. Generally speaking, the Toronto Women's Court was warmly received by a variety of court watchers, newspaper reporters, and public officials. Police Chief Grasset hailed it as "a step in the right direction."[7] Court reporter Robson Black saw it as "an omen of a general thaw" in police court treatments of crime.[8] And the usually anti-feminist journal *Jack Canuck* claimed that "[t]he new and humane order of things will work wonders in the reclamation of the unfortunate daughters of Eve who have, perhaps, taken the first false step ... The erring sister should be given a chance. It is the manly thing to do."[9]

The writer for *Jack Canuck* was not the only person to accredit the existence of the Women's Court to male chivalry. Magistrate Denison, said to be "at all times, in all places, and under all circumstances courteous to the gentler sex," saw himself as particularly instrumental to its formation.[10] Appointed to the police court bench in 1877, Denison was Toronto's most famous magistrate for forty-four years, until his retirement in the summer of 1921. According to one historian, Denison was "the living embodiment of the law in Toronto."[11] In his own *Recollections*, Denison prided himself on his role in the establishment of the Women's Court, claiming that he had facilitated the opening of the Women's Court in advance of provincial approval: "After this Court had been working for some time and had attracted a good deal of attention, the Attorney-General, Mr. Foy, meeting me casually said: 'What is this I hear about a Women's Court being established? How could that happen without my knowing anything about it?' I replied, 'You were busy, and I did not want to bother you, as it was no trouble to me to establish it ... and I was not bound to hold my court in any particular room.'"[12] Denison went on to describe the Women's Court as "an excellent regulation" and explained to his readers that his approval for the Women's Court was based in his belief that it would play an important part in "prevent[ing] a young girl from going astray."

Despite the echoes of the TLCW's court reform ideas in this last statement, Denison was by no means of a mind with Toronto's reformers. His various diaries and scrapbooks give no indication that he ever socialized with the women and men of the broader Toronto moral reform movement, of which the TLCW was an important part.[13] To the contrary Denison was "of the governing class"[14] and "one of Canada's leading supporters of British imperialism."[15] His position as senior police court magistrate in Toronto was due more to ties with the governing Liberal Party and his personal friendship with Ontario premier Oliver Mowat.[16] Although a lawyer, Denison evinced an interest in neither the causes of crime nor the law. He tended to view criminal behaviour through a deterministic lens that attributed disorderliness to the working class and through which vice was interpreted based on racial stereotyping.[17] He was also famous for his assembly line approach to justice and his contempt for legal niceties.[18] He preferred his own sense of British fair play and intuitive common sense to legal technicalities and proudly professed: "I never allow a point of law to be raised. This is a court of justice, not a court of law."[19]

As a result Gene Homel argues that a "whiggish view of history" that "[fails] to examine critically the disparity between reform pronouncements and actual accomplishments has contributed to what is probably an inflated assessment of reform advance in the court system."[20] John McLaren's survey of Denison's decision making with respect to prostitution-related offences confirms this view. Although inclined to be harsh with male procurers and pimps (recall that Frank M. received a harsher sentence than Bridget D. on the first day in the court), Denison remained unconvinced by various reform efforts to deal more harshly with bawdy houses.[21] Despite a moral campaign, led largely by the TLCW, to have bawdy houses treated more rigorously by the courts (a campaign discussed in more detail in Chapter 2) and subsequent changes to the *Criminal Code* that transformed bawdy house charges from summary convictions to indictable offences with proportionately greater maximum sentences, McLaren finds that "[t]hese changes seem to have [had] little perceptible impact on Denison's sentencing pattern [which] suggests that ... even when it was given legislative approbation, [Denison] continued to administer the law in the conservative and determinist spirit which had always guided him."[22] Homel reaches a similar conclusion. Noting Denison's "genial Toryism" and general paternalistic approach to crime and criminal justice, Homel argues that "[n]otwithstanding the evolution of separate trials for women and children, the addition of court translators, and the like, there was essentially little implementation of these reform goals in the police-court system while Denison presided as chief magistrate."[23]

Feminized Justice

Homel is partially correct. As later chapters will show, as far as women charged with a criminal offence are concerned, there is little evidence to suggest that the mere existence of the Women's Court had any great impact upon either their entry into police court or their exit from it. Indeed, apart from the exclusion of a public gallery, Denison's court did not entail any substantive changes in women's relationship to the criminal law. But Homel underestimates the significance of the Toronto Women's Court as an ideological event, especially for the local women reformers whose vision was what had been made real by its establishment.

Although paternalism has long been a feature associated with local judicial practices, the Women's Court was celebrated largely because it brought the values of maternalism to the low-level police courts. White, middle-class women purposefully adapted a familial model as an organizing principle for the court. In its original guise, this family was governed by Denison, who sat in as the paterfamilias. As far as the members of the TLCW were concerned, the existence of a father figure was only a temporary glitch, and they argued continuously for a female magistrate. The model of the family was also apparent in the Women's Court design, location, and function. Held not only as a separate court but also in a distinct location away from the other police courts, its architectural design and institutional setting helped to make it more than simply one more court in the system of police courts in Toronto. On the court's opening day, the *Telegram* reported that the proceedings in a committee room in City Hall operated without much formality and described the new site as "a large square room with softly covered and decorated terra cotta walls. There are pictures too, comfortable seats, and the railed dock is absent. Instead there is a wide open space in front of a long table, behind which Magistrate Denison sits."[24] Similarly, the reporter for the *Daily News* could not refrain from commenting on the "strange surroundings, so removed from the thought of crime or prison."[25] And the *Globe* remarked on the proceedings: "To the onlooker it seemed all as simple as being called to the teacher's table at school."[26] The home-like atmosphere, the informal hearings, the absence of any of the trappings of the adversarial trial process, the likeness to a schoolroom in which educative discipline was benevolently dispensed, these, along with the substitution of the public gallery with reform-minded women "who attended the court regularly and did their best to help the fallen girls and women," were what made the Toronto Women's Court unique.[27]

Nonetheless, under Denison's tenure the Women's Court was never just about women, and the court's docket included men charged with morals offences (a police category that distinguished public order offences from property crimes and crimes against the person) as well as women charged with all criminal offences. In this mandate the Toronto Women's Court borrowed from but also departed from emerging US models of specialized justice. In Chicago, for example, the development of a "morals court" was inspired not by a desire to create a gender-specific legal experience for lonely and impressionable city women but to deal with a specific array of offences, most notably prostitution, fornication, obscenity, pandering, and other "vices."[28] In other words, although the regulation of women's bodies was a central aim and function of these Progressive-era US morals courts, they were formally organized by criminal law categories, not gender, and they therefore enjoyed a legal scope wide enough to bring in a large number of male offenders. By contrast the Toronto Women's Court was meant to function first and foremost as a form of legal protection for women or, as Denison himself put it, to keep "female wrongdoers away from the mob."[29] Yet, because the Women's Court drew on the logic of US morals courts, its jurisdiction also extended to cases in which men were accused of morals crimes involving women (typically, bawdy house offences). This combination of gender-specific and morals cases made for a sometimes confused appearance. On the one hand, the Toronto Women's Court mirrored its US counterparts in the "expanded scope of state intervention and centralized administrative powers that [it] brought to public morals," powers that could be extended over men as well as women.[30] On the other hand, the Toronto Women's Court's decidedly more inchoate organization by gender, rather than by *Criminal Code* categories, meant that most men charged with morals offences other than those related to houses of ill fame were not shepherded into the court.

Adding to this confusion was the fact that men continued to be important players in the operation of the court, as clerks, witnesses, police officers, lawyers, and, of course, between 1913 and 1922, the magistrate. That the members of the TLCW were greatly disappointed that the court was presided over by a male magistrate is evident in the fact that, only three months after the court was established, the TLCW sent a delegation (headed by Margaret Patterson) to City Hall to "see about the appointment of a Judge of the Women's Court."[31] Given that Denison already sat on the Women's Court bench, one assumes they meant a female judge.[32] The placement of women in positions of authority within the criminal justice system – as magistrates, policewomen, matrons and wardens, parole and probation officers, and so on – was central to the politics of feminized justice.[33] Dorothy Chunn places this movement for women judges within the broader context of the movement for socialized justice, which was, in part, characterized by "the assumption that 'doing good' should take precedence over legal rights in the administration of family-welfare law."[34] Feminists, acting in accordance with these politics, expected women magistrates to bring a new perspective to the adjudication of women's criminal cases. Beverly Blair Cook refers to this perspective as "moral authority," a particular form of expertise that women brought to the courts that identified them with "the nurturing cooperative values attributed to feminist jurisprudence."[35] Accordingly, women activists favourably contrasted their moral authority to the judgements of "the average male Solon."[36] Whereas men tended to be interested in the crime, women were interested in the criminal; whereas men were tied to legal precedent, women advocated social casework in the courts; and whereas men were, at best, indifferent and, at worst, hostile to women's experiences, women could offer friendly and understanding counsel to "girls" in trouble.

In their efforts to secure a female magistrate, the members of the TLCW were likely influenced by developments in other jurisdictions such as Los Angeles, where Georgia Bullock had been named as judge in the Women's Court.[37] Bullock was a single mother and a graduate of the University of Southern California Law School who, while a law student, acted as a voluntary probation officer for women convicted in the police courts. The Los Angeles Women's Court had been established in 1913, in large part as a result of the lobbying efforts of California's newly enfranchised club women, who, like their Toronto counterparts, argued that women charged with a criminal offence needed a closed court to protect them from the morbid curiosity of male onlookers. The formal establishment of the court itself, however, was largely due to the amenable political sentiments of Thomas White, a police court judge. Judge White, clearly sympathetic to the idea that women had distinct legal needs, appointed Bullock as an assistant judge in the newly created Women's Court. Between 1914 and 1917, Bullock worked in this assistant capacity, without pay or formal status, while Judge White formally legalized her decisions. In 1924 Bullock was granted formal recognition as a paid judge in the Women's Court.

These parallel developments, however, seem not to have moved either Magistrate Denison or the provincial government. In a 1914 speech to the Social Service Congress about the Toronto Women's Court, Margaret Patterson noted, with pragmatic resignation: "This court is not yet all that we hope to see it, but it is a step in the right direction and an earnest of the time when we shall have a night court for women with a woman on the bench."[38] Once again this motion implicated developments south of the border. In Chicago and New York, the women's and morals courts that had emerged not only employed female officials as assistant judges, lawyers, policewomen, and probation officers but also operated as night courts. The logic of having courts run at night was based largely on an understanding of women's crime as almost exclusively prostitution-related. The Page Commission, empanelled by the City of New York to investigate the court system, reported in 1910 that night courts were an important development if women's cases were to be given the treatment they deserved. The reasoning used by the commission would have been intimately familiar to Toronto's reformers: "The establishment of a night court for women only will undoubtably [sic] limit the number of doubtful male characters who are seen from time to time among the spectators at the court."[39] Separate night courts for women were established in Manhattan and the Bronx in 1910, and they clearly provided another model for Toronto's court and moral reform advocates.

Nonetheless, the movement for a separate night court for women was no more successful than the efforts to have a woman appointed to the bench. The TLCW turned to another tactic. In January 1915 the council women engaged in an "animated discussion," during which they resolved "[t]hat this Council recommends the appointment of a woman physician for all cases in which women are concerned who shall be present at all trials of same and have full powers of interrogation of accused and witnesses on equal terms with the Crown Attorney or the presiding magistrate."[40] Although this resolution was not immediately successful, it, along with the other various efforts to reform the Women's Court, paint a clear and comprehensive picture. Toronto's maternal feminists did not trust men to implement woman-centred and woman-positive measures. Achieving formal legal change without the (female) personnel to oversee its implementation was only the first step. The appointment of Margaret Patterson – physician, feminist, and moral reformer – in 1922 was the essential second step toward the achievement of feminized justice.

The Appointment of Margaret Patterson

When, in 1920, Denison announced his imminent retirement, the TLCW "and kindred organizations" were quick to act, sending a deputation to the newly elected United Farmers of Ontario (UFO) and "asking for legislation providing for and, in due course, the appointment of a woman magistrate in Toronto."[41] In 1921 the UFO, attentive to the demands of its recently enfranchised female supporters, amended the *Police Magistrates' Act* to enable any Ontario city with a population over one hundred thousand to appoint a female magistrate.[42] On 4 January 1922, the government announced that it had selected Margaret Patterson to sit on the Women's Court bench.[43] Needless to say, the TLCW rejoiced at the news, declaring: "We worked for the appointment of a woman magistrate, we recommended the appointment of Dr. Margaret Patterson and now we will certainly stand behind her."[44]

The support of the TLCW was crucial, because the decision to appoint Patterson was controversial. The provincial government had overstepped its jurisdiction: the cities paid the salaries of police court magistrates, and they were, therefore, entitled to appoint them. Toronto City Council was initially opposed to Patterson's appointment, especially to having the appointment imposed upon it by the province. The City threatened not to pay Patterson the $3,500 per year salary (and even suggested she work without remuneration), and it acquiesced only in the face of a mounting female campaign in support of Patterson's appointment. A deputation of women's organizations, led by the Local Council of Women, called on the City Council to urge it to allow Patterson's appointment. The Woman's Christian Temperance Union also made it clear to the City that they would "back [Patterson] up and help her in this in any way we are able," including further actions against the councillors if they did not agree to more graciously accept Patterson as a salaried magistrate.[45] The City backed down from its challenge.[46]

Patterson herself stayed away from this debate, and other than to evince surprise at the announcement on 4 January 1922, she refrained from comment. She claimed to have first learned about her appointment when the press asked her for a statement about it and insisted that she had not sought out the position. At first, she said, she was not sure if she would accept it, demurring to her role as mother to a thirteen-year-old son, Arthur. "It wasn't until deputations kept coming that I took the matter seriously," she told the *Star* on 6 January. There is some reason, however, to doubt Patterson's passive role in her appointment. Patterson was one of the women elected by the TLCW to represent it in its lobby for a female replacement for Colonel Denison.[47] One month later Patterson withdrew from this committee. No reasons are given for her removal from the delegation, but perhaps her claims to having no idea that she would be selected for the magistracy and her insistence that she did not seek out the position are less credible in light of this withdrawal. Indeed, Patterson was nominated for president of the council that same year, and she withdrew her name from that nomination as well. In 1921 Patterson was chosen by the TLCW as its recommendation for the Women's Court bench. No reasons are given for this selection. The minutes tell us only that the TLCW considered three women for the position: Margaret Patterson, Charlotte Whitton, and Mrs. (Emma?) O'Sullivan: "After much discussion, Dr. Patterson was chosen as our nominee."[48] She did not withdraw her name from that competition.

Dorothy Chunn has argued that Patterson's appointment was the product of political pragmatism.[49] Pointing to a host of external factors, including a UFO government that was "unencumbered by legal knowledge," a premier and attorney general intent on enforcing the *Ontario Temperance Act*, and a constituency of rural men and women for whom Patterson's links to the Department of Agriculture's Women's Institutes, made her "not only the darling of urban, Protestant, middle-class women but also of farm women."[50] Chunn concludes that Patterson benefited from being "the 'right' woman in the 'right' place at the time."[51] Chunn's argument, however, is based on her premise that it was not Patterson who initiated the process. That is, Chunn argues that because Patterson did not seek the position, it behooves historians to examine who did decide to appoint her and why. The evidence presented above may indicate that this premise is in error and suggest, instead, that Patterson had grander designs than she admitted in public. This possibility does not necessarily detract from Chunn's overall arguments about the constellation of events that made Patterson's appointment a "timely coincidence of interests," but it does indicate that Patterson herself may have been one of those interests.[52] Unfortunately, the lack of historical records about how it was that Patterson came to be the TLCW's and the government's nominee makes it difficult to know with any certainty her own agency in the process. However it transpired, by 5 March 1922 Patterson was presiding over the Women's Court. For the next twelve years, Deputy Magistrate Doctor Margaret Norris Patterson would hear approximately two thousand cases per year, until she was removed from the bench in November 1934.

The "Right Sort of Woman"

"I am pleased," announced Doctor Augusta Stowe-Gullen upon hearing the news of the appointment of her colleague and friend to the magistracy, "because I feel Doctor Patterson to be so eminently fitted for the position. It is so necessary to have a woman to work among the women and children who come within the jurisdiction of the court, but more necessary that it be the right sort of woman."[53] This sentiment was echoed by many reform-minded individuals, who similarly commented on the unique suitability of Patterson for the post. Upon learning of her appointment, Dr. R.R. McClenahan, director of the Venereal Diseases Division of the Board of Health, wrote to Patterson to congratulate her and told her, "[Y]ou are especially well qualified for it. Personally, I am very well pleased that you are a physician because I realize that you will be better qualified to handle girls who are brought up for vagrancy and who are found to be infected with venereal diseases."[54] Ethel Chapman, writing for *MacLean's*, opened her article on Margaret Patterson within the same framework of the new magistrate's compelling credentials: "Just the matter of getting a woman appointed to the office of police magistrate might not be such a forward step. The thing that matters is that she be the right woman. If a woman could be appointed to such a place by virtue of her social prestige or her political influence or her marriage the result might amount to almost a tragedy. When she *grows* into it as Dr. Margaret Patterson has done, the work may be said to be fairly safe in her hands."[55] Patterson herself shared these beliefs about securing the right women for the work. Prior to, and then immediately after, the establishment of the Women's Court, she spent many hours organizing, and then monitoring, women volunteers for the court: "The women were rather carefully chosen – [Patterson] wanted no sensation-mongers in the court room and if any woman could not keep her appointment, instead of having her send a substitute, the doctor filled the vacancy herself."[56] Clearly, Patterson's qualifications for the magistracy did not flow from her essential qualities as a woman. To the contrary, it was her own experiences and political philosophies that qualified her for the job.

Knowledge of Patterson's personal background and diverse activities, therefore, is necessary to understand her appointment to and practices as magistrate in the Toronto Women's Court.[57] By 1922 Patterson had amassed considerable experience in a variety of works that led her supporters to believe that she was the right sort of woman for the post. In addition to being, as one newspaper reporter described her, a "wife, a mother, a doctor, and a trained nurse,"[58] Patterson had an extensive work history and background as a missionary, loyal imperial subject, teacher and author, social service worker, police court observer, patriotic war worker, and effective activist for women. It was all of these experiences that made her such an enthusiastically supported choice for magistrate.

Born Margaret Norris in 1874 to parents James and Sarah and into "one of the well-known Scotch farming families in Perth county, Ontario," she completed one year (1898) at the University of Toronto's Women's Medical Centre and then attended Northwestern University in Chicago, where she received her Master of Surgery degree.[59] After doing a one-year internship at the Detroit Women's Hospital, she joined the American Presbyterian Women's Mission Council and, in 1900, was sent to India as a medical missionary. There, she enjoyed an illustrious and "unusually interesting" career.[60] From 1900 to 1907, she was the director of the Seward Memorial Hospital in Allahabad, during which time there was an outbreak of the bubonic plague, and "she distinguished herself by organizing a system of plague relief camps, isolation camps and inoculation stations."[61] For this work she received the Kaisar-i-Hind Medal from King Edward VII at his coronation. Between 1903 and 1905, she acted as medical adviser to Lord Kitchener in an investigation of the social and moral conditions of the army in India. Her noteworthy activity was to open and supervise a rescue mission for camp followers. Additionally, between 1903 and 1910, she was a professor of obstetrics at the North India College of Medicine, and she wrote a textbook, used in public schools in India, on physiology and hygiene. On 1 January 1906, she married physicist John Patterson, a fellow Ontarian working as an imperial meteorologist for the Indian government. They had two children, one of whom died due to "the trying climate of India."[62] Because of John's ill health, the Pattersons – Margaret, John, and their infant son, Arthur – returned to Toronto in 1910.[63]

For reasons unknown, Margaret Patterson did not practise medicine again. She did, however, put her medical knowledge to use in her commitment to social service. During the war she garnered considerable respect for organizing Red Cross work, lecturing to St. John's Ambulance trainees, and taking charge of nursing at a convalescent hospital for returning soldiers.[64] After the war, an outbreak of influenza created a public health crisis and Patterson again rose to the occasion: merging her medical knowledge with her social service orientation, she became a member of the Ontario Emergency Volunteer Health Auxiliary and gave lectures to women volunteers at Queen's Park on how to treat people in their own homes. As one contemporary observer approvingly wrote, "[d]uring these years she was on duty practically day and night, training and organizing some thousand girls for voluntary aid work – going here and there to give instruction in practically every branch of Red Cross work."[65]

More broadly, Patterson devoted herself to Toronto's reform politics and became almost immediately one of its more energetic figures. She joined the Toronto Local Council of Women and the Presbyterian Social Service Council shortly after her arrival and quickly became involved in some of their central activities, including leading her self-sacrificing committee into the police courts.[66] In 1912 Patterson was elected as the convenor of the TLCW's Committee on Laws for Women and Children and as the council's vice-president.[67] In January 1913 she was elected as convenor of the TLCW's Committee for an Equal Moral Standard and the Prevention of Traffic in Women (EMS Committee). She served as the council's EMS Committee convenor only until 1915, when she was nominated by her council for, and won the position of, EMS Committee convenor for the National Council of Women of Canada, a position she held until 1920. Patterson ensured continuity on the EMS Committee in Toronto by nominating one Mrs. Woods as her successor. When Mrs. Woods could not attend TLCW meetings, Patterson spoke in her place. Patterson would maintain a keen interest in the work of this committee for almost as long as she was active with the council.[68]

Patterson was also an active member of the newly formed Women's Institutes, a government-sponsored organization for rural women whose mandate was to foster an acknowledgment of women's contributions to family farming and, thus, to national prosperity.[69] Loraine Gordon notes that between 1916 and 1919 alone, Patterson gave forty-one lectures to the Women's Institutes.[70] From 1920 to 1930, Patterson served as convenor of the Women's Institutes' Standing Committee on Health and Child Welfare, and from 1928 to 1930 she was the provincial chair of this same committee.[71] Indeed, in 1927 Patterson attended a special meeting of the TLCW as a representative of the Women's Institutes. She also once attended a TLCW meeting as a representative of the Social Service Council in 1917. Patterson was also affiliated with the Canadian Purity Education Association and the Young Women's Christian Association, for which she established a Department of Moral Health.

Patterson's appointment to the Women's Court bench on 4 January 1922 did not bring an end to her commitment to the council and its work. In that same year, on the recommendation of the TLCW, she was sent as one of Canada's representatives to the Pan American Criminology Conference in Baltimore, a trip that delayed her taking the Women's Court bench until May.[72] In 1923 she became the convenor of the Committee on Mental Hygiene, a position she held until 1932. By 1926 Patterson was being celebrated by the council members as an exemplary member. In that year the Provincial Council of Women moved that Patterson be made an honorary member of the National Council of Women.[73] In 1927 members of the TLCW moved that they would "recognise the work of our woman magistrate, Dr. Patterson, and give a luncheon in honour and appreciation of her work."[74] This luncheon was to be organized by the EMS Committee. In January 1929, in the midst of a scandal over her court (see Chapter 6), Patterson again received the full support of the council, which "tender[ed] to Dr. Margaret Patterson their thanks and appreciation of her wonderful work during her seven years on the bench."[75] It was not until 1932 – two years before Patterson's forced removal (at the age of fifty-eight and after twenty-two years of active social service work in Toronto) from the Women's Court bench – that Patterson disappears from the council meeting records.

Margaret Patterson's Court

In addition to her long career in reform politics, Patterson managed to effect some significant changes to the Women's Court during her twelve-year tenure on its bench. To appreciate her achievements, it is important to recognize that Patterson inherited quite a different court from the one established by her predecessor, Colonel Denison. As an incoming magistrate, Patterson was assigned a broad-based jurisdiction that encompassed "[a]ll women accused of crime and men jointly charged with women. All sexual offences in which a woman was in any way involved. All prosecutions under the Venereal Diseases Act. All Domestic Relations Cases."[76] This mandate was distinct from the one that Denison had undertaken in two ways. First, this mandate swept more men into the Women's Court, focusing as it did on women as accused *and* as victims. Second, Patterson's jurisdiction over domestic relations cases expanded her reach and allowed her to "try all cases of domestic infelicity, from a bad temper to bigamy."[77] Thus, immediately upon taking the bench, Patterson effected what Denison would, or could, not: she made the court a site of redress for women as well as the venue for the hearing of their criminal cases.

More important than the fact of her jurisdiction, however, was the way in which Patterson followed through on this mandate. She reorganized the Women's Court into two parts: the first continued the practices of her predecessor, that is, trying criminal cases that involved women; the second served as an informal domestic mediations court in which women complainants could bring cases of "domestic infelicity" to a sympathetic judge. Patterson signalled her feminist intentions by making it clear that domestic cases were her priority as an incoming magistrate. In all of the newspaper interviews about her appointment, she iterated that she did not see her mandate as "bench work only"; rather, she repeated, "I shall want quiet office hours that I may be consulted."[78] The domestic mediations court was the result of these private consultation sessions: "The Court was always cleared of both spectators and press before hearing Domestic Relations cases as any publicity is detrimental to re-establishing the home."[79] If Colonel Denison had been the living embodiment of the law in Toronto, then Margaret Patterson was the living embodiment of feminized law in Ontario.

Patterson's domestic mediations court was never a formally constituted court. Rather, it should be viewed as a streamlined caseload. Dorothy Chunn has written extensively about Patterson's approach to this caseload, noting that the informality, the closed courtroom, and the increasing use of supervision and follow-up work with troubled households were all consistent with, and offered concrete ground for experimentation with, socialized justice.[80] The movement for domestic relations courts was growing at a rapid pace by the early 1920s and emerged as one of the central demands of the national and local social welfare movements across North America. On 16 May 1922, at its regular monthly meeting (and shortly after Patterson had begun her work in the Women's Court), the TLCW passed a motion that indicated its inclusion in this movement: "Resolved: 'That a Court of Domestic Relations be established in all large cities in Canada.'"[81] In February 1923 an article that appeared in the journal *Social Welfare* described exactly what the term *court of domestic relations* was to mean: "[T]he term is used to denote a court established to deal with cases of non-support and difficulties between man and wife. Such a court implies the consideration of the family as a unit ... The Court of Domestic Relations exists ... not for the purpose of preventing families from becoming a public charge ... but for the purpose of rendering active assistance to families in order that they may find their own normal place in the community."[82] This reform impulse focused on switching family court matters to "the attitude of Rex pro the accused, and not Rex vs. the accused."[83] Relying heavily on non-legal experts, such as social workers, probation officers, and psychiatrists, those who advocated domestic disputes mechanisms hoped to uphold and make it possible for even poor and working-class families to achieve the middle-class model of the nuclear family as loving, interdependent members working together toward a unified goal.[84] Not surprisingly, one of the most committed proponents of this ideal was Margaret Patterson, whom Chunn describes as "a vocal proselytizer for socialized police court work."[85]

Although domestic relations courts are rightly seen as progressing out of the juvenile courts of the 1910s and 1920s, Patterson's practices in her own, informal, domestic relations court also advanced the cause of socialized justice.[86] Patterson described her work to the readers of *Social Welfare* in 1925: "Some idea of the extent of the work in this Court may be gained from the fact that during the past year over sixty thousand dollars was collected from husbands who were trying to shirk their duty. The chief object of this Court, however, is not to collect money, but to re-establish homes, and much valuable work has been done in this connection and many families re-united."[87] Domestic relations cases were also those that were most amenable to an explicitly feminist world view. In the domestic relations side of the Women's Court, women could seek sympathetic legal protection, even when the legal and social status of wives placed them at a considerable disadvantage. As a magistrate, Patterson was able to put into practice her own ideas about marital equity:

> Perhaps the greatest cause of domestic unhappiness is the economic position of the wife. As long as the wife and mother is regarded as non-productive in a commercial sense and dependent upon the charity of her husband for her food and clothes, to say nothing of any spending money she may receive, it is surely an unbusinesslike partnership. The wife is in partnership with her husband in the conservation if not the production of the wealth that supports the home, and as such is entitled to some part of the profits of that partnership ... At his death she is entitled to one-third of his property, why not during his life?[88]

For those women in search of legal remedies for husbands who either failed to support or deserted them, the existence of a domestic mediations court, with a feminist magistrate on the bench, must surely have been a welcome innovation.

Given her commitment to the practice of hearing cases of a domestic nature and her pioneering work in this regard, Patterson was all the more insulted when, in 1929, the province announced that it was removing her jurisdiction over domestic relations cases and, instead, formally establishing a separate Domestic Relations Court (DRC) in which Patterson was, at best, to play a minor part. Judge Hawley S. Mott (formerly of the Juvenile Court) was appointed to the bench of the new court, and Margaret Patterson was offered a position in the court, but one that would be under the direction of Mott. Even worse, in its original guise, the DRC was planned as a substitute for the Women's Court. Members of the TLCW were outraged and passed the following resolution:

> Whereas the reasons for the creation of the Women's Court still exist, namely: *First* – that there is need for a place where women wronged by men may give their evidence before a woman magistrate and unembarrassed by the presence of men not connected with the case. *Second* – There is need for a place from which men not necessary to the trial are excluded to prevent the likelihood of such men annoying them later. *Third* – There is need for a place where the court has sufficient time to enter into all the detail necessary to settle satisfactorily Domestic Relations troubles, And, whereas a woman who has been wronged is more worthy of consideration than the man who has wronged her ... Therefore be it resolved that this meeting of the L.C. of W. – representing 63 organizations of women in the city of Toronto – expresses its appreciation of the work done by the Women's Court and strongly protest against any curtailment of its power and scope.[89]

This threat to the court and the potential demotion of Patterson also engendered the opprobrium of other Toronto reform groups, including the Ontario Liberal Party Women, the Ontario Conservative Party Women, the Toronto Ministerial Association, and the Bloor Street United Church. The Toronto Board of Control and Mayor McBride soon added their voices to the outcry.[90] So vigorous was the protest against replacing Patterson and the Women's Court altogether that, when the Domestic Relations Court opened on 15 June 1929, the attorney general, Colonel Price, spoke about it during the dedication ceremony: "Right here, I would also like to clear a little misapprehension. Magistrate Dr. Patterson had a chance to come here, but she preferred to stay in the Women's Court. She believes there is work there for her to do, and there is."[91] Patterson herself was notably absent from the opening ceremonies.

But for all that the adjudication of domestic mediations cases was innovative, explicitly feminist, and publicly proclaimed as a chief virtue of Patterson's magistracy, this was only one aspect of the work of her Women's Court. Patterson was still responsible for trying the criminal cases that involved women. Loraine Gordon's survey of Patterson's decisions reveals that her "reputation for being somewhat harsher than her male counterparts in Toronto was at least partially true. Her sentences appear to be similar to those meted out by Police Magistrates in a number of cities and towns outside of Toronto, suggesting that she agreed with the prevailing norms of small-town Ontario."[92] Overall, Patterson attempted to implement a policy in which she was lenient with first-time offenders and strict with repeat offenders and with men who harmed women. Although the practices and philosophies relating to women charged with a criminal offence will be discussed in greater detail in the chapters to follow, it is important to recognize the relationship between Patterson's two jurisdictions, the separation of which facilitated her larger vision of feminized justice. Importantly, in the domestic relations court, women could come to Patterson for aid as victims of legally constituted inequalities based on their sex. That is, when women complained about the various inadequacies of their husbands and marriages, Patterson could point to the man-made legal structures that patently discriminated against women and for which she, *as* a woman, could offer sympathetic redress. Conversely, those women who found themselves before Patterson because of a criminal charge tended to be viewed with suspicion about their agency. Patterson seldom questioned the assumption that women's arrests arose from some act or behaviour that fell outside the norm and, thus, brought them to the attention of the police. Rather, she understood her job to be a process of offering them aid *after* the fact. This aid, of course, could also be denied.

The experiences of George A. and his (unnamed) wife, who appeared in both parts of Patterson's court in 1925, illustrate this point. George and his wife had a troubled marriage marked by infidelity and violence. George's wife had previously laid a complaint against her husband for assault, and this charge had been heard in the domestic court. True to her ideals about trying to keep families together and the utility of supervised release, Patterson had instructed the couple to try again, with the proviso that a police officer would monitor their relations. But during the "one exception" in which the policeman was absent, George assaulted his wife "as a result of which she is now in the Western Hospital." In this case the police laid charges against George, and he appeared in the women's police court, where he was remanded in custody to await trial. Patterson admitted that George had a decent defence, declaring "that George had a certain amount of right in adopting summary measures when he found Mrs. A. kissing a man on their verandah." Mrs. A., obviously not present in court, was thereby denied the sympathy of a magistrate well versed in the unequal position of the wife in marriage. Her own actions placed her outside the realm of victim. Rather, this "case of in flagrante delicto" resulted in the weight of magisterial sympathy shifting toward the husband. The concrete organization of the Women's Court into domestic cases and criminal cases thus also acted as a material and institutionalized manifestation of the distinctions that Patterson made between women as victims and women as agents and upon which her vision of feminized justice depended.[93]

The inherent instabilities of this vision ultimately cost Patterson her job. Her appointment was not renewed in 1934, when the recently elected Hepburn Liberals, fulfilling an election promise, restructured Ontario's court system.[94] On 21 November 1934, as she sat on the bench, Patterson was handed a three-line letter that informed her that, although the Women's Court would continue, her services would no longer be required.[95] Thomas O'Connor, KC, was named to the Women's Court bench (at nearly twice the salary that Patterson had received); Patterson was offered a job as a Justice of the Peace.[96] The Liberal government insisted that this was not an anti-woman initiative and claimed that, should Patterson accept this position, it would still qualify as "the most important position in the gift of the government enjoyed by any woman in the City of Toronto."[97] Patterson, rightly seeing this as a demotion, replied: "[A]s you have seen fit to dismiss me as a magistrate, I decline to accept the position of justice of the peace."[98]

Meanwhile, a women's movement that had "fizzled" was unable or, possibly, unwilling to help her.[99] The Liberal Women's Association could not decide whether to send a deputation to the government in protest: while some argued strongly in favour of defending Patterson and opposing a male replacement for her, others wondered about "the wisdom of sending a deputation at the present time when the appointment had already been made."[100] The TLCW's efforts were considerably less than might have been expected from a once energetic and influential group. It forwarded an emergency resolution to the Provincial Council of Women that was passed at its annual meeting on 6 December 1934. It read, simply: "That the Council petition Government to continue this principle and appoint a woman as Magistrate to preside over the Women's Court in Toronto." Similarly, on 21 November 1935 (one year to the day after Patterson's dismissal), the Provincial Council of Women carried the following emergency resolution: "The Toronto Local Council of Women deplores the dismissal of the first woman Magistrate in Ontario, whose appointment the Council urged for so long, and the renewal of the policy of the exclusion of women from this most important office many of the duties of which women are especially qualified to perform, and appeal to the Provincial Council of Women to continue its efforts and take all possible measures to obtain the appointment of another competent woman Magistrate."[101] It may be noted that this was no spirited defence of Margaret Patterson specifically. There were no further references to her removal from the bench or to the principle of a female magistrate in either the TLCW minutes or the minutes of the Provincial Council of Women. Margaret Patterson retired to private life, and the ideal of a woman-specific police court, in which women were the principal actors, disappeared as a significant component of Toronto women's politics.

Conclusion

This overview of the Toronto Women's Court demonstrates its ideological and institutional significance to the organized women of Toronto. It also illustrates the inseparable relationship between local women's political strength and police court reform. At the height of its influence, the TLCW, which was linked through political and personal associations with women around the country and around the world, was able to not only imagine but also bring into effect criminal justice reforms that mimicked reforms south of the border. Yet, in some ways the Women's Court could be considered something of a failure. In its first nine years, Colonel Denison remained intransigently resistant to the reform goals that the TLCW hoped that the Women's Court would advance. In addition, the Toronto Women's Court was not a night court like the New York Courts, and unlike the Los Angeles Women's Court, it did not start out with a female magistrate. Instead, the TLCW had to work hard, and wait almost a decade, before a provincial government sympathetic to social reform and dependent on female voters made this vision possible.

But even if the court was not always what they had envisioned, the members of the TLCW did not see it as a failure. To the contrary, it remained for them a site for experimenting with feminist criminological ideas. These ideas included an informal domestic mediations court, which Patterson began immediately upon taking the bench. As Dorothy Chunn has noted, "[a]dult members of problem families, particularly women, had not been exposed to the horrors of the ordinary police court in Toronto since her appointment to the Bench in 1922."[102] This was no small accomplishment, and it represented a decisive feminist victory in the local court system. Indeed, although the Toronto Women's Court shared a great deal with similar developments across North America, including the desire to shield women from the morbid curiosity of unscrupulous men and create a legal forum that allowed women activists to shape the nature of female justice through a logic of maternalism and female moral authority, it was also unique. Not quite a morals court and not simply a domestic mediations court, the Toronto Women's Court, especially under Patterson's tenure, existed somewhere between these two experiments in feminist jurisprudence. For the organized women's community of Toronto, this was part of its allure and its potential. As they described it, the Women's Court was, limitations notwithstanding, "an untold boon" in the development of more humane treatments of female crime.[103] The significance of the court to the TLCW's politics of reform should not be underestimated. The next chapter turns to these politics and to a closer examination of the court's material and ideological importance to the TLCW's complex politics of legal, moral, and sexual equality.

Feminism, Moral Equality, and the Criminal Law
The Women's Court as Feminized Justice

In 1918 an article decrying the *Criminal Code Amendment Act,* authored by Mrs. Edith Lang, appeared in the pages of the National Council of Women of Canada's journal, *Woman's Century:*

> The recent debate in the Federal Parliament on the proposed amendments for the Criminal Code has brought to the fore the old, old injustice of the legalized double standard of morals. The long-looked-for bill to amend the clauses re crimes against morality has been brought in, but it falls far short of the oft-expressed desires of the organized women ... It does not recognize that there should be one standard of morals for both sexes ... As I think of the proposed injustice, my blood is so hot and my indignation so seething that I can hardly write these words that you will read.[1]

At the heart of Lang's scathing critique was anger that the amendments had failed to provide for the equal treatment of male and female moral trespasses. Among the list of injustices detailed by Lang was the fact that the age of consent had not been raised above fourteen years, even though women's groups had lobbied to have it increased to at least sixteen years.[2] Men were immune from a charge of seduction until they were twenty-one years of age, while women could only press a seduction charge if they were under the age of eighteen. "By what right," she asked rhetorically, "did a Government ... bring a bill legalizing a man to be immoral until he reaches 21 years of age, while only protecting the girl until she is 18 years old?"

The insults to women did not stop there. Adultery was no longer a criminal offence: "[A] man may live openly with any number of women, but so long as he only goes through the marriage ceremony with one of them and so escape the charge of bigamy, the law can have no hold on him."[3] A variety of minor amendments gave the keepers of immoral houses, their landlords, and property owners legal defences that rendered charges against them "practically useless." Penalties for procuring and living on the avails of prostitution were no greater than, and in some cases less than, property offences. This disparaging comparison of the value of offences was a principal outrage and a recurrent theme for feminist critics. Elizabeth Becker, writing an article subtitled "The Double Standard Shown in the Criminal Code" in an earlier edition of *Woman's Century*, led her readers to contemplate the following: "We would ask you to compare the possible sentences for crimes against property and crimes against morality: For instance, compare sections 213 and 349. If an employer takes advantage of his position to seduce an employee under twenty-one years, the maximum penalty is two years – *but*, if an employee steals anything from his employer the maximum penalty is fourteen years."[4] Criminal statutes spoke volumes to maternal feminist reformers. Lang's final message to her readership was clear: "Hitherto we [women] have not been responsible for these things. But if we tolerate them now that we are voting citizens we put ourselves on record as being in favour of them and ours will be an equal guilt." Denied the franchise for so long, women could look to the *Criminal Code* as being literally manmade. But their analysis ran deeper than that: as Lang pointed out, winning the vote was not, in itself, sufficient. It was women's responsibility to act out against "the legalized double standard of morals." This was feminism in action.

These impassioned recitations of injustice speak to a profound, but unfortunately undertheorized, aspect of the maternal feminist agenda, namely, the politicization of the criminal justice system as a key moral reform. This chapter explores this field of political action. By making direct links between criminal justice mechanisms, injustices to women, and moral standards, council women such as Edith Lang and Elizabeth Becker were drawing on a long tradition in feminism in which the law and women's own sense of justice were juxtaposed. As a result, women's activism was directed toward reconciling these into a "moral code" (as they called the *Criminal Code*) that was both legal and just.[5] The members of the Councils of Women had a vision of "justice" that was both ideological and practical. At the ideological level, it referred to their idea of sexual equality for women, which was articulated as the equal moral standard. In practice, this philosophy of moral-sexual equality found its most direct expression in the criminal justice system, which council women held to be the practical application of the standard of morals of the country as a whole. I refer to this triangular relationship between morality, sexual equality, and the criminal terrain as feminized justice.

This chapter deconstructs the concept of feminized justice through an examination of the politicization of the criminal justice system. Through this exploration, I demonstrate that the criminal justice system was, simultaneously, a feminist strategy and a political goal. Moreover, the fact that the disciplinary authority granted to some women to govern other women was actively sought out and welcomed by feminists indicates not only the degree of slippage between moral politics and punitive politics but also that the two existed so comfortably that *moral* and *criminal* could be used coterminously. I begin with an overview of the broader philosophy of the equal moral standard that helped to define early feminist organizing, and I pay special attention to its application to criminal law, where the politics of prostitution offer the paradigmatic case study. I then turn to the work of the Toronto Local Council of Women's (TLCW's) standing committee that bore the name of this important articulation of feminism: the Committee for an Equal Moral Standard. It was through this committee that Toronto's maternal feminists conceptualized, developed a strategy for, and acted upon the processes of the criminal justice system: crime, policing, trials, and sentencing. The final section of the chapter introduces some of the fissures, or weaknesses, of this moral-coercive agenda and opens up for closer scrutiny both the effectiveness and limitations of feminized justice.

The Equal Moral Standard and the Criminal Law

The desire to achieve an equal moral standard – "the new sexual morality in which men lived by the same ethical precepts as women" – defined the early white women's movement in Britain and North America.[6] *The double moral standard* was the term used by turn-of-the-century women to refer to the existing state of affairs that unfairly discriminated against women. The expression carried a similar meaning for first-wave feminists as *the sexual double standard* did for second-wave feminists of the latter half of the twentieth century. The difference between these generational deployments of the double standard is that second-wave feminists argued for women's right to enjoy the same sexual liberties as men, whereas first-wave feminists "interpreted equality in the sexual realm not as equal sexual freedom for women but as equal sexual restraint for men."[7]

Importantly, the politics of the equal moral standard offered feminists the opportunity to articulate an often searing critique of male sexuality.[8] Through this politicization of male sexual prerogatives, early feminists collapsed the categories of sex, sexuality, and gender: the sexual liberties of men were conflated with the power of masculine hegemony. Thus, as Alan Hunt has pointed out, the principal targets in the political struggle to achieve morality – that is, an equal moral standard – were men.[9] It was male sexual licence, male lasciviousness, and male appetite that were the targets and objects of a great deal of reform aimed at (re)moralizing social relations. As long as male misconduct was acceptable or tolerated, a double standard would continue to prevail. This was not merely a politics concerned with the negative. Embedded in this philosophy, as the very name suggests, was a positive standard by which to gauge both the public and private behaviours of the citizenry. The moral standard to which women were held – piety and faithfulness, familial belongingness and modest deference, chastity before marriage, and monogamous conjugal relations in a private setting – was the goal and measure of moral reform. It was the failure of the equal application of these expectations that not only spelled out a double moral standard but also formed the basis of inequality between men and women. This philosophy is captured in a 1918 *Woman's Century* editorial entitled "Equal Moral Standard": "If society expects a low standard of morality from men it does by that very expectation undermine their mental resistance to temptation. Good conduct is largely the response of the individual to the expectation of society. Women have been helped and sustained in virtuous living by the standard required of them. Why not set this standard as a help to men?"[10] It was by setting out to achieve this "standard" that white, middle-class women established their claim to public political activism.

Prostitution was the central metaphor for the equal moral standard. Within the politics of the moral standard, prostitution was not simply an occupation that involved some women: it functioned as a powerful symbol of all women's victimization to male prerogatives and as an analogy for the harms inflicted on women by male sexual licence. Feminists in Britain and North America tirelessly argued that women who prostituted themselves carried almost all the burden for the evils of commercialized sex. Reversing the masculinist logic that positioned women as temptresses of innocent (if fallible) men, women reformers saw prostitutes as women who had been disadvantaged from the outset, as women forced to battle a host of sexual depredations too freely enjoyed by men and who found themselves in prostitution as a last resort, only to be blamed socially (as outcasts) and legally (as criminals) for this "choice."[11] This political view was more than a statement on sexual discrimination: it was also a critique of the law. As Philippa Levine notes, by the late nineteenth century there was "an increasing equivalence in ... popular thought between the prostitute and the woman criminal."[12] Prostitution also captured a larger legal problem. Levine offers the additional insight that the prostitute embodied the very contradictions that middle-class women were seeking to redress: as a public woman, the prostitute was "legally vulnerable as opposed to legally invisible, the more usual status accorded ... women at this juncture."[13] Contained within the politics of prostitution, then, was a full-scale legal reform project. Feminists acted to correct the over-visibility and over-regulation of women on one end of the spectrum and to flesh out women's legal rights and visibility on the other end.

This perspective did not necessarily make early women activists sympathetic to the *occupation* of prostitution. But it was even more troubling to them that the double standard was abundantly manifest in the prosecution of prostitution-related offences in the courts. Men who found themselves in court after availing themselves of the services of prostitutes were, more often than not, discharged or had their charges withdrawn in exchange for giving evidence against the prostitutes or the bawdy house in which the services were available. The women who sold the services, however, were typically convicted and either paid a fine or went to prison. And how could it be otherwise? women activists asked, when men made the law, policed the streets, and adjudicated the cases.[14] How could women ever hope to redeem themselves from a life of prostitution (for, certainly, few women reformers saw prostitution as a viable occupation, and were much more likely to see it as the last step on a road of victimization) when men continued to exonerate and protect themselves at the direct expense of women? Through this politicization, not only of sexuality but also of the criminal law processes, early feminists developed what Estelle Freedman calls "a sexual interpretation of crime"[15] that identified men, and the law, as the real perpetrators of the injustice borne by women: "[I]n the opinion of these reformers, the system of justice appeared more criminal than the acts of prostitution for which women were arrested."[16]

Given this world view, early feminists argued for a complete overhaul of prostitution-related laws. Their end goal was the total suppression of the trade. Their target was men. Their method was criminal regulation. If laws could be devised that stemmed the male demand for prostitution, they argued, the supply would cease to exist. In Canada a variety of amendments to the *Criminal Code* were crafted to more sharply delineate crimes specific to men as profiteers in the prostitution industry, while also increasing the penalties for morals offences. In 1913 amendments were introduced that created new summary offences for being a landlord or proprietor of a property used as a bawdy house. Also introduced was a reverse onus clause for men charged with living on the avails of prostitution.[17] Newspaper headlines such as "New Laws for Protection of Women" indicate the degree to which these amendments were enthusiastically welcomed by reformers, precisely because they were seen to target those who had long profited from prostitution but had not been held to legal account for women's ruination.[18] Over the years a series of amendments increased the penalties for these various offences, with especially severe punishments for those convicted two or more times for the same crime.

Prostitution, conceptualized as both the symbol of and evidence for a politics for an equal moral standard, was simultaneously a moral and a criminal issue. Furthermore, crime and its treatment became the necessary terrain on which feminists worked to achieve the broader goals that were crystallized by prostitution. The sexual interpretation of crime also gave women reformers a feminist interpretation of the criminal justice system. Within each of its component areas, and as a system as a whole, feminists saw problems that required their intervention. As Lang argued in her 1918 indictment of the *Criminal Code* amendments: "[I]t does seem as if women must be the apostles of a better and more stringent moral code. Men have been legislators for so long and they have got into the way of believing that Governments exist chiefly to protect property that it seems hard for them to widen their vision."[19] The remainder of this chapter explores the ways in which Toronto's maternal feminists theorized the criminal justice system as a site for their intervention and envisioned the use of the criminal law as a strategy to implement moral-sexual equality for women. Not incidentally, the bulk of this work was undertaken by their standing committee, entitled the Committee for an Equal Moral Standard.

The Committee for an Equal Moral Standard

> The work of your Moral Standards Committee covers so many different aspects
> of life that it is difficult to know within just what limits it should confine its activ-
> ities. Fundamentally it concerns the maintenance of ideals and standards, the de-
> velopment of all that is finest and best in life and the suppression of that which is
> evil or which tends to the lowering of standards or the disintegration of character.
> – Toronto Local Council of Women (Grace G. MacGregor, Convenor),
> "Report of the Moral Standards Committee"[20]

Mrs. Grace MacGregor's annual report on the TLCW's Committee for an Equal
Moral Standard fits neatly with observations about moral regulation. Moral
regulation refers to "the process whereby some behaviours, ideals, and values
were marginalized and proscribed while others were legitimized and naturalized."[21] As developed by Canadian feminists,[22] moral regulation scholarship
draws heavily on Foucauldian theories of power, knowledge, and discourse and,
especially, on Foucault's insistence that power is neither wholly monopolized
by the state nor exclusively repressive but is, instead, also productive, constitutive, and exercised through the discursive and diffuse construction of know-
ledges. In particular, the Foucauldian principle that discourse is, in and of itself,
regulatory is key to most moral regulation studies. Rather than focusing on
whether any particular reform "worked," moral regulation draws our attention
to the constitutive powers of reform goals themselves. For example, Mariana
Valverde argues that members of the English Canadian moral reform movement, of which the TLCW was a part, "did not intend simply to stamp out one
or more vices. They had a larger vision of how people ought to pass their time,
how they ought to act, speak, think and even feel. This vision ... I will here call
'positive' not because it was necessarily good, but to distinguish it from negativ-
ity, from mere prohibition."[23] This is not to suggest that proscription, or coercion,
had no role to play in this project. Rather, as Mary Louise Adams has put it,
"moral regulation ... encourages us to recognize that subjection is not only a
product of armies and prisons."[24] An analysis of discursive constitutions of
morally good subjectivities is what binds *moral* with *regulation,* resulting in an
approach through which regulation is itself done through the production of a
"positive vision" that is, in turn, articulated through a discourse of morality.

More recent moral regulation scholarship, however, has been critical of the
overemphasis on non-state forms of regulation and of the centrality of discourse

in these formulations. A central point of contention in these critiques is that narrowing the focus to discursive forms of regulation replicates the much lamented "expulsion of law" from Foucauldian theorizations and fails to address the historically specific ways that moral discourses were often enacted through coercive measures.[25] As Mary Odem has argued, histories of feminist reform have paid "far less attention [to] the extent to which women reformers also relied on legal coercion ... The distinction between 'environmental' and 'coercive' strategies, between preventive and institutional solutions, is not as clear as some historians have suggested."[26] Joan Sangster's research on the use of criminal law to regulate women and young girls similarly demonstrates that some populations that were targeted in moral regulation schemes "experienced a more *repressive* version of regulation."[27] That is, for some, subjection *is* a product of armies (or, at least, police) and prisons.

In an effort to resolve this debate, Alan Hunt helpfully suggests that "moral regulation has a dual character as both externally regulative and internally constitutive."[28] This more inclusive definition is a good characterization of MacGregor's own approach to the work of her Committee for an Equal Moral Standard. As she declared in her report, the "constructive and affirmative side of this work is particularly emphasized." The ideal goal of the committee was to encourage those practices and ways of life that were consistent with upstanding citizenship. In this particular example, MacGregor told her fellow council members that her committee was focusing its attention on encouraging "the reading and study of good books [and promoting] the publication of clean, wholesome stories" (this against the long identified problem of the movies, which the council members were sure were promoting "false standards and wrong attitudes toward life"), as well as healthy forms of entertainment and "the proper use of leisure."

On the surface this agenda appears to be benign, perhaps hopeful, and possibly quaintly traditionalist in its values. Certainly, the public focus of these campaigns was on "internal constitution," that is, on the making of the self into a morally upstanding social citizen, or what many moral regulation scholars have referred to as the making of ethical subjectivity.[29] But read in its entirety, and in the context of two decades' worth of work by the Committee for an Equal Moral Standard, this call to wholesome pastimes was less innocuous than it may, at first, appear. Although she admitted that the promotion of a good life was her priority, MacGregor spent the better part of her report detailing those activities that more closely resembled "the suppression of that which is evil."

Promoting good books meant the "suppression of pernicious literature"; encouraging the better types of entertainment involved the "supervision and control of vaudeville" and "severe restrictions on the use and sale of intoxicating liquor." Her committee had also met to discuss "drastic legislation" for assaults on children and to study the *Criminal Code*, and it had held conferences with the heads of the police department regarding "young men and women drifting into a life of crime," recommended the appointment of "more police women and a closer supervision of public parks, beaches and all places where ... offences occur," and established a subcommittee to investigate the treatment of women prisoners "and conditions obtaining in local corrective and punitive institutions." In sum, the promotion of good citizenship required serious and time-consuming attention to the more seamy side of urban life. "The suppression of that which is evil," including through the externally regulative mechanisms of criminal law, was an essential task in the achievement of an equal moral standard.

The Committee for an Equal Moral Standard was but one of a series of standing committees that constituted the collective work of the TLCW.[30] Between 1913 and 1934, the TLCW's committee structure did change somewhat in response to local demands and new points of interest for activist women, and the Executive Committee of the council always had the power to convene ad hoc committees as necessary. Overall, however, the division of labour within the council retained a structural consistency that ensured a continuity of attention to those public affairs deemed important to the council. Table 1, below, provides a list of the standing committees for the years 1914, 1924, and 1934. Together, these various committees constituted the work of the TLCW.

The work of the Committee for an Equal Moral Standard encompassed a far-ranging set of goals and targets, as MacGregor's speech indicates. But this mandate was neither exclusive nor fully defined and the committee often worked with other standing committees, including the Citizenship Committee, the Committee on Laws for the Protection of Women and Children (Committee on Laws), and the Committee on Objectionable Printed Matter (with which it sometimes merged). For example, in 1919 the Committee on Laws raised in the council meeting the matter of a court case dealing with a crime against a fourteen-year-old girl. The council, on motion, directed the Laws Committee to work with the Committee for an Equal Moral Standard on this issue and to "join in sending a deputation to confer with the judge in this connection."[31] This type of cross-over was both necessary and expedient, as Margaret Patterson

Table 1

Standing committees of the Toronto Local Council of Women, 1914-34

1914	1924	1934
Advertisement	–	–
Agriculture	Agriculture	–
–	(see Fine Arts)	Arts and Letters
–	–	Child Welfare
(see Objectionable Printed Matter)	(see EMS Committee)	Cinema, Printed Matter, Radio
Citizenship	Citizenship	Citizenship
Conservation	–	–
Custodial Care of Feeble-Minded	(see Mental Hygiene)	–
Education	Education	Education
Employment for Women	(see Professions and Employment for Women)	(see Professions and Employment for Women)
Equal Moral Standard and Prevention of Traffic in Women	Equal Moral Standard and Objectionable Printed Matter	Equal Moral Standard
Finance	Finance	Finance
–	Fine Arts	(see Arts and Letters)
–	Household Economics	Household Economics
–	Housing and Town Planning	Housing and Town Planning
Immigration	Immigration	Immigration
Laws for Women and Children	Laws for Women and Children	Laws for Women and Children
(see Custodial Care of Feeble-Minded)	Mental Hygiene	–
Objectionable Printed Matter	(see EMS)	(see Cinema, Printed Matter, Radio)
Peace and Arbitration	–	–
Pensions (Mothers')	Pensions (Soldiers and Sailors)	Pensions (Soldiers and Sailors)
Press	Press	Press
(see Employment for Women)	Professions and Employment for Women	Professions and Employment for Women
Public Health	Public Health	Public Health
–	Taxation	Taxation

Source: AO, F 805-1, container no. 1, Toronto Local Council of Women, Minutes, 1903-38.

(then convenor of the National Council of Women's Committee for an Equal Moral Standard)[32] noted: "The work of this Committee is so closely linked with other committees viz. 'Laws affecting Women and Children,' 'Care of the Feeble-Minded,' 'Public Health' and 'Immigration' that often after having investigated and collected necessary data, it is found necessary to hand the case over to one of the above committees to deal with it under its department."[33] There was, then, some fluidity within the general division of labour that was the council's committee structure. Nonetheless, although the work of moral regulation, most broadly defined, was a concern of all of these committees, what distinguished the Committee for an Equal Moral Standard from the other committees, such as those on laws or public health, was its primary focus on those reforms that targeted criminal justice institutions.

The committee was originally called the Committee for an Equal Moral Standard and the Suppression of the Traffic in Women. The "white slave" traffic had been brought to popular consciousness by the sensationalist "Maiden Tribute of Modern Babylon" series by William T. Stead in the *Pall Mall Gazette* in 1885.[34] Because of the multivalent discourses surrounding the sexual slavery of the Empire's (white) daughters by foreigners, immigrants, and dastardly men, the boundaries between prostitution and sexual slavery became so blurred that it was next to impossible for middle-class reformers to imagine that women ever entered the sex trade voluntarily. This panic over the traffic in girls and women re-emerged in the 1910s and became a priority for Canadian feminists after the International Council of Women held its 1909 Quinquennial Convention in Toronto. The National and the Toronto Local Councils of Women expressed embarrassment that Canada was not doing its part to stem the international traffic in women. Council women resolved to dedicate themselves to this cause, particularly through their standing committee on moral standards.[35] Indeed, it was because of fears engendered by the traffic in women narratives that the TLCW, through the Committee for an Equal Moral Standard, pressed for "the establishment of a Vice Commission ... to investigate the moral conditions in the City," a resolution that resulted in the Toronto Social Survey Commission.[36]

But, as heightened a panic as white slavery was, by 1915 the committee had dropped its lengthy title and became more commonly known as the Equal Moral Standard Committee (EMS Committee). And, importantly, as significant as the white slavery narratives were to the moral reformers' discursive constructions of urban vice and danger, they also brought these same reformers, feminists foremost among them, to one pressing conclusion: "Shoulder to shoulder, let us attack this evil, and attack it at a vital point – the law."[37] The 1913 amendments to the Canadian *Criminal Code* reflected this strategy: among the additions were such specific offences as abducting an immigrant girl to a brothel, exerting control over women for the purposes of prostitution, and concealment in a bawdy house.[38] Although historians have usefully deconstructed the white slavery panic as an exemplary instance of moral discourses and their ability to constitute a universe of meaning, less theoretical attention has been paid to the strategic choices through which these meanings were translated into action.[39] The same cannot be said in the TLCW's case. Subordinating the specific goal of stopping the slave traffic to the more broad aim of "the development of all that is finest" and "the suppression of that which is evil," the EMS Committee sustained an ongoing critique of the criminal justice system.

Not surprisingly, then, it was the TLCW's EMS Committee that took an active interest in the Toronto Women's Court. It was Margaret Patterson, as convenor of the Toronto EMS Committee, who gave the first formal report on the Women's Court to the TLCW one month into the court's operation. She urged her fellow council members to make sure that "each society take a day or month throughout the year and have a lady represent [sic] there, thus showing we were in earnest regarding our Women's Court."[40] In May 1913 Patterson, again in her capacity as convenor of the EMS Committee, was named to the deputation to City Hall to inquire about a female judge for the court.[41] In early 1916 a subcommittee of the EMS Committee, led by its new convenor, Mrs. J.N. Wood, organized a visiting roster for the Women's Court and produced a report on the court later that year.[42] In 1925 it was, again, the TLCW's EMS Committee that announced that the Toronto Women's Court was one of its great achievements.

But the Toronto Women's Court was not the only, or even the most time-consuming, aspect of the work of the EMS Committee. Rather, over the period under examination, this committee dedicated itself to a broad number of causes, all linked by their criminological content. Each stage of the criminal justice system was identified, politicized, and acted upon by the members of the TLCW, most especially by members of the EMS Committee. Examining these reforms in criminological sequence – that is, from policing through to court appearances, sentencing, and prisons – illuminates the broad scope of this reform agenda.

In the TLCW's effort to reframe the definitions of crime and punishment, a key stage was policing. Of course, police officers are the front line of the criminal justice system: it is they who patrol the streets and make the arrests that land women and men before the courts. Consistent with their sexual interpretation of crime, feminists did not trust that male police officers could deal adequately with women's moral-criminal dilemmas. To feminist reformers, "asking a policeman to stamp out vice was like asking a wolf to guard sheep."[43] The solution was to grant women the authority to patrol the streets, with the important difference being that women would act to protect women, not men. Buoyed by the politics of the moral standard, women police officers brought with them an entirely different philosophical approach to policing.[44] Their social work perspective was much more concerned with proactive measures that would prevent crime from taking place than with the masculinist crime control model that reacted to situations after the damage was done. Toronto newspaper headlines welcomed the appointment of policewomen to the Toronto Police Force in these very terms: "Police Women Use Dusters Instead of Batons"[45] and "Policewoman Is Prevention Ounce"[46] are telling indicators of the highly gendered understanding of these new public roles for women.

In her analysis of early policewomen in the United States, Janis Appier argues that these philosophical differences between policemen and policewomen resulted in a direct and concerted power struggle between two decidedly gendered approaches to law enforcement, one that women eventually lost.[47] Male police officers actively resented and resisted the presence of female police, not because they were women per se but because they threatened to undermine a particularly masculinist definition of authority. The reaction to the introduction of policewomen to the Toronto Police Force suggests a similar struggle over male prerogatives. After much lobbying by the TLCW,[48] the police commissioners agreed to the appointment of policewomen during the same 5 February 1913 meeting in which they approved the establishment of the Women's Court. The EMS Committee went straight to work to find the appropriate candidates. At their next meeting, on 19 February 1913, they interviewed, and recommended, Mary Minty, a matron at the Mercer Reformatory, for the job. Despite Police Chief Grasset's declaration that "recommendations from local women's organizations will not carry much weight with us. The Police Board ought to be independent of outside influence,"[49] Minty was hired and began work with Maria Levitt on 2 June 1913. Chief Grasset maintained his cautious outlook and stressed the gender-specific boundaries of policewomen's work on the force. One year later he wrote: "[A]s they acquire experience their services become increasingly useful. They have been employed in the supervision of dance halls, and their visitations there have a good moral effect."[50]

Despite the police chief's grudging acceptance of policewomen, the members of the TLCW were delighted with these appointments. The EMS Committee consistently monitored policewomen's work and their working conditions, and it lobbied for them to be allowed on night duty;[51] to engage more regularly in dance hall patrols;[52] and to be put on active duty in downtown districts, where young girls were most likely to be in need of protection.[53] The committee also supported policewomen in their "request for a more suitable monetary recognition of their excellent service to our city."[54] Most importantly, committee members argued that women should be appointed to police forces across the country:

> Whereas in the present practice of law, women offenders are arrested by men, tried by men, before men, and
>
> Whereas in many cases disastrous results follow, which easily might have been averted by contact with women officials, and
>
> Whereas the Standing Committee of the National Council of Women on Equal Moral Standard [sic] is of the opinion that the ideals for which it stands would be more quickly attained if ... Policewomen [were appointed],
>
> Therefore, this Provincial Committee recommends that the National Council of Women advocate the establishment of this valuable moral agency in every community where they do not already exist.[55]

Clearly, if men perceived the intentions of the "moral agency" of policewomen as a slight to their capacities as law enforcers and to their crime control models, it was because they were meant to. Women police officers were necessary because men could not be trusted to be just in their handling of women's moral-sexual urban problems. The causes of women's crime were perceived as being sufficiently distinct from men's to warrant a feminized response.

Toronto feminists' concerns with female crime carried over into the courts, and the EMS Committee closely monitored women's court appearances. It was this committee that attempted to intervene in the trial of Carrie Davies, a domestic servant who shot her employer in 1915,[56] as it had done on behalf of Angelina Napolitano, who was convicted of killing her husband and sentenced to hang in 1911.[57] This monitoring of the courts also led them to argue for women's right to serve on juries. Although Ontario women would not win this right until the 1950s, the Provincial Council of Women argued as early as 1920 that "in view of the fact that women are now automatically qualified to act on juries, and that their presence there would be of great advantage in cases relating to young girls and women, the National Council of Women urge upon all Local Councils to have women appointed as jurymen in their respective locations."[58] Toronto feminists were also highly vigilant, and vocally critical, of newspaper coverage of crime stories, especially those involving young people and women. They persistently argued against the "unnecessary detail with which certain cases were reported in some of our daily papers" and moved "that the Local Council of Women ask the managing editors of the newspapers to use their influence for the purification of the daily press," especially as this pertained to court cases.[59] Using arguments markedly similar to those presented to justify the specific reform of a separate court for women, feminists continued to conceptualize the public humiliation that accompanied an open and reported trial as damning for women defendants and as a block to their path to redemption. Protecting women from unwanted exposure was a central feature of feminized justice.

Equally important was the range and purpose of sentencing on conviction in the police courts. The TLCW was particularly condemnatory of the fining system, arguing that it did nothing to suppress the prostitution trade. In 1916 Margaret Patterson, speaking for the EMS Committee, read the following report to fellow members of the council:

> [T]he system in vogue in the Toronto Police Court of imposing fines or short terms of imprisonment in cases of persons charged as keepers, inmates or frequenters of houses of prostitution is objectionable in that:
>
> 1 It is a modified form of license of the social evil;
> 2 It makes the public treasure a sharer in the profits of the business of prostitution;
> 3 It accomplishes nothing in the direction of the prevention of the spread of venereal diseases;
> 4 It does little or nothing for the reclamation of the offenders;
> 5 It does not carry out the spirit of the law but on the contrary tends to demoralize public sentiment and to bring the law into contempt.[60]

Following this report the TLCW unanimously carried a motion urging the attorney general "to instruct the Police Magistrates of Toronto to enforce the law with a view to the suppression of houses of prostitution." Importantly, resolutions such as this make it clear that feminists were not opposed to using the criminal law to solve social problems: to the contrary, they argued that better criminal enforcement would lead to social change.

To this end, feminists also scrutinized the very purpose of sentencing and challenged the practices of the police courts, which they understood to be imposing punishments without a view to ending crime. This politicization of sentencing led to a broad critique of masculinist justice as well as a specific, and not well-veiled, critique of the Women's Court's presiding magistrate, Colonel Denison. Denison was (in)famous for his speedy justice: one wonderstruck commentator noted that "in his daily duty, it is not uncommon for the Colonel to smooth out two hundred and fifty cases in one hundred and eighty minutes."[61] To the feminists this was nothing to brag about: "The police records show that the same people come before the court again and again, and each time more confirmed criminals than before ... The sentence is given as a punishment, not as a means of reform ... The trouble with our present system is that we think only of the offence, and not of the offender. We deal with cases, forgetting that each case represents a human being with an immortal soul. These cases cannot be diagnosed and prescribed for at the rate of thirty per hour."[62] Feminized justice, in this regard, involved a wholesale philosophical change to extant police court processes. It was not simply specific magisterial decisions about sentencing options that needed fixing. The very foundation of the court required examination and fundamental change.

A key indicator of the lack of justice in sentencing was the short sentence (less than six months).[63] The members of the TLCW argued against the short sentence as "a system of compulsory education in crime."[64] In its place they argued for the indeterminate sentence, which allowed magistrates to impose sentences of up to two years less a day on any summary conviction. The time was to be remitted on the basis of good behaviour of the inmate, thus securing a central role for rehabilitation in sentencing.[65] In combination, the fining system, the short sentence, and the evident lack of interest in the redemption of the offender added up to a system of profound injustice. The lack of a relationship between the crime, the criminal, and the punishment was, for the feminists, an absurdity that necessitated their intervention: "For instance, a girl charged with theft of the most petty kind was sentenced to a term of imprisonment, as the law did not allow the crime of theft to be punished by fine. On the other hand, the most horrible cases of immorality were charged under the term vagrancy and punished by a small fine."[66] This "iniquity" proved the criminal justice system to be unjust: it neither engaged in "corrective measures" nor "deterred immorality."[67] In other words, the courts provided further evidence of the juxtaposition of criminal law and justice: feminist intervention was aimed at a reconciliation.

In the interest of combatting immorality in the name of justice, the TLCW also took an active interest in women after sentencing, particularly in the forms and the conditions of their imprisonment.[68] Indeed, although they were the last stage in the criminalization process, jails and reformatories were the site of some of the earliest campaigns, and first successes, of the organized women's movement and its long-held practices of woman-centred criminological reform.[69] The reform of local jails was an important concern for the TLCW. In October 1914 it drew up a twelve-point recommendation for jail reform that was based on "results of reports brought to us in our work." The concerns that were identified ranged from the lack of clothing and undergarments supplied to prisoners to the need for a female physician on site and the lack of any policy regarding "diseased women" cooking meals and washing dishes.[70] The TLCW was partially successful in these agitations: a separate municipal jail farm for women was established in Concord, Ontario, in 1914. At the provincial level, the Mercer Reformatory had opened its doors in 1880 as "an institutional setting [in which a] mother's love coupled with her power could become the ... model of reform and control."[71] Of all the criminological reforms undertaken by early feminists, the reformatory movement has received the most scholarly attention, and the debates about the sentencing of women to women-run institutions are discussed in more detail in the next chapter. Here, it will suffice to place this movement in context: middle-class women's prison reform, like their other sex-specific interventions into each stage of the criminal justice system,[72] was consistent with the strategic application of a politics for an equal moral standard, inasmuch as prisons were, at one and the same time, a site for women's enactment of criminal justice and a critique of malestream applications of legal authority.

Taken together, these reforms illustrate how the politics of the moral standard led women reformers to a coherent idea of feminized justice. In this sense the politics of the equal moral standard was both a philosophy and a strategy. The initial feminist focus on prostitution – itself a manifestation of, and evidence for, the politics of the moral standard – led white, middle-class women reformers to a broader world view that linked together a variety of causes and holistically connected a number of campaigns. Feminists saw the criminal legal system as an interconnected entity that required reform at each and every stage. Because of this world view, women reformers lobbied for amendments to the *Criminal Code* to make men more legally culpable for a range of prostitution-related offences as well as for women police officers and jurists, feminized judicial venues, therapeutic sentencing practices, a social work approach to law enforcement and administration, and sex-specific jails and reformatories. All of these political interventions shared common aims: to protect women from sexual exploitation, to eliminate the male bias and self-protection embedded in law enforcement, and to create for women in conflict with the law an environment shaped by women's understandings of sexual injustice. In short, the central and cohering goal of these various campaigns and struggles was to end the practical effects of the double moral standard.

The Limits of Feminized Justice

"I will ask you to come with me to our 'Women's Court' in Toronto." With this invitation, Margaret Patterson took her 1914 Social Service Congress audience on an "imaginary visit" to "an average morning in court."[73] There, Patterson offered a series of paradigmatic problems that summed up the campaign for feminized justice. Her narrative introduced the audience to a female keeper of a house of ill fame, three men charged with frequenting, and three women charged with being inmates. "The keeper of the house of ill fame is tried first. The men who are there give evidence that they have paid her money for immoral purposes. She is convicted and probably sentenced to $30.00 or 60 days." Patterson made it clear to her audience that a conviction did not necessarily penalize the keeper: "Often the fine is paid, but sometimes they 'take time' ... as it was always easy to get a hold of some fresh, healthy girls who were in jail for shoplifting and other such charges. This is a favorite way of procuring girls." Patterson did not comment on which of these equally bad outcomes followed on this average day, leaving her audience to ponder this no-win situation.

She next turned her attention to the "girls" charged with being inmates of the bawdy house. "Again, the men give evidence that for a monetary consideration they have been allowed to dishonor the girls. The girls are convicted and sentenced to $20.00 or 30 days." Once again, Patterson invoked the multiple outcomes of this type of sentencing. Two of the women could not pay their fines, and so they went to jail, where the conditions were "unspeakable" and the conversation "vile" and where they were "indiscriminately herded with other women of all ages and guilty of all manner of offenses." Meanwhile, the third woman "has the money and pays her fine [and] goes out to continue her life of shame until again hauled before the court." So common was this, and so ineffective the legal system, that "a few mornings ago a comparatively young looking woman was called to answer a call of this kind. The lady beside me asked one of the court officials if it were her first offence and was told 'not the first, the thirty-first.'" On this ominous note, Patterson concluded her guided tour of the Women's Court.

As I have argued in this chapter, a strong sense of injustice, perpetuated at nearly every turn, underwrites Patterson's imaginary visit. Men who have committed moral trespasses by frequenting a house of ill fame are allowed to go free at women's expense, a point that is made not once, but twice, as the men give evidence against the keeper and then again against the women inmates. Women of highly suspect moral character treat their legal experiences lightly. The keeper-procuress received money for "immoral purposes," and the law could do little to stop her. She might breezily pay the fine, or she might take time to procure "fresh girls" to her undeterred business. Those women already in her employ are similarly unaffected by their day in court. One pays a fine and is freed to continue to endanger herself and the public. The women who go to jail personify another unresolved political problem. The jail environment provides "nothing to uplift" them, while their very presence is a threat to the "innocent lambs" jailed for shoplifting and other negligible, if regrettable, transgressions. Margaret Patterson's imaginary visit to the Women's Court makes clear that each stage of the criminal justice system – from definitions of crime to policing mechanisms, from trial procedures to sentencing options – was a political issue that evidenced problematic gender relations. In every one of these moralized problems, the law appears as the weak link in the struggle for good. Achieving a more moral society meant reforming the mechanisms of criminal justice.

Moreover, there is truth in Patterson's narrative. There were women in the courts who were there "not for the first, but the thirty-first time." As I will discuss in detail in the next chapters, there were women who kept houses of ill fame who did find themselves in the Women's Court, where they often paid the fine, and there were male frequenters of their establishments who were typically released after giving evidence against the house and the women who worked in it. These women were regulars in the court, and they frequently could not pay their fines. The local jail was roundly condemned as being unspeakably vile and for its failure, which was largely architectural, to properly separate and classify prisoners.[74] The legal system evidenced the double standard time and again. And, as this chapter has shown, the TLCW was indefatigable in pointing out these deficiencies, and it was largely successful in effecting a variety of piecemeal changes to legal institutions, operations, and infrastructure to diminish the impact of these manifest problems.

At the same time, Patterson's imaginary visit and, in particular, her use of a typically middle-class urban voyeur technique as entrée to the Women's Court reveals the limits of feminized justice. The tradition of urban tourism deployed by Patterson was characterized by middle-class entry into and commentary on those sites "of vice and poverty respectable people would never otherwise visit."[75] The travelogues that were produced as a result of these urban descents had the appearance of detached scientific observation, through which middle-class observers "mimicked anthropologists reporting discoveries of exotic tribes."[76] For her part, Margaret Patterson felt it necessary to defend herself against "accus[ations] of going [to the police courts] from 'morbid curiosity.'"[77] To the contrary, she explained, she was "collecting information [that] gave us some very good material in support of reforms we were asking for."[78] But despite the veneer of pedagogical and scientific value, these urban voyeur missions were organized through highly subjective narrative conventions tailored to preconceived notions held by the middle class. In her examination of this phenomenon in mid-nineteenth-century New York, Christine Stansell argues that the descent of middle-class women into the neighbourhoods of the labouring class may have made reformers more aware of poor women and their travails, but they did not necessarily lead them to "thoughtful responses." Rather, these encounters were filtered through "certain conventions of the imagination."[79] Stansell argues further that the specific ideas held by the middle classes about women's criminality were also filtered by what they did *not* see. A large portion of poor women's lives remained invisible to middle-class reformers interested in women's court experiences and criminality precisely because only those acts or behaviours that drew women into direct engagement with the law were available in open court for public view. Women's acts of kindness, solidarity, and support to one another and mutual and complex exchanges in their small neighbourhoods went unnoticed by middle-class observers, while acts of public pugnacity and "immorality" were repeatedly on view in the court system.[80] Middle-class women reformers thus framed their views of women's criminality in the context of these limitations and imaginative conventions.

Margaret Patterson's imaginary visit to the Toronto Women's Court is fuelled by these filters. Convinced that women's criminality was a "problem" of sexual-moral proportions, Patterson's guided visit to the Women's Court draws public attention to particular issues, but not to others. The entire thrust of her narrative casts "bad" women, in partnership with a legal system that did nothing "but harden and corrupt" and which allowed men to go free while creating a vicious cycle for women's immorality, as the targets of action. This, of course, was entirely consistent with the politics of the equal moral standard.

But as much as Patterson's guided tour indicates the significance of criminal law reform to the maternal moral reformers, it does not tell us much about the actual practices in the court or about the women who were paraded before a magistrate to answer to charges about their public, and often troublesome, conduct. Indeed, for all that the feminists politicized the criminal terrain as a moralized site that warranted their intervention, their insistence on the *sexual* subordination of women precluded an analysis of any other cause of female crime. Moreover, although the politics of the unequal moral standard stressed male sexual misconduct (and its toleration by officialdom) as the cause of women's subordination, it did not, in itself, offer a politics of female sexuality. To the contrary, an autonomous female sexuality was denied and replaced with an image of women enslaved by male sexual excess. In other words, a conceptualization of women as sexually passive victims was a component part of the re-imagining of the new moral ethos. As Patterson's imaginary visit to the court makes clear, the punishment of "bad" (sexual) women was as important as the promotion of "good" (sexually innocent) womanhood. Consequently, although feminist reformers critiqued male sexual licence and attempted to set a single standard in law to hold men accountable for their behaviour, their emphasis on women's victimization, and the attendant suspicion with which they held women's sexual agency, led to the creation of institutions, such as the Women's Court, that over-regulated *women's* sexual-moral conduct.[81] As a result, the TLCW's positive assessment of the Toronto Women's Court as a great achievement was not likely shared by the criminalized women who appeared there: as the site of their own criminal sanctions, the court was, often, an unwelcome intervention into their personal lives. In itself this, too, was largely a product of the politics of the equal moral standard.

Conclusion

Understanding the links between morality, sexuality, and crime is key to appreciating the larger picture of a more moral society that the TLCW envisioned. For Patterson and the organized women's movement, the problems that were visible in the police court system combined to form a concrete reform platform that reveals the extent to which the TLCW politicized the terrain of the criminal as an articulation of the terrain of the moral. That the Toronto Women's

Court would emerge as a great achievement within this platform is, in large measure, because the court was a central point from which the feminists' other projects came into view. As Patterson's imaginary visit indicates, and as the work of the EMS Committee confirms, the TLCW did not believe that the problem of female crime or its solution began and ended at the Women's Court. Rather, just as the court was the central setting for Patterson's narrative, so too was it imagined as the central site from which to radiate a variety of solutions to the problem of women, crime, and injustice.

The resultant politics of feminized justice simultaneously offered a searing critique of an androcentric criminal justice system and was implemented through a forum that issued, authorized, and legitimated moral pronouncements about "good" and "bad" women (and men). In this way, the Women's Court fits neatly with observations that emerge from moral regulation scholarship. Moral reclamation may have been the positive vision embodied in the Women's Court, but criminal sanctions were the chief tool used to achieve it. Rereading the term *moral* not only as a discursive device but also as a reference to coercion captures the fullness of the court as it framed a significant component of the TLCW's overall agenda for reform. A survey of the specific work of the EMS Committee offers further insights into the conceptual and instrumental links between morality, sexual equality, and criminality in maternal feminist and urban reform history. To those active in feminist moral reform, the goal of producing good citizens necessarily meant keeping an eye on, organizing action around, and effecting changes to the various workings of the criminal justice system. Law, and particularly criminal law, was the site by which feminists judged the existing moral state of affairs. To this end they engaged in a comprehensive criminological program of reform to exorcize the criminal terrain of its masculinist demons. Although they were instrumentalist in their approach to the state and the law, members of the TLCW were, nonetheless, adamant that these formal structures should mirror their own sense of justice.

Through the framework of feminized justice, the Toronto Women's Court can be understood not simply as an extra court in the network of police courts in Toronto but, rather, as a direct feminist intervention in the moral conditions affecting women in the city and as a living experiment in feminist ideals. Being able to put the law to use to achieve a moral standard meant balancing "the development of all that is finest" with "the suppression of that which is evil." The Toronto Women's Court was celebrated because, as a criminal court, it could achieve both. At the same time, however, the coercive morality that the court encapsulated was its chief weakness. Insistent that women's crimes could be translated into a moral universe, feminists initiated top-down criminological reforms that filtered out a great deal of women's crime and translated women's criminality into a language they could understand and act upon. Moreover, the moral tones through which coercive regulation was justified were often the very problem that criminalized women faced when they confronted the mechanisms of justice. To understand these dimensions of the Women's Court, it is necessary to look beyond middle-class women's presentation of the problem of female criminality. The next chapter charts the crimes that led mostly poor and marginalized women into the Women's Court and traces how feminized justice was put into practice through the "suppression of all that is evil."

"The badness of their badness when they're bad"
Women, Crime, and the Court

Oh, the gladness of their gladness when they're glad!
Oh, the sadness of their sadness when they're sad!
But the gladness of their gladness and the sadness of their sadness
Are nothing to the badness of their badness when they're bad.
— Harry S. Wodson, "Woman, Lovely Woman"[1]

Despite poetic homages and judicial venues established in their name, "bad" women have been few and far between in Canadian history. "The outstanding feature about female crime in Canada," observes D. Owen Carrigan, "is not that there was so much of it but that there was actually very little."[2] This was particularly the case when the Toronto Women's Court opened in 1913, during a period when women's crime rates were dropping, as they had been doing since the mid-nineteenth century. In 1840 women accounted for 27 percent of all arrests in Toronto;[3] by 1913 they represented only 6 percent of arrests made by Toronto police.[4] Declines in the incidence of official female (and male) crime were consistent across the board.[5] In the category of violent crime, women's rates dropped from 524 arrests in 1872 to 26 arrests in 1924. In 1862, 1,416 women were arrested for property crimes, while in 1924 a mere 167 women were so arrested. Even public order offences fell considerably, although "arrest rates for both sexes are heavily influenced by the preponderance of arrests for drunk and disorderly conduct."[6] In 1862, 6,964 women were arrested for public order offences; by 1935, that number had dropped sharply to 161. A variety of explanations are offered for these steep declines in official criminality. The growth of Toronto meant the city was more integrated and offered more networks for its inhabitants to lean upon (or hide behind). In addition, the emergence of the social purity movement, the development of alternative recreations, the increasing efficiency and effectiveness of the urban police force, and the expansion of the economy, especially of employment opportunities for women, are all offered as explanations for the drop in women's arrest rates.[7]

Low crime rates among women are a defining characteristic of the period under study. More than the repressive effect of the feminists' politicization of sexuality, this is a chief contradiction of the "great achievement" of the Toronto Women's Court. Moreover, despite middle-class women's ideas about the substance and causes of female criminality, women charged with keeping or being inmates of a house of ill fame were not the majority of female defendants in court. Looking at the Toronto Women's Court through the lens of the local jail registers, which recorded demographic and committal information about each woman held overnight because of an arrest by the police, a very different picture of criminal women emerges. Numerically speaking, drunkenness was, far and away, the single most frequent charge that led women (and men) to an appearance in court. Despite Patterson's view that it was the legal system's failure to deal properly with "the social evil" that led to the possibility of some thirty-one appearances by one individual, drunkenness accounted for the lion's share of recidivism.

The next most frequent charge laid against women that resulted in an appearance in court was the extremely vague and flexible charge of vagrancy. Although the vagrancy section, especially the female-specific streetwalking subsection, of the *Criminal Code* was one of the only prostitution offences available to law enforcement agencies from the 1910s to the 1930s, it would be a mistake to confuse all vagrancy charges with prostitution or to read them as evidence of a flourishing sex trade. From time to time, a warrant of committment from the Toronto Women's Court would specify the nature of the vagrancy charge (for example, "unlawfully was a vagrant, by soliciting men on the streets"), but the simple phrase "unlawfully was a vagrant" or the only slightly more prosaic "having no visible means of support, failed to give a satisfactory answer when called upon to do so by a police officer and was thereby a vagrant" was the norm.[8] Moreover, this was often all there was to the offence. For example, on an evening in June 1915, Clara M., newly arrived to Toronto from Galt, was asked to explain herself to a police officer who saw her standing outside the YWCA building on Elm Street. She had neither a job nor lodgings, but sure she had done nothing wrong, she refused to answer the policeman. She was charged with vagrancy, and ultimately spent fourteen months at the Mercer Reformatory. Ironically, the convicting magistrate justified the sentence by saying that Clara had no friends or relatives in Toronto and that her best interests would be served by sending her somewhere "where she will have to work." Clara's protests that she had been looking for lodgings and work when interrupted by the inquisitive police officer fell on deaf ears.[9] In addition to the wide-ranging powers of arrest under the *Criminal Code* vagrancy provisions, police could also arrest women under the City of Toronto's 1904 "public morals" bylaw, which made drunkenness and vagrancy (whose definition was even more vague than in the *Criminal Code*) municipal offences.[10] Together, drunkenness and vagrancy accounted for 42 percent (2,006) of the 4,781 collected charges against women heard in the Women's Court (see Table 2).

Table 2

Most common charges against women in local detention, Toronto, 1913-34

Year	Total charges	Drunk	Vagrancy	Theft	Keeping[a]	Inmate[b]	BOTA/ BCLA[c]	Top 5 charges as % of total[d]
1913	951	361	228	73	81	84	n/a	87
1916	568	105	107	87	113	86	(0)	88
1919	336	20	130	57	18	28	(10)	75
1922	615	110	93	76	69	92	(49)	72
1925	845	129	131	(81)	141	129	119	77
1928	622	162	91	98	49	(30)	112	82
1931	458	92	112	47	48	(23)	61	79
1934	386	107	28	55	35	(19)	49	71
TOTAL	4,781	1,086	920	574	554	491	400	76

a "Keeping" combines keeping a house of ill fame, bawdy house, or disorderly house.

b The specific charges relating to those discovered in an illegal house changed over the years, so that "inmates" and "frequenters" became "found-ins." However, jail clerks used all three terms coterminously over the period of study. The houses have been combined, as above.

c "BOTA" is breach of *Ontario Temperance Act*; "BLCA" is breach of *Liquor Control Act*, enacted in 1927.

d This is based on a count of the five top charges in each year; the average does not include the offence listed in brackets, which falls outside of the top five.

Source: AO, RG 20-100-1, series A, Toronto (York) Jail, Jail Registers.

Four other charges made up the remainder of the majority (76 percent, including drunk and vagrancy) of criminal charges against women that led to at least one night in the city cells. Overall, theft was the third most common offence; keeping a bawdy house, house of ill fame, or disorderly house was the fourth most common offence; and frequenting, being an inmate of, or being found in a bawdy house was the fifth most common offence. The order in which these ranked in relation to one another varied by year (see Table 2). After the passage of the *Ontario Temperance Act* in 1916 and its replacement, the *Liquor Control Act,* in 1927, liquor violations displaced theft (in 1925) and frequenting (in 1928, 1931, and 1934) from the top five most common reasons for an appearance in court. With the exception of theft charges, these main offence categories were punishable by a fine, in default of which a prison term was mandated. The majority of convicted women were unable to pay these fines. Because a great number of women's prison terms were produced by poverty, and because so many of women's offences were rendered invisible in Patterson's "average day" in court, it is necessary to look beyond middle-class presentations of the "problem" of women's criminality for information about the actual practices of the Women's Court. This chapter offers an overview of some of these practices, while Chapters 4 and 5 focus on specific crimes and their varied implications for women appearing in a court ostensibly established in their names.

Overview of Women's Crime

Those few women who were arrested and detained at least one night in local custody were largely charged with public order, or morals, offences that "criminalized social status as much or more than specific behaviours."[11] Table 2 shows the charges that drew women into the Women's Court and the city cells in each of the eight years surveyed. As is evident from this table, the vast majority of women's offences were concentrated in six charges that, with the exception of theft, were victimless morals crimes. Fifty-four percent of all women held in local custody were Canadian born, and 80 percent of the women were born in Canada (54 percent), England (12 percent), Scotland (7 percent), or Ireland (7 percent). Roman Catholics were disproportionately represented. Constituting 13 percent of the Toronto population in the 1910s and 1920s,[12] Roman Catholics represented 33 percent of all women detained and 40 percent of all repeat offenders.[13]

Determining criminal women's occupations based on the information contained in the jail registers is an inherently difficult task. It is, of course, impossible to tell if women were gainfully employed in the field they listed at the time of arrest. Furthermore, many of the women probably listed false occupations to hide sex-trade work, whether as a full-time job or as a means by which they supplemented otherwise meagre incomes. In 1913, 94 women, entered in the jail register on 171 occasions, listed prostitution as their trade (although only 34, or 20 percent, of these arrests were for vagrancy). Eighty-six of these 94 women were repeat offenders, but in other appearances they were also entered as laundresses, charwomen, domestics, and housekeepers. It is difficult to ascertain whether this means they moved in and out of the sex trade as necessary, whether the jail clerk entered the trade he thought appropriate, or whether the women were attempting to be strategic about their own self-representations to the court and jail officials. After 1913, although many of the same women continued to spend at least one night in the city cells, prostitution is no longer listed under "occupation." Nick Larsen suggests that World War I ushered in a new phase in attitudes toward prostitution, one in which growing hostility toward camp followers and a tendency to shift blame for venereal disease among soldiers to women meant that prostitution came under increasing social opprobrium.[14] This may explain the abrupt disappearance of prostitution as an entry in the jail ledgers.[15] If so, this might suggest that the women listed their own trade when asked by a jail clerk and, in a changing public climate, strategically chose to downplay their participation in an increasingly derided occupation. However, in his study of the Mercer Reformatory in its first two decades of operation (1880-1900), Peter Oliver also detects a pattern in which fewer women were officially listed as prostitutes over this time period, from 29.7 percent of incarcerated women in the 1881-85 period to a mere 5.6 percent of incarcerated women in the 1896-1900 period. He speculates that this may be most "logically attributable to a labelling change as authorities became increasingly reluctant to dignify prostitution by calling it an occupation."[16] Following Oliver's observations, what we see in and after 1913 may well be the close of a longer pattern of officials distancing themselves from a formal recognition of prostitution as a profession.

Notwithstanding some of these difficulties, what is most apparent from the listed occupations of jailed women is their general economic vulnerability. The largest occupational category listed was housewife (37 percent). This was followed closely by domestic (25 percent). If other, specific, domestic occupations are included (such as cook, general servant, housemaid, laundress, and so on), then the proportion of women engaged in low-waged, domestic employment rises to 35 percent. These two types of domestic labour – unwaged and waged – far outstrip any other occupation listed. The next single largest occupational category was waitress, but waitresses accounted only for 6 percent of all women entered. Factories employed 3 percent of detained women, and a variety of professions (such as nurse, stenographer, clerk, bookkeeper, and "saleslady") accounted for another 4 percent. The 171 prostitution entries for 1913 alone account for 3.5 percent of all occupational designations. Women held in custody prior to, or because of, a trial in the Women's Court were not, in the main, women with much economic autonomy.

The jail registers had a column for "color," but this was never filled in. Mercer records sometimes included a notation on the race of an inmate, if she was not white, but they did not always do so. The lack of regularized notations about race, however, does not mean that race was not a salient factor in women's experiences with the criminal justice system. The disproportionate number of Catholics detained in local custody testifies to the structure of opportunities in Orange Toronto. Furthermore, if newspaper accounts are anything to go by, race was always a salient factor. Press reports about non-white, especially black, women made clear links between their race and their charge. When Pearl B. was arrested for vagrancy after allegedly picking a pocket on College Street, the *Telegram* reporter went overboard to describe the case against this black woman: "Dark was the night on College street. Dark were the faces of two colored ladies who accosted V.M. Roberts ... Dark were the thoughts of the scandalized man when, a few minutes later, he missed $15 out of his pocket."[17] Although seemingly few in number, women who were not white were nearly always identified by race by the police court reporters: black women were described variously as "dusky maidens," "colored ladies," "mulattos," and "negresses," while First Nations women were routinely identified as "Indians." Through this form of identification, it was always implied, but never directly said, that some essential relation existed between their race and their criminality. Because I examined the jail registers in three-year intervals, it is not possible to determine patterns of racialized justice.[18] However, as will be discussed in the chapters to follow, specific cases indicate that whiteness was a core element in the definition of respectable womanhood, and it played an important role in both legal and extra-legal determinations of women's criminal justice outcomes.

If arrest rates for women in general were low, conviction rates were even lower. These low rates are even more dramatic given that those in the city jails had either been convicted or were most likely to be convicted. Only 51 percent

Table 3

Sentences for convicted women in local detention, Toronto, 1913-34

Year	Cases	Convictions[a]		Sent to		
---	---	---	---	Local jail	Concord	Mercer
1913	951	480	(50%)	264	n/a[b]	95
1916	568	323	(57%)	115	93	22
1919	336	329	(98%)	3	97	11
1922	615	248	(40%)	14	158	22
1925	845	380	(45%)	28	194	51
1928	622	333	(54%)	48	172	25
1931	458	189	(41%)	33	85	18
1934	386	159	(41%)	59	52	16
TOTAL	4,781	2,441	(51%)	564	851	260

a   Includes those who paid a fine, as well as those jailed.
b   The Concord Municipal Jail Farm for Women did not open until 1914.
Source: AO, RG 20-100-1, series A, Toronto (York) Jail, Jail Registers.

of all charges leading to an appearance in the city jail resulted in conviction, and in 1922, 1931, and 1934 closer to 40 percent of charges resulted in conviction (see Table 3). Moreover, of those convicted to a prison term, the vast majority served short sentences, of five months or less, either in the local jail or, after 1914, the Concord Industrial Farm for Women. Only 12 percent of all convicted women (and only 5 percent of all women) surveyed were committed to the Mercer Reformatory; 21 percent of convicted women were able to pay their fines, either in court or from jail; and the remaining 67 percent served short sentences in default of payment at the local jail or, more commonly, the Concord.

Most histories of women's crime in early twentieth-century Ontario, as well as middle-class women's theories of criminality, have focused on the provincial Mercer Reformatory.[19] There are good reasons for this: the Mercer kept excellent case files that offer a variety of subjective and quantitative information about women, crime, and the methods employed by early women reformers to deal with them in a uniquely feminist way. However, as the aggregate figures from the jail registers make clear, a reformatory sentence was anomalous in the overall treatment of women's crime. Court decisions about what kind of criminality and which type of female offender would most likely benefit from a reformatory sentence predetermined the population at the Mercer and, thus, has overdetermined the criminological history of the relationships between women offenders, female criminalization, and feminist penal institutions.

The increasingly narrow range of women incarcerated at the Mercer is specific to the time period under examination. When the Mercer first opened, in 1880, it was meant to be a model reformatory that would offer a uniquely female correctional treatment to what was seen as a uniquely female crime problem. It became immediately clear, however, that the aims and the actual practices of the reformatory were at odds. In large part the early failures of the Mercer were attributable to the difficulties of attempting to apply maternalist philosophies to a coercive institution.[20] But the Mercer also faced difficulties from without. Magistrates routinely sentenced women charged with drunkenness and bawdy house offences to the Mercer for short terms. As late as 1913, Emma O'Sullivan, superintendent of the reformatory, complained in her annual report that these kinds of offenders, and these kinds of sentences, undermined the entire point of a female reformatory:

> Eighty-one inmates with sentences of six months, and twenty inmates with sentences of less than six months from the total number one hundred and thirty received, leave but thirty-one inmates with terms sufficiently long to enable us to do something towards fitting them to become respectable citizens. Since this institution was opened in August, 1880, the absurdity of such short sentences here has been pointed out – the positive failure is reflected in the statistics that show repeaters serving their seventeenth term in the Reformatory, in addition to the numberless short terms of a few days served in gaols and the terms avoided by payment of a fine.[21]

The following year, O'Sullivan would get the institutional change she was seeking, in part through the introduction of indeterminate sentencing (see Chapter 2), but also through the establishment of the Concord Industrial Farm for Women.

The idea of a municipal jail farm for women was originally conceived as an addition to the correctional infrastructure, specifically designated for first-time offenders. The Toronto Local Council of Women (TLCW), looking south to the United States for inspiration, called informally upon the provincial secretary, William J. Hanna, in March 1913 to request a jail farm. The TLCW's convenor of the Agricultural Committee, Mrs. Hamilton, "acting not so much officially as in her personal capacity," explained to Hanna the success of a female farm in Darling, Delaware County, Pennsylvania, the good work it offered to "college women and their success in reforming erring girls," the benefits to women's overall health of productive outdoor farming work "adjusted to women's strength," and "ask[ed] that girls and women in the jails, the Mercer Reformatory, the Alexandra Girls' School, etc., be emancipated from the cooped-up surroundings, and as their knowledge of men's society has been the worst, that they be transferred to women's society of the best."[22] At one point the government considered using a women's jail farm, located outside of Toronto, as a holding facility "for women who have been arrested for the first time who have not been tried and found guilty. It is not fair to herd them together at the jail with hardened criminals."[23] This, obviously, was not feasible, if only because of the costs of transporting women from the downtown city police stations to beyond the city limits and back again for trial. When the Concord opened in September 1914, it became the alternative to the city jail.[24] That is, those women who, in 1913, would have served their short sentences at the local common jail were now sent to the women's farm.

As Wendy Reumper found in her comparison of women detained in local custody in northern Ontario and those sentenced to the Mercer, there was no definitive relationship between the offence and the sentence. However, "women who were younger, who were given indefinite sentences, or who worked as domestics" were those most likely to be sentenced to the reformatory.[25] Loraine Gordon's statistical surveys of the Concord and the Mercer reveal a similar pattern, especially with respect to age. She calculates that the Concord's population of eighteen to thirty-five-year-olds was roughly 60 percent of that of the Mercer: this key age group ranged from a high of 62 percent (1920-25) to a low of 35 percent (1930-35) of the Concord's inmate population. By contrast, eighteen- to thirty-five-year-olds constituted 84 percent of the Mercer's population in the years 1918-33.[26] Kelly Pineault's thorough examination of the records of the Concord draws even more precise conclusions about who was incarcerated there. She found that the majority of sentences were under five months and that most of the inmates were older, repeat, and predominantly Catholic offenders. Slightly less than half (47 percent) of the inmates at the Concord were Canadian-born. This contrasts with the Mercer population, which Gordon calculates as 75 percent Canadian-born.[27]

My own records show that more than three times as many women were sent from the city cells to the Concord as to the Mercer. They confirm Pineault's finding that just under 40 percent of all women sentenced to the Concord were recidivists. In contrast, none of the women sentenced to the Mercer in 1919 and less than 5 percent of those sentenced in 1922, 1928, and 1934 were repeat offenders. It seems clear that, for officials, the Concord became the repository for women deemed to be unreformable. Consequently, the existence of the Concord made it possible for the Mercer to begin to approximate its ideal as a model female reformatory.[28] By 1914, 58 percent of all inmates at the Mercer were serving sentences of one year or more, a drastic increase of 17 percent over the previous year. By 1917 half of all inmates at the Mercer were serving indeterminate sentences.[29] Reformatory demographics changed along with the sentencing patterns. Whereas between 1899 and 1917 Mercer inmates were, on average, over thirty years old and most likely to be widowed or married, between 1918 and 1931 inmates were, on average, twenty-five years old. Fifty percent of them were single, and 88 percent were first-time offenders.[30] Within a few years, O'Sullivan's 1913 complaint had become largely redundant. This dramatic transformation of reformatory demographics is, in itself, a testament to the political influence of women's reform groups and their ability to secure for themselves the daughterly subjects they were convinced they should help.

Toronto's "Jailbirds"

Although paying attention to broader patterns of arrest, sentencing, and incarceration is important, aggregate data reveal only part of the story of female criminality in early twentieth-century Toronto. Judith Fingard's detailed study of the dark side of Victorian Halifax reveals a subculture of jailbirds whose repeated, if mostly minor, criminality was the product of "a loud, boisterous, hard-drinking culture that spilled out of the taverns and dance halls into the streets," where it was easily detectable and an affront to a middle-class sense of propriety.[31] Mary-Ann Poutanen's study of "the homeless, the whore, the drunkard, and the disorderly" in Montreal between 1810 and 1842 reveals the existence of a similar subculture of public women who made frequent court experiences.[32] Her survey of 2,528 arrests of women for vagrancy revealed that 32 percent (233) of the arrested women accounted for 68 percent (1,724) of the total female vagrancy figures.[33] These repeat offenders were often street prostitutes, but they were not necessarily arrested for soliciting men, nor was their profession their only defining characteristic. These women were often also chronic alcoholics, homeless and destitute, and/or participants in a street culture in which "women and men were attracted to the numerous drinking establishments, public buildings and brothels" that were regularly targeted by patrolling police officers.[34]

The Toronto jail records for 1913 to 1934 reveal a similar jailbird population whose repeated appearances in the local courts had a marked affect on aggregate crime statistics. Of the total selected cases (4,781), one-third (1,563) are attributable to 186 women. Because my sampling of the jail registers is in three-year intervals, this number likely underestimates the rate of recidivism in Toronto. Moreover, securing the identity of female petty criminals is a fraught task. As John Pratt has argued in reference to the "dangerous classes" of the nineteenth century, "[t]heir very rootlessness, their ability to shrug off one identity as it suited them and then assume another, rendering them, as it were, 'unknowable,' confirmed their status as dangerous."[35] Toronto's jailbirds likewise shifted their identities, and many of them used aliases in their recurrent appearances in jail: for example, one woman, regularly convicted for drunkenness, once offered the (false) last name "Mercer," revealing, perhaps, a sense of ironic humour about her fate.[36] Notwithstanding these difficulties, I have been able to track the appearances of those women who appeared at least twice in the jail records.[37] Among a total of 183 repeat offenders, there are 40 women who form a core group of especially frequent offenders. This subgroup appeared at least six times and in at least three of the years that I studied, which means that their appearances in a criminal court spanned a time period of at least nine years. Nearly three-quarters of the 40 women (29) were tracked for twelve or more years, including 7 women who appeared across the entire time period, that is, at least once in every third year between 1913 and 1934.

In addition to having long careers, many of these women appeared with remarkable frequency in any given year. For example, the dubious honour of the most local jail entries by any woman goes to one Lizzie C. Although she can be traced only for nine years (1922 to 1931, or for four counted years [1922, 1925, 1928, and 1931]), Lizzie appeared twenty-four times.[38] A sampling of her record may be used as an example of the distinct patterns of criminality and the general demographic and criminal traits that were shared by this group of offenders.

Lizzie first appears in my survey of the jail records in February 1922.[39] This was just after the retirement of Colonel Denison from the police court bench and the official appointment to the Women's Court bench of Margaret Patterson but before Patterson began sitting as magistrate (which she did not do permanently until May of that year). Magistrate Jacob Cohen sat on the Women's Court bench when Lizzie was brought to court on 24 February. Lizzie was listed in the jail register as follows: born in Ireland, resident of Canada for seventeen years, forty-eight years old, single, literate, and Roman Catholic. Her occupation was listed as "housekeeper," an occupational designation that was often deployed as a thinly veiled euphemism for keeper of a bawdy or disorderly house.[40] This, however, was not the charge against her. Lizzie was charged with drunkenness, as she would be on all but two of her twenty-four charges. For this offence, the magistrate sentenced her with a fine of $13.25 (or, $10.00 and costs) or thirty days' imprisonment. As on nearly every occasion in her long list of charges, Lizzie was unable to pay the fine, and she served her thirty days at the Concord Industrial Farm for Women.

Having finished her jail sentence in late March, Lizzie, regardless of whether she was sober, was able to stay away from the attentions of police for two weeks or so. On 7 April 1922, she was again arrested for drunkenness, tried in the Women's Court by Magistrate Cohen, found guilty, and fined $13.25, in default of which she would spend another thirty days at the women's jail farm. This time, Lizzie was able to pay her fine, and she was released from jail thirteen days later, on 19 April. On 30 April she was back in the Women's Court, found guilty of being drunk, and returned to the women's jail farm on 1 May 1922 for yet another thirty-day sentence. This sentence must have also been cut short by the payment of the fine, for Lizzie was back in court, once again for being drunk but this time before the newly seated Margaret Patterson, on 10 May.[41] On this fourth charge in as many months, Patterson sentenced Lizzie to serve three months at the women's jail farm, perhaps in the hopes that this might offer Lizzie some time to dry out. If so, this effort to remove Lizzie from the temptations of alcohol was unsuccessful. Almost exactly three months later, Lizzie was sentenced to the Concord again, again for drunkenness but this time for six months. This pattern continued until June 1931 when, at the age of fifty-seven, Lizzie was sentenced to a psychiatric hospital and does not reappear in my survey of the jail records.

From this sad record of less than one year in Lizzie's life, it is possible to draw out some features of the lives and characteristics of many of the female recidivists, especially of that core group of the forty most frequent offenders. Although few women offended as often and with so little time between arrests as Lizzie, her demographic characteristics and the sentencing pattern were hardly unique to her. First, it should be noted that much of her incarceration was due to poverty: many women were jailed for not having the money to pay fines for various disorderly behaviours. Another common trait among these women was that they tended to be over the age of thirty: Lizzie, at forty-eight (in 1922),is typical, and some women were in their sixties or more. The average recorded age of recidivists was consistently higher than that of first-time offenders. Indeed, some commentators hinted that these women either lied about or did not know their age. Mercer's superintendent, Emma O'Sullivan, suggested one of these possibilities in a report on a prisoner who was routinely convicted for drunkenness and, in 1921, serving her nineteenth term: "She claims to be forty five years of age, I think ten years might be added to that."[42] Economic marginality, routine drunkenness, and sequential prison terms clearly took their toll.

Furthermore, as Table 4 shows, as the same women continued to appear over the years, the age gap between recidivists and one-time offenders increased. What this growing age polarization seems to mean is that there were, at least, two groups of offenders being brought before the courts after a night in jail. First-time offenders tended to be younger women, and in 1919 and 1922 many women were well below the age of thirty. Repeat offenders, however, tended to be over the age of thirty, and by 1928 many of them were in their forties or older. As noted earlier, the difference in the age between first-time and repeat offenders has a counterpart in sentencing patterns. Significantly, after 1914 older repeat offenders were much less likely to be sentenced to the Mercer Reformatory than were young first-time offenders (see Table 5).

Even for those recidivists who were sent to the Mercer, little information is available. The forty most frequent offenders, who were responsible collectively for 396 appearances in the Women's Court, muster among them only thirty-three Mercer sentences in the entire twenty-one-year period under study. This number includes several women who were committed there more than once. Twenty-two of these forty offenders have left no files (Mercer, parole, court investigation, etc.) whatsoever.[43] Of the thirty-three Mercer commitments, only seventeen include case files that detail any information beyond a warrant of commitment and the date of release. For example, although Nellie W. appeared ten times in my records between 1928 and 1934, and was sentenced to the Mercer in 1929, her inmate record from the reformatory includes only her warrant of commitment and the Mercer inmate intake form. Aside from knowing that she served nine months and fifteen days of an indeterminate sentence of twelve months less one day for vagrancy, the only thing that can be learned about Nellie is that she was of insufficient interest to her keepers to warrant any official documentation.[44] With the exception of the local jail entries, repeat offenders like Nellie are most notable in their absence from official commentary on women's criminality.

Table 4

Comparison of average age of female recidivists and one-time offenders in custody, Toronto, 1913-34

Year	Number of cases	All (female) offenders[a]	Recidivists[b]	One-time offenders
		Average age		
1913	951	36.0	37.0	35.9
1916	568	32.6	34.6	32.0
1919	336	26.7	32.0	25.9
1922	615	30.0	33.0	29.0
1925	845	31.6	33.0	31.4
1928	622	33.2	38.8	32.4
1931	458	31.5	37.2	30.8
1934	386	34.1	41.7	33.2
TOTAL/AVERAGE	4,781	32.0	35.9	31.7

a   All averages are rounded off.

b   Recidivists were counted only once in each year that they appeared. Where ages for any one woman are listed differently in the same year, I have chosen the most likely one (for example, if a woman was listed as 32, 34, and 35 in 1916 and appears as 37 in 1919, I have chosen 34 as her age for 1916).

Source: AO, RG 20-100-1, series A, Toronto (York) Jail, Jail Registers.

Table 5

Comparison of average age of women sentenced from local custody to Mercer Reformatory or Concord Industrial Farm for Women, Toronto, 1913-34

Year	Number of cases	All (female) offenders	Recidivists	One-time offenders
		Average age		
1913	951	36.0	37.0	35.9
1913	951	36.0	32.0	n/a
1916	568	32.6	31.0	32.0
1919	336	26.7	28.0	26.0
1922	615	30.0	24.0	33.0
1925	845	31.6	27.0	33.8
1928	622	33.2	21.0	37.9
1931	458	31.5	19.5	35.0
1934	386	34.1	31.0	38.0
TOTAL/AVERAGE	4,781	31.9	26.7	33.7

Source: AO, RG 20-100-1, series A, Toronto (York) Jail, Jail Registers.

Fortunately, jail registers do provide us with some general information about the material conditions of repeat offenders. As a group, recidivists were poor women who lived a precarious existence on the margins of society. Over two-thirds (70 percent) of the 183 repeat offenders listed a trade other than housewife, and nearly half (45 percent) were employed in some form of low-waged domestic service.[45] By contrast, 40 percent of one-time offenders were non-waged housewives, and less than one-third (30 percent) were employed in domestic service. Of the 1,563 entries for recidivists, some form of factory work is listed as an occupation only twenty-four times, and there are only seven entries for saleswomen, eight for stenographers, and six for nurses. Overall, although most of the repeat offenders worked for a living, very few of them were employed in the expanding female workforce that was one of the characteristics of this period. As noted earlier, however, it is impossible to know whether the women were, in fact, gainfully employed in the trade listed at the time of arrest. Indeed, as Fingard notes about the Halifax jailbirds, "people who were frequently institutionalized were on the fringes of the casual labour market and seldom able to cope with its demands."[46]

Perhaps even more telling is the information available about the street addresses of members of the core recidivist population. Like their counterparts in Halifax and Montreal, these women were drawn from the streets, alehouses, and disorderly or bawdy houses known to police. In particular, they were residents of the Ward. Technically, "the Ward" was shorthand for St. John's Ward, a neighbourhood originally bounded by Queen and Bloor streets to the south and north and by Yonge to College streets (now University Avenue) to the east and west. In 1901 the Ward became a slightly larger geographic area known as Ward 3. But to early twentieth-century Torontonians, the Ward was less a geographic location than it was "a condition, an attitude of mind toward life, a standard of living"[47] and a "subjective shorthand designation for Toronto's foreign quarter."[48] The Ward housed 99 percent of the city's Jewish population,[49] 78 percent of the black population, 75 percent of Italians, and 62 percent of Toronto's Chinese residents. As these populations – and the core repeat offenders – moved west of University Avenue in the 1910s, they brought the term *the Ward* with them to their new location.[50] As a 1918 investigation into the Ward put it, "not only is the inhabited part of 'the Ward' becoming more congested ... it is 'boiling over' into adjacent areas and new 'Wards' are springing up sporadically."[51] Popular references to the Ward did not mean the entirety of specified municipal blocks but rather the inner network of cramped streets and alleyways in which the lines between public and private were blurred and that were assumed (not wholly without cause) to be breeding grounds of disease and criminality.[52]

The compressed neighbourhoods within sight of City Hall were characterized by poverty and squalor. In a 1911 report on slum conditions in Toronto, the chief medical officer of health, Dr. Charles Hastings, focused almost all of his attention on housing in the Ward. He wrote of one house that "could be reached only by a curious tunnel-like passage from the street, down a dark and precipitous stairway, and up again into a back yard" and of many overcrowded houses and rental units that lacked water, light, privies, and access to sewage drains.[53] A 1918 investigation judged the interior spaces of these houses to be no better: "In many cases, these are infested with vermin and generally dirty. Plaster has fallen from ceilings and walls and often there is little attempt at sanitation ... [T]enants are behind in their rents or are paying such a nominal rent that they hesitate to ask repairs for fear of ejection."[54] Bursting with cramped tenant dwellings, "teeming with backstreets and lanes," alive with a multiplicity of languages, and housing any number of legal and illegal businesses, "to outsiders, [the Ward] was a disorderly region set quite apart from their norm."[55] And it was here, in the midst of this "foreign," poverty-stricken, and (to the middle class) disturbingly vibrant neighbourhood that most of the city's most frequent offenders lived, drank, worked, and were arrested.

In this small neighbourhood, criminalized women knew one another and often shared resources, although sometimes the insular and close quarters of the Ward could lead to friction. For instance, Minnie H., "a comely young Jewish mother," was sentenced to ten days in jail for assaulting her tenant, Lizzie G. Minnie had approached Lizzie's upstairs apartment to let in some workmen, but Lizzie thought she was coming for the rent and pushed her down the stairs. Minnie picked herself up, and "when the subsequent tumult and the shouting had died, and the loose hair had been gathered up," Lizzie had to be taken to hospital and Minnie was convicted of assault.[56] That Lizzie acted as the complainant in this case supports those studies that focus on the ways that the poor incorporated the criminal justice system into their own dispute resolution remedies.[57] However, they also depended on their own resources. When Mike D. repeatedly exposed himself to young girls and women passing by the window of his lodging house in the Ward, "women to the number of two hundred turned out with sticks and stones, and tin pans, and rolling pins, and iron bars, and garden rakes. One busy little bee pushed a lawn mower; another a savage-looking pair of grass clippers." Police who arrived on the scene were lionized by the press for having "saved [Mike's] head from many a crack and the other end from many a pinch with the grass clippers."[58] Crime-ridden as the Ward may have seemed to outsiders, its residents were clearly not without a sense of justice.

The jail registers make it clear that Toronto's jailbirds lived together, were arrested in groups, and led semi-itinerant lives, often moving from one known bawdy house to another.[59] In her twenty-four recorded appearances in the city jail, for example, Lizzie C. gave nineteen different addresses, including five places in which other convicted women had lived. Three times she shared an address with other women well known to the police and court officials.[60] Kate C., who was often charged but rarely convicted and who appears in the records only in 1913, is yet another example. In the first year of the Toronto Women's Court, Kate appeared seven times, all but once for drunkenness. Like Lizzie, she was of Irish birth but a long-time resident of Canada (twenty-eight years), widowed, and forty-three years old. Her occupation was listed variously as prostitute, houseworker, charwoman, domestic, and dayworker. She rarely gave the same address with each arrest. In May she was living on Sheridan Avenue; two weeks later, upon her next arrest, she was living on Terauley Street (now Bay, north of Queen). By June, when she made her next appearance, her address had changed to Wellington, and it is likely that this was a bawdy house, because this address was also given by four other women, all of whom were repeat offenders and two of whom were listed as prostitutes in the jail register. One month later, on 4 August, Kate, once more in court, was living on Jarvis. Two days later she was living at 51 Duke Street, another common address and likely a house of ill fame. The day after her release from jail on this drunk charge, Kate, picked up again for drunkenness, gave the address on Terauley Street that she had given four months earlier.[61] It is possible that, with each appearance in court, Kate was instructed by the magistrate to find alternate accommodations as a condition of her discharge. Or perhaps her arrests were the product of raids on and (temporary) closures of known bawdy houses, which left her with no home to which to return. Whatever the reason, Kate claimed that she lived in five separate places, not including the city jail, over the course of five months.

Poverty, homelessness, and itinerancy were taken into account in the police court, and it was no secret that the jails were sometimes used by street women for housing, food, medical attention, and, occasionally, as a place to die. When Jane D. – sixty-eight years of age, homeless, and with no job – was sentenced to pay a fine of $1.25 or spend six months in prison for vagrancy in the winter of 1913, in all likelihood the court's concern was her well-being, rather than her punishment.[62] In this way, and in advance of its formation proper, the criminal justice system acted as a quasi-welfare net.[63] Although, in all probability, health problems were not their underlying reason for going to jail, several of the most itinerant repeat offenders did receive important medical assistance while they were incarcerated at the Mercer: Alice D. (1916-25) had her eyeglasses, which she had broken prior to her incarceration, replaced;[64] Florence B. (1914-22) received an orthopaedic shoe because "one leg is shorter than the other which causes her pain in legs and back";[65] and Lizzie C. (1922-31) and Daisy H. (1913-34), who had only six cents in her possession at the time of her commitment to the Mercer in 1917, were both taken to the dentist to be fitted for artificial teeth.[66] These various services were paid for by the province, as were any medical services received by inmates who could prove that they were destitute.[67] In addition to indicating the degree to which incarceration might hold some advantages (welcomed or not) for some, these incidents also point to the sheer poverty of many members of the core recidivist population.

This poverty compelled some women to actively seek out such assistance. On a cold evening in the winter of 1921, fifty-three-year-old former inmate Mabel P., "hungry, dirty and exhausted," knocked on the door of the Mercer Reformatory and "begged us to allow her to remain here until it was time for her to work in the fields."[68] She was taken to the Women's Court the next day and committed for three months on a charge of vagrancy. On 5 January 1923, Margaret H. appeared in the Women's Court after her arrest for smashing a department store window. Having been without work for the past three months, Margaret had briefly been in the care of the Salvation Army, but it had "been unable to keep her employed" and Margaret became desperate. "She told the court that she knew she would be punished, and was willing to take the penalty the magistrate wished to impose." Margaret Patterson sentenced her to three months plus an additional indeterminate sentence of up to six months "so that she would be taken care of for the rest of the winter."[69] Similarly, in 1925 "neither home nor money had Elizabeth K.," who explained to the court her destitution: "I've slept in parks for a long time. I've eaten where I could. Sometimes it has been hard." When Margaret Patterson, "glancing down at the frail over-coated figure before her," sentenced her to an indeterminate period at the jail farm, "wearily, Elizabeth picked up her little bundle of belongings, and faded umbrella, passing out in the care of friendly hands."[70]

In one very compelling story, repeat offender Meg H. (1913-16), serving her twentieth term at the Mercer, mostly for drinking offences, requested that she be transferred to the House of Providence, a Catholic home for indigents. Meg was described by O'Sullivan as being "in a very frail and worn condition of mind and body," and the superintendent supported her request on the basis that "she does not give much promise of improving in any way by a longer stay here and perhaps might benefit a little and be happier by a change of surroundings ... She is homeless." Edwin Rogers, inspector of prisons, acquiesced to this humanitarian request, and Meg was transferred to the home on 24 March 1916. However, on 5 April Meg tried to move herself to the hospital. She "got as far as Church Street and asked an officer to take her to the Court Street station to see Miss Kelly, the Police matron, whom she hoped would get her transferred to the hospital." Unfortunately, the police officer thought she was drunk and took her to the jail cells. Brought up to court the next day, and in evident ill health, the court officers (probably at Meg's request) finally telephoned the Mercer superintendent, who sent Field Officer Letitia Scott to pick her up. Back at the reformatory, Meg repeated her request to be taken to hospital: "I think she fears she is dying and does not want the stigma attached to her name of having died in prison." This last wish of Meg's was carried out, and she died at the Toronto General Hospital on 1 May 1916 at the age of forty. Rogers instructed that she have a decent burial, at the province's expense.[71]

With no resources to her name, Meg used the criminal justice and correctional infrastructure as a helping system, and she evidenced a familiarity with, and well-placed reliance on, the kindness of various prison and court officials that belies any one dimensional assessment of criminal justice as something "done" to the poor. These examples of compassion, assistance, and cooperation with the prisoners and among criminal justice agents indicate that not all instances of arrest and incarceration were coercive: sometimes they were the most humanitarian thing that could be done. However, I concur with Poutanen, who argues that "[n]otwithstanding the benevolent use of incarceration towards some vagrants, the treatment of ... vagrant women at the hands of the criminal justice system illustrates the ... coercive nature of the state."[72] Indeed, sometimes even humanitarian intentions could go awry, revealing the problematic effects of imprisonment as a form of welfare.

In the summer of 1931 – when Toronto, like elsewhere, was in the grip of the Depression – Lucy Ratcliffe, elderly, homeless, and destitute, walked into the temporary police station at the Canadian National Exhibition at 11:00 p.m. and asked for protection. When the officers appealed unsuccessfully to the Salvation Army and Neighbourhood Workers to take Ratcliffe in (both organizations said the hour was too late), the police transferred her downtown to the Court Street police station "on a technical charge of vagrancy." Apparently both they and Ratcliffe expected that she would be held overnight and that further welfare would then be sought for "the unfortunate woman" the next day. In the Women's Court, however, Margaret Patterson convicted Ratcliffe and sentenced her to six months at the jail farm. Ratcliffe and other observers were outraged. Ratcliffe "protested that she was not wicked and had done nothing wrong," while police officers, Salvation Army representatives, the Provincial Secretary George H. Challies, the *Globe,* and the "many citizens [who] telephoned the newspaper" expressed their concern over this harsh sentence for a "homeless and friendless aged lady." Margaret Patterson was not asked to explain herself in the press, but one of her supporters, Dr. Laura Hamilton, called the *Globe* to explain that "at the time there was no other place than the Jail Farm for her to go. She was old, feeble, and needing care ... therefore she was sent to a place where she would have a woman doctor, a nurse, and good food and shelter."[73] However, using the (feminized) correctional infrastructure as a welfare mechanism was clearly not considered benevolent in this instance, and Patterson's sentence appeared more punitive than kind. More than anything, what cases like these reveal is that making sense of overall arrest and commitment patterns from the Women's Court is a complex but worthwhile task.

Conclusion

As this overview of women's crime rates demonstrates, different women had different relationships to the criminal justice system, and even the same charge or sentence could have divergent meanings in different circumstances. In particular, although they did not constitute a majority of offenders, recidivists in the Women's Court merit careful attention, and their presence warns against making overgeneralizations about patterns of women's criminality. Recidivists were a subgroup within the criminalized population that had specific patterns of arrest and disposition and whose members shared certain demographic and material characteristics. Their existence means that it is necessary to think in terms of at least two streams of women targeted by the law. Recidivists, responsible for one-third of all examined appearances in court, were sometimes objects of pity or compassion, but as a group they were hardly the material for reform circles. Their lives were entangled with the criminal justice system, and they moved in and out of police stations, courthouses, and jails with startling frequency. Their crime patterns and the theories of female criminality expounded by the TLCW were often two distinct things.

With this in mind, the next chapters break down the different major offences that brought women (recidivists and one-time offenders) into the Women's Court in order to disentangle the divergent points of entry and departure for women offenders and their shifting significance for women whose experiences could differ from one another in important ways. Despite the claims of the TLCW that women as a group had interests that were sufficiently distinct from men as a group to warrant a specific criminal venue (to which, not incidentally, they sometimes referred in the singular as the Woman's Court), the next chapter looks at how other factors – most notably, the reasons for arrest, previous criminal experience, and subjective interpretations of what constituted "respectable" womanhood – meant that different women experienced the court in some importantly different ways. And a caveat: although the following chapters break down the aggregate crime statistics by specific charge (drunkenness, vagrancy, theft, etc.), for some women, as we have begun to see, these distinctions were not very significant. Repeat offenders were arrested for a variety of minor offences; consequently, while they predominate in arrest and detention figures for drunkenness, they also appeared in court charged with vagrancy, theft, and bawdy house offences. In and of itself this fluidity is an indication of their precarious living conditions and the strategies of survival that they pursued. It was also something that the maternal feminists could not, or would not, understand.

4

"What chance is there for a girl?"
Vagrancy and Theft Charges in the Women's Court

When Benedictine Wiseman left her husband in Montreal in 1913, cropped her hair, donned her brother's clothing, and became Jimmy, who worked during the day at a Toronto factory and at night singing at a nickelodeon, she clearly hoped to build a new life for herself. She was, therefore, understandably upset when she was discovered and arrested for vagrancy: "'Why did you not leave me alone?' she had cried passionately ... 'I was a good boy. I was earning my living. Now you make me walk the streets.'"[1] Her unmasking had led to her losing her jobs and, thus, made her status as a "loose, idle, or disorderly person" a self-fulfilling prophecy.[2] It also piqued the curiosity of the Women's Court reporters, who wished to know more about the "noble little amazon" who was so "fearlessly defiant of law and order":

> "I suppose you never played with dolls when you were little?" a sympathetic voice queried ...
>
> "Huh!" snapped Benedictine, "I had fifteen of my own" ...
>
> "But, you'll go back; you'll be a girl?"
>
> "What chance is there for a girl?" said Benedictine: "You are girls, yes" to the reporters and the [Salvation Army] deaconess, "But me, I am not such a girl. For me there is no chance."[3]

For obvious reasons, Benedictine/Jimmy was keenly aware of the requirements of being a girl, requirements that she could not and did not aspire to meet. "The trouble with Benedictine," reported the *Star,* was "that she was too independent": she was "of the 'Master of my fate and captain of my soul' type, not having lived long enough to learn better."[4] It was this transgression of "order" that made Benedictine a criminal before the law. For her own good, the Women's Court would teach Benedictine the important lesson of accepting her womanhood.[5]

The newspaper accounts of Benedictine's transgressions fit neatly into the formula identified by Alison Oran in her analysis of popular press stories of women cross-dressers in Britain in the early decades of the twentieth century.[6] Central features of these stories included the sensational revelation that a presumed male was, really, female, a discovery that was usually made because the woman came into contact with the authorities; an account of her crossing of gender boundaries, typically signified by such things as physical transformations, usually a cropping of the hair and male clothing, often stolen from a brother; a description of her success at male social habits, including both homo- and heterosocial relationships; and, finally, a search for motive, which was often economic, for instance, job or personal mobility. Even upon discovery, Oran argues, the cross-dressing woman was given credit for her audacity, her daring, and her success (if only for a time) at performing a recognizable masculinity, in much the same way that male impersonators on stage were enjoyed, by both male and female audiences, for their ability to dramatize gendered behaviour.

Benedictine's story contained all of these elements. She was "discovered" by a police officer searching for a missing girl from Montreal, after having successfully passed as a boy for three months. During that time she had been employed in male labour, without arousing the suspicions of her workmates. To pass as a boy, she had taken her brother's clothes, and the reporter made a great deal of her cropped hair, depicting Benedictine as a comedic figure who was eventually returned to court dressed as a girl, but whose hat did not stay on her head because there was no hair to pin it to. This indication of failing girlhood may even signal some acceptance of Benedictine's defiant vow that "they shall not keep me."[7] Her success as a boy had been demonstrated not only by commanding a boy's wages but also by winning a singing competition for male youth and by an ability to "fight a man's battles with men, and scorn the associations or assistance of her own kind."[8] As Oran argues, women like Benedictine were received with some admiration and awe. But they were also disquieting: "Within a familiar story formula, they were safety entertaining, yet sowed the seeds of the insurrectionary idea that gender was not innate but a social sham."[9] Indeed, Benedictine's story reveals that alongside female reformers' naturalist references to womanliness was the concern that gender was something that required constant reinforcement and policing.

Ultimately, the insistence that Benedictine "go back" and "be a girl" underscored the fundamental role that the Women's Court was to play in reclaiming women from a life of moral endangerment and waywardness. In a court explicitly established to help restore women to respectability, choosing not to be a woman was not a viable option. But, being a "girl" was not as straightforward as it might have appeared: more than simply an embodiment, respectable femininity was to be performed properly and maintained vigilantly. As a result, many women would find themselves in the Women's Court between 1913 and 1934 trying to defend themselves against charges that had a great deal to do with what kind of girl they were. Many of them may have inwardly repeated the same lament that Benedictine had: "What chance is there for a girl?" The interplay between female criminality and particular definitions of womanhood was consistently in evidence in the Women's Court.

This chapter is about this interplay, as seen through an examination of the crimes that engaged and fuelled the imaginations of members of the Toronto Local Council of Women (TLCW): vagrancy and theft. These two offences, ranked second and third as the most likely reasons for an appearance in the Women's Court, tended to bring in the girls the TLCW imagined helping. Thus, these offences, including as they were reported by the press, typically augmented the maternal feminists' arguments about the benefits of a separate venue to try women's criminal cases. But even within these crime categories, important differences appear between those deemed worthy of the court's maternal guidance and those who needed to be punished in the name of the reclamation of a broader womanhood. Paying attention to these differences helps to illustrate the complexities of adjudicating female crime.

Disaggregating the major routes by which women came into the Women's Court has some disadvantages. Space limitations mean that only the broad strokes of these charges can be examined, likely to the exclusion of some interesting nuances. Additionally, it must be acknowledged that the categories I use – vagrancy, theft, drunkenness, and bawdy house offences (these latter two are discussed in the next chapter) – are made distinct by the law itself. As indicated in the previous chapter, in many criminalized women's lives, these categories blended together as part of their day-to-day culture of survival. Some vagrant women were repeatedly drunk; they sometimes turned to the sex trade, where they were arrested; and from time to time, they engaged in petty theft as a way to make do. To say that these categories are important, then, is in some way to deny both the flexibility with which they were enforced and the actual experiences of many women for whom they were a continuum, rather than neatly compartmentalized and discrete events.

At the same time, this type of disaggregation of criminal categories does have its advantages. First, looking at charges such as drunkenness and theft fleshes out analyses of female crime beyond prostitution or suspicions of prostitution and opens up the terrain of the regulation of sexuality beyond explicit sexual "deviance." Second, paying attention to different types of crimes offers glimpses into the workings of gender in the lives of ordinary women, including as it intersected with race and class. Additionally, the varying meanings attributed to distinct types of offences offer up instructive lessons on the ways that gender was viewed by the reforming classes and in the courts. Finally, this breakdown illustrates the complex bases of legitimacy upon which the Women's Court was grounded. In these ways the differences between, and within, women's main criminal offences help to answer Benedictine's poignant question regarding what chances there really were for women who appeared in a court established to sort out that very problem.

Vagrancy: "Good-Time Girls" and "Automobile Experts"

Technically, the vagrancy provisions of the *Criminal Code* were meant to target street prostitution, particularly through the female-specific subsection that defined a vagrant as "any loose, idle, or disorderly person who being a common prostitute or night walker, wanders in the fields, public streets or highways, lanes or places of public meeting or gathering of people, and does not give a satisfactory account of herself."[10] But, aside from the gender-specific language of this subsection, a vagrant was also, among other problematic behaviours, any loose, idle, or disorderly person who "loiters on the street, road, highway or public place, and obstructs passengers by standing across the footpath, or by using insulting language, or in any other way causes a disturbance in or near any street, highway or public place, by screaming, swearing or singing, or by being drunk, or by impeding or incommoding peaceable passengers."[11] The sweeping discretionary powers allowed to police to determine who was a vagrant, which were informed by prevailing ideas about appropriate sexual deportment, meant that a diverse range of behaviours was targeted by this catch-all provision and that vagrancy could mean different things for women and men. As Mary-Anne Poutanen observes, although the particular trespasses engaged in by those charged with vagrancy were usually trivial, vagrancy provisions, because they regulated the public sphere, were a direct manifestation of the power of the state in the lives of the popular classes.[12] For women arrested for vagrancy, this often meant a direct contest over their very presence in public places.

There was a substantial amount of interchange between vagrancy, disorderly, and drunkenness arrests, and some women were routinely arrested for these (and other) offences. This interchangeability was largely due to the broad discretionary powers of the police, who enjoyed considerable flexibility in the charges they could lay. For example, in July 1928 Susan W. (1913-34), whose previous convictions were said to number "somewhere in the sixties," broke a window while drunk in a public place. She was charged with drunkenness but was let off on the condition that she pay for the window, which she did.[13] Mary S. (1913-16), another regular in the court, who also "thrust her fist through a pane of glass" while intoxicated, was arrested for being disorderly. She was also discharged.[14] Meanwhile, women who were found drinking with men might as easily have been arrested for vagrancy. Sadie S. (1913-34), a known prostitute, was charged with drunkenness when she was discovered at 2:00 a.m. in a wash house on King Street West, "guzzling suds" with two men. She was sentenced to a week at the Concord jail farm.[15] Similarly, first-timer and eighteen-year-old Vera M. was charged with drunkenness after being found in a Dundas Street taxi garage with three young men at 2:30 a.m. She had had one drink.[16] On the same day, Irene A. (1928-34), a Women's Court regular for drunkenness, was charged with vagrancy for being drunk in a taxicab.[17] Given this interchangeability, official arrest and detention figures need to be treated with some caution.

Despite this caveat, the vagrancy statistics available from police and jail sources do tell an important part of the story of women and crime. Vagrancy was the second most common charge leading to arrest and at least one night in the city cells between 1913 and 1934. Of the total 4,781 counted charges against women, 922, or nearly one in five arrests (19 percent), were for vagrancy. More importantly, vagrancy was a highly gendered crime. In 1913 women constituted only 6 percent of all arrests made by the Toronto police, but they made up a full 24 percent of all vagrancy arrests.[18] This pattern is consistent throughout the period under study. Women never accounted for more than 10 percent of the total arrests made by Toronto's police force each year, but they did constitute, on average, approximately 25 percent of all vagrancy arrests. Overall, vagrancy had a conviction rate of 39 percent, which was just more than 10 percent below the general conviction rate for detained women (see Chapter 3). Eighty-five percent of these convictions were meted out to one-time offenders. Perhaps even more telling, the average age of female vagrants was considerably lower than that of women charged with other crimes, most notably drunkenness. Women arrested for vagrancy were, on average, twenty-eight years old, although the ages ranged from fifteen to eighty-five years. Between 1913 and 1934, 71 percent of all women detained as vagrants were under the age of thirty.

The gendered and targeted nature of vagrancy has attracted the attention of many feminist researchers, precisely because, as a discretionary status offence, vagrancy neatly encapsulates ideas about what women should, and should not, do or be. Various social anxieties about women's sexuality, respectability, and increasingly public role can be read in the discourses about, and arrests for, vagrancy. Therefore, a growing feminist body of research has focused on vagrancy and what it can tell us about gender in the city. More specifically, feminist research has linked the feminization of vagrancy with fascination with the "girl adrift" and the 1910s and 1920s.[19]

The girl adrift – the young, single, working woman tempted by a variety of new sexual and economic opportunities in a new urban youth culture – was the target of, and the reason for, a politics of urban uplift across North America. Her dangerous independence, her heterosociability, and her participation in a new and vibrant youth culture generated considerable consternation among feminist urban reformers who feared that extra-familial activities in an anonymous city posed moral hazards to women that required swift action. The Toronto Social Survey Commission, initiated in 1913 at the request of the TLCW and mandated to investigate vice and moral conditions in the city, reported that this problem was a serious cause for alarm.[20] Most troubling to the commissioners was the discovery of what they called "occasional prostitution," or the propensity of young women to barter sexual favours for some form of financial gain or, worse, "for a good time." According to the commissioners, the difference between the professional and the occasional prostitute was that the latter had a deceptive alter-ego, one that was engaged in honourable work or ensconced in a respectable home when she was not out being a good-time girl. The consequences of this newly discovered social problem were clear to the commissioners: the new "thoroughly commercialized immorality" existed "in such a form that those engaged in it are not a segregated and despised class, but outwardly respectable, and with a definite standing in the world of business and industry." This meant that "the innocent and pure-minded of either sex may have to be in daily and hourly association with the corrupt."[21] The danger of contamination and defilement was clear. All women, especially single women in the city, came under suspicion of being good-time girls.

The identification of the girl adrift – who was perilously close to losing her respectability, while simultaneously imperilling the morality of the city in which she lived – gave urgency to the deployment of the criminal justice system and the need to strengthen its correctional infrastructure. There can be no doubt that, in large part, the Toronto Women's Court was welcomed because it was conceived as a mechanism that could address the problems posed by, and to, single urban women. Vagrancy charges were the most readily available instrument to achieve both aims. But the enormously wide scope of the vagrancy provisions meant that an equally wide variety of women arrived in the Women's Court. Sorting out the overlap between "public women" and women in public, determining the difference between women endangered and dangerous women, and knowing how to tell the difference between the occasional prostitute, the "professional prostitute," and women wronged by men was both key to the legitimacy of the Women's Court and an enormously difficult task to accomplish.

In some instances vagrancy was a street prostitution offence. In 1915 Gussie J. and Ethel S. were thought to "require a rest from their labours" when they appeared in the Women's Court for vagrancy.[22] Also sent to the Concord "for six restful months" were Annie Y. and Lena K., who "were shown to have turned their nights into garish days and their days into 'moonshine' nights."[23] These "rests" were often an unwelcome part of the trade. When Annie M. and Florence K., "whose charms have lured impressionable night hawks to their rendezvous on Thompson street," were sentenced by Magistrate Denison in the Women's Court, "they flung their thanks at Plainsclothesemen Forbes and Dunn. A brick would have hurt less."[24] But, welcomed or not, arrest and detention were a part of the risk assumed by working prostitutes. Thus, Lillian S. and Jennie C. "were sent down ... after their good time on Saturday."[25] Myrtle L. and Bertha D. were sentenced to the jail farm for being "automobile experts."[26] And "flowers from the same valley," Bella M. and Verbina L., "attired in the height of fashion, plumes, dust coats and white shoes," found themselves in the Women's Court to "explain why they chose midnight and the early hours of morning for constitutional walks on King Street." When it was further shown that, on these

Feminized Justice

constitutionals, "the girls bade gentlemen good night in most affectionate tones," their pleasantries earned them each a sentence at the jail farm.[27]

These charges did not, however, necessarily result in conviction. When Ellen F. was arrested for "walking the streets exchanging compliments of the season," Magistrate Denison asked if there was any further evidence against her. When none was presented, Denison discharged Ellen, saying, "[I]t's not enough. The air is particularly pleasant these days, and if a sociable lady like Miss F–, who I know loves air and freedom, does nothing worse than that I cannot convict."[28] Denison's decision to discharge Ellen was not simply the whim of a paternalist magistrate. To the contrary, his view that there was no harm in Ellen's seasonal greetings was consistent with that of many in the police force and beyond. Police departments throughout North America (albeit to differing degrees) preferred a policy of containment to suppression when it came to prostitution.[29] But even the social survey commissioners, who were themselves fascinated with the sex trade (real and imagined), evidenced a worldly complacency about the existence of the professional prostitute: "The out-and-out prostitutes, as a class, are known to have existed always, and in a large city their presence in considerable numbers is more or less to be expected. This condition, therefore, however serious, is at any rate nothing new."[30]

Indeed, the rather mundane existence of prostitutes and their semi-regular appearances in the Women's Court threatened to undermine the legitimacy of this special criminal venue. Harry Wodson noted the ill fit between prostitution-related charges and the claims of the Women's Court in a typically acerbic fashion: "[T]o-day the women – mere girls many of them – laugh and talk gaily with the profligate rakes who sit near them. For some obscure reason these offenders, male and female, are given trial in private; their crime is sheltered, while the unfortunate man whose reason has fled, is forced to stand in the dock, exposed to the glare and curiosity of an open court, and to the laughter his strange conduct and speech might produce. Some day this injustice may cease."[31] Small wonder, in light of these juxtapositions, that reformers focused more of their attention on the single woman who seemed, for the time being, to have lost her moral compass. After all, this was what the Women's Court was meant to address.

In stark contrast to Wodson's characterization of "the daughters of the night" as central characters in the court, the TLCW drew attention to the young women whose lives might have fallen into irretrievable disrepair were it not for the intervention of the Women's Court. Margaret Patterson, for instance, painted a different picture of the vagrant woman. In Patterson's view a vagrant woman's appearance in the sheltered environment of the Women's Court could prove to be a turning point in her life:

> One day a girl with a baby in her arms was called to answer a charge of vagrancy. One of the ladies present offered to take her and give her the opportunity of earning an honest living. The girl gratefully accepted, and to use a modern phrase, "made good." She is now married to the father of her child, and they are getting along very well, and living together most happily. Had there not been a sympathetic woman in court to give her this chance, one dreads to think of how different life might have been for that girl to-day.[32]

This was a radically different portrait of vagrancy than that presented by police court reporter Wodson, although it was no less ideologically informed. In fact, most women fell somewhere between these two characterizations of female vagrancy. But they had to fend against the negative impacts of both. It would not do for a woman to be equated with prostitution, but the hyperfamilial notions of respectable womanhood against which arrested women were compared could prove to be just as damning.

Most commonly, women charged with vagrancy were women caught up in minor trespasses who were, importantly, deemed to be in the wrong place at the wrong time. Flora S. and Delia B. found themselves in the Women's Court after joyriding in a stolen car with two young men. The "lads" had invited the young women, whom they had not met before, to "go for a spin." The young men were charged with stealing an automobile, and the women were charged with vagrancy, although the women were eventually discharged.[33] It would appear that the "joyriding" of which Flora and Delia were accused differed from the charge of being "automobile experts" put forward in the case of known prostitutes Myrtle and Bertha. These euphemisms offer important clues as to the gradation of, and meanings of, vagrancy charges for different women.

Even still, joyriding was not always seen as a more benign form of the car date, and young women could find themselves in serious trouble for their casual relationships with young men. Accepting a ride from two boys resulted in a Mercer Reformatory sentence for vagrancy for Eva C.: "Accused said that she was out with two boys in a car on Tuesday night about 10:30 p.m. in the Roxborough Ravine. Asked if she knew the boys before she said she did not, that she had only gone for a ride with them. She said that she had not been doing anything, and she thought it very strange that the police did not arrest the boys when they arrested her."[34] The same sense of injustice may have been experienced by two young women who claimed to have been locked out of their home when they came home too late from a party and who were found in the company of two young men at the ferry docks at 1:30 a.m. They were discharged after a court appearance for vagrancy. There is no information as to whether charges were laid against their companions.[35] Olive T. likewise found herself facing Margaret Patterson on a vagrancy charge after she had been found spooning with a boyfriend in a park at 3:00 a.m. The couple had been at a party and stopped off in the park on the way home. When Patterson asked why they had stopped for so long, Olive "blushed, very faintly" and replied, "I hadn't any place to go and I thought it was a nice place to stay with John." Although both John and Olive were fined ten dollars and costs or ten days in prison, John's fine was paid by a relative, "presumably his father." Olive served her sentence in the local jail cells.[36] The broad strokes of the vagrancy provisions, the preoccupation with the girl adrift, and the varying gendered interpretations of a "loose, idle, or disorderly person" meant that young women walked a very thin line between dating and criminal behaviour.[37]

Some women openly flaunted this line. In her study of the criminalization of young women's behaviour in early twentieth-century New York, Ruth Alexander suggests that the incarcerated women themselves should be credited with agency, rather than being conceptualized as victims of top-down control.[38] In other words, young women acted, and middle-class reformers reacted. However one reads this equation, the differential power relations associated with each side are unmistakable. Although records do show that some young women were making autonomous decisions about how they wished to live their lives (decisions that were clearly untenable and unsettling to reformers), for those who were caught up in the carceral net, the same records also indicate that this was often a struggle that young women could lose badly. For example, nineteen-year-old Ruth T., sent to the Mercer for vagrancy in 1925, seemed to confirm the social survey commissioners' findings about the existence of occasional prostitutes. Officially listed as a seamstress, Ruth was convicted by Patterson because she did "not have any visible means of support and lives without employment." This was not an entirely accurate statement. Ruth explained to her warders that "she desired more money than she was getting at Eaton's store and sold her virtue to get it, and set a high price on her wares." This rational reasoning struck a chord with Mercer officials, who determined that this declaration proved that she was not feeble-minded, as they had originally suspected. Rather, they noted, in somewhat awestruck tones, "she shows the shrewdness of the modern man of business with the moral lack of the irresponsible type."[39] Ruth's clear statement does suggest a woman exerting her own agency within the context of known choices. With this characterization on her record, however, it is hardly surprising to learn that Ruth served nearly the entirety of her indeterminate sentence of two years less a day. Surely this was not an option she would have chosen for herself.

Beatrice D. was likewise not predisposed to behave in the way that reformers hoped she would. Beatrice appeared before Margaret Patterson after being found "wandering abroad" at 8:15 p.m. on 20 July 1931 without a satisfactory explanation. Since this was her first appearance, Patterson gave her a remanded sentence under the care of the Salvation Army, which sent her to "a position" in a respectable home. For the first few days, this seemed to be a suitable arrangement, but at some point Beatrice clearly decided that this was not a life for her. Margaret Patterson included the following report with Beatrice's commitment papers to the Mercer:

> She stayed out one night and the next day refused to get up, lay in bed smoking cigarettes and reading a magazine. Her mistress phoned the Army and asked them to remove her. One of the Army officers went, but the girl refused to get up, said she was going to stay where she was as long as she liked. After coaxing and reasoning with her the Army officer called in a policeman. Still the girl refused to get up until the policeman removed her from the bed by force and she fought so that it took the policeman and Army officer over an hour to get her dressed. When this evidence was given in Court regarding her and I asked her why she acted in this way she told me because she wanted to.[40]

Beatrice's lack of workplace discipline and intransigent behaviour continued while she was incarcerated at the Mercer, where she was often punished for refusing to work and using profane language. After serving one year and eight months at the Mercer, she was transferred to the Orillia Psychiatric Institution. Her commitment form stated that she was "an unstable moron with poor judgment and wholly undesirable sex attitudes." Her refusal to fit within the prescribed boundaries of proper womanhood was clearly incomprehensible to criminal justice officials. But, ultimately, her fierce independence did her few favours. In contrast to Patterson's story of the vagrant woman who made good,

Beatrice's case illuminates how a summary conviction offence like vagrancy could spiral into something powerfully dangerous for women who rejected its social meanings.

In addition to regulating women's public, heterosocial behaviours, vagrancy provisions played a role in patrolling racial borders. Relationships between white women and Chinese men were treated as de facto grounds for an arrest. For example, on 8 May 1915, a "young and prepossessing white girl" appeared in the Women's Court after having attempted to cross into the United States with her Chinese fiancé, in whose restaurant she had worked. Customs officials at Windsor stopped the couple, detained the man, and sent the young unnamed woman back to Toronto. She was given a suspended sentence on the charge of vagrancy, "after promising to have nothing to do with any Chinaman."[41] In addition to disciplining the young woman for her choice in lovers, this sentence also implicitly limited her employment options.[42] In another instance Jean G., "a striking blond girl," was given a two-year indeterminate sentence for vagrancy after the police "found her entering a house occupied by a Chinaman." When Jean protested that she had only been picking up a girlfriend with whom she had a movie date and that she had a job (and, thereby, visible means of support), Margaret Patterson responded that the sentence would enable Jean to get "a proper perspective on life."[43]

The 1930 appeal case of Violet Davis, more so than any other case, illustrates the relationship between vagrancy, race, and gender.[44] Davis, a white woman, had been convicted of vagrancy by Patterson in the Women's Court after having lied to the police officer who found her sitting on a fence at 6:00 a.m., after having spent the night going in and out of restaurants with both "colored and white men." Thus, she had been found "wandering abroad" and had failed to give a satisfactory account of herself when called upon to do so. The substance of Davis's appeal, however, was that the third requirement for a finding of vagrancy – that is, that she had no visible means of subsistence – was not satisfied. She did have a means of support, in the form of her live-in lover, a black railway porter, who willingly provided for her. She was, therefore, appealing her conviction.

Judge Denton, hearing the appeal on his own, acknowledged Davis's cohabitation and wrote in his judgement, "While he chooses to cohabit with her, I suppose we may take it that she is able to subsist. She has no steady employment; no other means of livelihood. The porter may abandon her at any time." The question to be answered, then, was whether this constituted a visible means of subsistence as intended by the *Criminal Code*. Denton allowed that the vagrancy provisions of the *Criminal Code* were meant to target prostitution, and "whatever suspicions one may have in the case, there is no evidence that the accused, who is a white girl, had anything to do with more than this one man, the colored porter." Nonetheless, although he could not find that Davis was a prostitute, Denton's interpretation of the case law was that the means of support had to be not only lawful but also honest and reputable, which was defined by Denton as "such as is generally recognised as not subject to condemnation by the ordinary moral standards of the community." Davis's non-marital, interracial relationship failed this community standards test. Thus, ruled Denton, "while it has not been shewn that this girl is a prostitute, in the sense that she had to do with many men ... it has been shewn that she does live with this colored man, who seems to provide, for the present, her only means of subsistence, and this sort of subsistence is not the kind that is contemplated by the vagrancy section of the *Criminal Code*." Denton also considered the source of the conviction to arrive at his ultimate conclusion. Noting that Patterson had been the convicting magistrate, Denton reasoned that "a woman magistrate knows quite as much, if not more, than a man what is the best to be done with a girl of this kind ... A girl living as this girl does is better where she is than out on the streets of Toronto." Davis's appeal was dismissed.

These examples provide only a small glimpse into the world of vagrancy, but they illustrate the broad range of conduct targeted by the vagrancy law and its explicit role in regulating the "ordinary moral standards of the community."[45] Nonetheless, despite the clear intention to regulate women's sexual activities, women and men continued to have sex. One palpable consequence of this was the spread of venereal disease, which was taken as de facto evidence of "immorality." However, using VD as proof of deviant behaviours was a stretch even for the vagrancy law. In 1917 Justice Middleton quashed a woman's vagrancy conviction because "the whole proceeding suggests that this woman was sent to prison, not because of the acts of immorality, but because she is diseased ... The question of the prevention of the spread of venereal disease is no doubt of prime importance, but the remedy must, it seems to me, be found not in the Criminal Code, but under the Public Health Act."[46] In 1918 the *Telegram* reported again on the inefficacy of the vagrancy law in preventing what it saw as an impending public health disaster. Under the subheading "Menace to Society," the police court reporter told the story of four young women arrested for vagrancy: "The accused were fair to look upon, chiefly on account of a lavish use of paint, and the fate of one of the quartette [sic], Margaret, left onlookers wondering where the law begins and ends." Margaret had a venereal disease, "but because she was regularly employed in a restaurant, of all places in the world, and the police couldn't prove that she made her living by prostitution, she was discharged." Only one of the women, Annie, who shared the same story as Margaret but about whom "police had sufficient evidence of other industry," was convicted.[47]

These alarmist warnings from the Women's Court timed perfectly with the Ontario Commission on Venereal Diseases, which was empanelled in 1917 in the face of distressing numbers of cases of venereal disease among soldiers and which reported in 1918.[48] In his 1918 interim report, Commissioner Justice Frank Egerton Hodgins echoed many of the concerns articulated by Toronto's social survey commissioners, identifying immorality in general, and occasional prostitution in particular, as a principal cause of the spread of VD, which was represented as a threat to the health of "the race."[49] Thus, the final report of the commission advised that "[t]he protection of girls is a matter which in a large city requires a great deal of machinery both of a legal and social nature."[50] Following these recommendations, the Ontario government passed *An Act for the Prevention of Venereal Disease* (the *VD Act*) in 1918.[51]

The *VD Act* allowed authorities to physically examine any person who was under arrest or in custody or who had been convicted of an offence and was in a city or provincial jail or reformatory whom the medical officer of health believed was, or might be, infected or had been exposed to infection.[52] If found to have a venereal disease, the person was then obligated to undergo any course of treatment prescribed by the medical officer, including detention, until such time as the medical officer gave him or her a clean bill of health. Not surprisingly, and despite the gender-neutral language employed in the Act, women, especially young women, came under increased, authorized, surveillance as a result of this Act.

The relationship between the girl adrift and the ostensibly protective mandate of the Women's Court was explicit in the enforcement of the *VD Act*. The Act gave authorities another means by which to criminalize the long suspect good-time girl. Indeed, according to police court reporter Harry Wodson, "the police share the opinion that the most assiduous disseminator [of the terrible disease] is the girl in her teens who thoughtlessly rushes into sexual vice, via movie shows, dance halls, and joy rides."[53] This combination of police opinion, the legal search for the girl adrift, and the medical search for VD sufferers was so powerful that in 1919 the average age of *all* women in custody dropped from its usual average of over thirty to twenty-seven. Although it is difficult to tell how many vagrancy charges in general in 1919 were linked to the medicalized obsession with occasional prostitutes, release information tells an unambiguous story: twenty-one women arrested for vagrancy, eighteen of whom were aged seventeen to twenty-four, were discharged from the court by the medical officer of health. Officials were on a fishing trip, and young women were the catch. Although only thirty-five women between 1919 and 1925 were detained in local custody for breaching the *VD Act*, twenty-nine of these detentions resulted in sentences of six months or more, and only five of these sentenced women were over the age of thirty.

The criminalization of young women on suspicion of venereal disease, which was itself seen as scientific proof of occasional prostitution, was a clear articulation of the politics of the girl adrift, which was near and dear to reformers' hearts. At the same time, the gendered enforcement of the law gave reform-minded women cause for alarm. Once again the double standard of morality was in evidence. In 1924 Helen Gregory MacGill, celebrated judge (among feminist circles) of the Vancouver Juvenile Court,[54] lamented the bad enforcement of a good law to the readers of *Social Welfare:* "[H]ow curious that usually male patrons are allowed to go, or to pay their forfeitable bails or fines, even when taken in the same raid where the women are required to submit to medical examination ... The pity of it is that both man and woman should not stand at least equal in the eyes of the law."[55] Some women, perhaps in agreement with MacGill, found ways to elude the intrusive laws that over-regulated their bodies and practices. Nellie C. was sentenced to the Mercer because she was found to be a "person infected with Venereal Disease and having been notified by the Medical Officer of Health to undergo proper medical treatment and to produce to him such evidence that you are undergoing such medical treatment did neglect to do so." However, after suffering through the painful treatments at the Mercer, Nellie was released, on the promise that she continue her treatments in Hamilton, where she was discharged.[56] Mercer and public health officials flew into a flap when they discovered that the address Nellie had given them turned out to be the Hamilton cemetery and that Nellie could not be found.[57]

More commonly, however, many women found their detention time increased because they were infected with a venereal disease, regardless of whether this was the original reason for arrest. Twenty-year-old Marjory L., for example, was convicted as a vagrant in 1924 after a policeman who thought she was a common prostitute because she was wandering the public streets without satisfactory explanation arrested her. The mother tried to secure her daughter's release by telephoning Prison Inspector Dunlop to explain that Marjory was "in no sense a vagrant, but was working in Eaton's store and was coming home from a night party when she was arrested by a detective without any evidence whatever of improper conduct." Dunlop was prepared to support Marjory's early parole "if it is found that the penalty was too severe." However, Superintendent Emma O'Sullivan, in consultation with the Mercer's doctor, Edna Guest, denied Marjory the possibility of early release upon discovering that she had gonorrhea, "which will make it necessary for her to remain many months in this Institution for treatment before she is released." Ultimately, Marjory served seven months and four days of a sentence originally set at six months' imprisonment.[58]

Marjory's extra detention time was such a common outcome of the *VD Act* that it became a matter of concern for prison and public health officials. In 1921 Prison Inspector Dunlop, Public Health Doctor McCullough, and Deputy Crown Attorney Bayly exchanged letters about the "fertile field of discontent when patients are kept over their sentence on account of venereal disease." The solution the trio came up with was to advise magistrates to sentence *all* women to indeterminate sentences, rather than short and definite ones, to avert this "discontent."[59] The restraining powers allowed by the *VD Act* enabled authorities to bypass Judge Middleton's 1917 qualms about the over-elasticity of the vagrancy provisions.

The legal definition of vagrancy, the extra-legal concerns with the girl adrift, the medicalization of crime, and women's changing public roles combined in a variety of ways in the Toronto Women's Court and led to scores of women, mostly young women, defending themselves against official questions about just what kind of girl they were. Held up against typologies of oversexualized or overvictimized women, and held to account for the "ordinary moral standards" of the community, a multitude of women confronted a magistrate to explain their behaviour in automobiles, in dating relationships, at work, and in the streets, parks, and other public places of the city. The good times sought out by urban women could be extremely costly. Although some of the vagrant women were sex workers, most were guilty of bad luck or poor judgement, and a few were openly defiant. In all cases, however, the power of the law was brought to bear upon their nonconformist behaviour. Moreover, vagrancy cases were regularly reported in the press, and this probably acted as a general warning to all women that they must chart a very careful path in a changing city, where a great deal of blame for social ills was placed at the feet of women in public.

"Kleptomaniacs" and "Apparently Useless Thefts"

Women's theft cases were equally amenable to reformers' narratives. Theft was the third most common offence to land women in the city jail cells. Between 1913 and 1934, 574 arrests (12 percent) leading to local detention were for theft, 86 percent of which involved one-time offenders. The conviction rate for theft was 46 percent, which was lower than the general conviction rate of 51 percent over the entire period under examination. But theft charges rarely resulted in either a reformatory or an indeterminate sentence. Most convictions were short-term and definite (without option of a fine), and they were served either at the local jail or the Concord. Sentences for theft typically ranged from as few as five days to the more typical ten days in the city jail to thirty or sixty days at the jail farm. Only forty-three women convicted of theft served sentences of one year or more at the Mercer. The *Criminal Code* distinguished between theft under ten dollars and theft over ten dollars to determine between petty and more serious crimes, but gender prescriptions played an important role as well. As they did in vagrancy charges, extra-legal considerations affected court determinations about what to do with thieving women.

Theft is an underexplored aspect of the history of female crime. This is surprising. Because theft occurred in a variety of places (on the streets, in department stores, and in domestic service employment relations), theft charges offer a glimpse into women's daily routines in the early decades of twentieth-century Toronto. In addition, theft charges offer another window to view prevailing gender ideologies at the turn of the century. Different kinds of theft were narrated differently by the press, and this, in and of itself, can tell us something about idealized notions of women, gender, and propriety. Street crimes were associated with women's sexualized public presence and were seen as a particularly female way to prey upon unsuspecting men. Shoplifting from department stores, on the other hand, was constructed as quintessentially feminine. Because of these gendered dimensions, theft charges often played out in the newspapers as parables about familial relations, especially ideas about good and bad motherhood.

Although theft is officially categorized as a property offence and, thus, as distinct from crimes against either the person or morality, for some offenders a continuing pattern is evident and, from time to time, theft charges, especially as a street offence, appear to be interchangeable with vagrancy and disorderly conduct. Lena E., "a young girl who stayed out late last p.m. and took a room at a hotel," was charged with theft of "a picture, towel and a feather from the sleeping chamber." The articles were recovered, and Lena was given a suspended sentence and a warning from the magistrate "to hurry home at night, because Toronto was a big city, filled with pitfalls for simple little things like herself."[60] Although Lena was technically charged with theft, her case, which appeared under the subheading "Maiden Out Late," comes across in the press as being very similar to the "girl adrift" story. By contrast, in 1920 a "dusky maiden" who had picked the pocket of one Ike Rockstein outside Union Station was convicted of disorderly conduct after, it was implied, what had been an illicit proposition by her.[61] No doubt the race of each of these minor thieves influenced the different perceptions of their acts: Lena was constituted largely as a danger to herself; the dusky pickpocket, meanwhile, appears as a racialized and sexualized threat to an ordered city.

The blurry line between a variety of disorderly behaviours and property crimes is further exemplified in the 1913 case of repeat offender Hazel W. (1913-17). Because Hazel refused summary conviction and elected trial by jury (a selection she later changed to trial by judge without jury), a paper trail of her case exists. Her criminal case file includes the complaint made by the victim, Nick N., of 125 Centre Street, to the police: "[Complainant] will say that def. called to him from basement of house on Terauly [sic] near Elm. He went down. She caught him around the waist and began hugging and dancing around him and asking him if he loved her. His money was in his inside coat pocket[,] he told her he did not love her and pushed her away from him and saw his pocket book on the floor. The money $5.00 was gone[,] he caught her[,] and another Italian coming along at the time went for the police. She gave back the money." Hazel was found guilty of theft from the person by Judge Morgan and convicted to two weeks in the local jail.[62]

Each of these women's crimes seems to have had as much to do with suspicions of prostitution as with theft. It is, then, even more noteworthy that men appear as victims rather than as participants in, or seekers of, casual sexual encounters (why *did* Nick go to the basement with Hazel?). Indeed, the potential victimization of hapless men at the hands of beguiling women was sometimes the object lesson in newspaper accounts of street theft cases. In 1918 "over-friendly" Frances J. was sentenced to thirty days at the jail farm for theft after being found guilty of meeting William L., "a lonely French-Canadian, near a downtown hotel" and "abstracting $50 from his pocket."[63] William appears as a victim, and his loneliness is presented as sufficient explanation of his encounter with a woman at a city hotel at night. In 1920 Frances appeared again in the Women's Court on a similar charge:

> Eleven-thirty p.m. on Parliament St. George W–, an eminently respectable man, hurrying home with a plug of tobacco and – supposedly – $30 in his pocket. Young son with him. Fluffy young lady, Frances J–, with French accent, steps up and engages Pa in conversation. Boy discreetly moves on about 100 yards. After the interview, which lasts about three minutes, Pa tears himself away and joins boy. Feels in his pocket. Still has tobacco, but money is gone. However, there wasn't enough evidence to prove that Frances had taken it, and the charge of theft against her was dismissed.[64]

George W. hardly comes off well in this story, but he was, nonetheless, the complainant in this case, victimized by Frances's audacity. Tried variously through disorderly conduct and theft charges, and recorded by the press in narratives that most closely resemble tales of vagrancy, street crimes by women were established, discursively at least, as an offshoot of their suspect presence on the street in the first place. Women who were out and about in Toronto at night were associated with prostitution, and theft was yet one more charge, no more or less accurate than any other, by which to regulate their public presence.

By contrast, women who shoplifted, women who were typically one-time offenders, offered an entirely different storyline. Elaine Abelson's history of shoplifting demonstrates the ways in which kleptomania emerged simultaneously with the department store itself.[65] Indeed, the very term *kleptomania* was invented in the nineteenth century as a way to distinguish middle-class shoplifters from their poorer counterparts like Hazel W. and Frances J. It was received medical wisdom in the late nineteenth and early twentieth centuries that women, bedazzled by the opulent displays of the new shopping culture, could not help themselves from taking what they were meant to desire. In other words middle-class women had a "sickness" that they could not control and that made them victims of their very femaleness, rather than deviants from it. Recall Margaret Patterson's condemnation in 1914 of the lack of separation of different types of offenders at the city jail, an oversight she believed resulted in the moral endangerment of the "innocent lambs who were in jail for shoplifting."[66] The ability to distinguish between female deviance and female weakness was another crucial and legitimating feature of the Women's Court.

The femininity of shoplifters was continually reinforced in the Women's Court and by the press. Women stole from department stores regularly, and they stole distinctly female items. Thus, Sadie F. and Mary L. were each sentenced to jail for twenty days because they "had a little sport in Simpson's store, picking up various little articles that happened to please their dainty tastes."[67] Annie I. was sentenced to four months at the jail farm for "stealing a blouse, silk handkerchiefs, a muffler and a vest from the Robt [sic] Simpson store."[68] Jean R., "an elderly widow," was remanded for a week after she "admitted she took a $19 dress from a departmental store."[69] Annie B. received concurrent thirty-day sentences at the jail farm after being arrested "in Simpson's wearing a fur coat which she had just picked up without paying for it" and for having other stolen goods from Eaton's found in her possession.[70] Kate P. spent ten days in jail "for the theft of a piece of dress goods and a bar of chocolate from the R. Simpson Co."[71] From extravagant items such as a fur coat, to small luxuries such as a bar of chocolate, to everyday items such as dresses, skirts, blouses, and undergarments, Toronto women often helped themselves to the new and desirable goods of an emerging consumer culture.

Most of the women who were tried for shoplifting in the Women's Court were working-class women. Thus, they did not resemble the ideal kleptomaniac constructed by medical discourses. Nonetheless, given its association with a distinctly middle-class femininity, women who appeared before the court on a shoplifting charge could often mitigate the consequences of their crime if they could show that they were otherwise decent women. Lydia R., mother of two small children (one of whom was ill), who had stolen a diamond ring valued at one hundred dollars from Simpson's, wept openly while she explained to the court that her husband "had been out of work for quite a while, but recently found some, and things had begun to look up a little." She was remanded to her husband's care "for [her] child's sake."[72] Mary, a middle-aged woman recently arrived in the city and a stranger to "shopping etiquette," offered up a paragon of country matronhood undone by the sensation of the department store phenomenon:

> When Mary went down to Simpson's to buy some clothing she found the clerks too busy to attend to her. Two of them were waiting for their change to come up the chute, two of them had been at a dance the night before, and one who hadn't

was listening, and the last in the circle was serving a bona fide customer. Mary didn't want to interrupt the dance seance, even if she had the nerve, which she hadn't. So she went round and gathered up the three articles she wanted from the underwear counter, put them in her big shopping bag, and started for the paying office in the basement to pay for them. She told two of the court workers this and they believed it but the store detective didn't, so he had her arrested.[73]

The juxtaposition of farm-raised Mary's traditional femininity against the temptations of the modern city – symbolized by the "busy dance" of the department store and embodied in the young, self-absorbed female salesclerks – is a tale of urban gender anxieties. Needless to say, the story had a happy ending for poor, bewildered Mary. Her "round shouldered husband came in in time to learn that she might go home free on condition that such carelessness was not allowed to occur again. He understood at once, but it won't probably be till Mary arrives safe at home in her own little hall that she will really believe she won't have to wear stripes and handcuffs for the rest of her natural existence." Mary's passive femininity both landed her in the Women's Court and resulted in her release.

Mary's story, although extreme in its narrative and ideal types, is typical of the recurrent familial theme that characterized women's department store theft cases in the press. In this way, incidences of shoplifting served as a legitimating tool of the Women's Court itself. Perhaps most paradigmatic of this device is the story of mother and daughter Hannah and Annie Allison. On 4 February 1918, the Allisons appeared in the Women's Court after they were caught stealing two pairs of underwear from Simpson's. Upon hearing of this typical female offence, Magistrate Denison prepared to send the mother to jail, reasoning that she had been the instigator of the crime and a poor influence on her apparently guileless daughter. At that moment, the daughter stepped forward and, in a "quiet, clear tone," offered herself in place of her mother. It was a sensational moment that "g[a]ve onlookers the sort of thrills you get at the movies." Rising to the occasion, the Crown attorney suggested to Denison that he "let the mother go for the sake of her daughter's request, and give the girl her freedom because of her willingness to sacrifice herself to her mother." The magistrate chose not to stand in the way of proper respect for one's mother and agreed to release them both. "Was it not a beautiful scene?" asked the reporter for the *Telegram*, and then answered, "Yea, verily."[74]

Feminized Justice

The foundational values of the Women's Court found expression in this simple case of shoplifting. In the sequestered surroundings of the Women's Court, removed from the foul atmosphere of the "regular" police court and the cold hand of masculine justice, a small family drama could be played out to its satisfactory conclusion. The redeeming value of family relations and, even more specifically, the moral correctness of daughterly devotion and exemplary motherhood, embodied literally in the Allisons, could take centre stage and be both cause and effect of feminized justice.

The values of motherhood could also be presented in cases in which the biological maternal figure was suspect. Thus, under the headline "Mothers and Girls Caught Shoplifting," we learn about "five women from Stratford, looking just like one more family party," who had come into Toronto for the day, ostensibly to shop, but who had engaged in a shoplifting spree. The two mothers, their daughters, and one young friend had collectively taken "four knives, three souvenirs, four packages of hairpins, three spoons and four forks," which were valued at less than two dollars, from Knox's and "ladies' clothing, plumes, jewelry [sic], and cutlery," valued at between three hundred and four hundred dollars, from Eaton's. In the Women's Court, Denison set bail for the young friend, Mabel, at two hundred dollars, while the four other women were to pay five hundred dollars each. After securing her own bail, Mabel was released to secure bail for the others, and she shocked the court when she said that she would get the two thousand dollars from *her* mother. The reporter concluded: "So the two daughters who looked like summer magazine covers, and the two mothers, who would deceive a casual observer into thinking their worst thought to be making the best apple pie for the fair, retired to the prisoners' bench to wait, until Mabel did what she could to free them from the necessity of going to jail with the other inhabitants of the bench." Ultimately, it was only the mothers who were tried, and found guilty, of theft.[75] Motherhood was a tricky thing. By design the Women's Court offered the opportunity for more astute judgement than that of a "casual observer," and good maternal values could triumph over bad mothers.

Another typical way to steal from department stores was through petty fraud.[76] Some women walked out of department stores with merchandise and then attempted to use the store refund policy to get the cash equivalent for the goods. Although technically different from the medicalized definition of kleptomania, a disease which was said to be about the uncontrollable desire for the displayed goods themselves, petty fraud cases enjoyed much the same treatment as kleptomania cases in the Women's Court. Thus, Marie R.'s sentence of fifteen days for fraud was reduced to two days after arguments were made that "she has for months been caring for a sick relative, and sometimes has not known which way to turn."[77] Harriet W. was given only five days by the County Court Judges' Criminal Court after being found guilty of "trying to get a refund [from Simpson's] on a skirt [valued at $22.30] which she said she had purchased a few days previously" but for which she had no receipt. Because "she was very demure and apparently very penitent," the judge "declared that he would make the sentence as light as possible."[78] Similar lenience was granted to a young woman who pleaded guilty to having "stolen a new dressing case worth $5, had taken it back to Eaton's store where it was bought, and had received the money in return." Magistrate Denison agreed to a light sentence of five days when her counsel explained the circumstances: "She had been out of work, had just obtained employment in a restaurant, and needed the money for a room."[79] Clearly, department store fraud was a more forgivable way of earning needed cash than the obvious and feared alternative of becoming a good time girl.

Women who engaged in theft from their employers were much more suspect. For the reformers, this was personal. The middle-class community that was interested in urban uplift was generally troubled by the relationship between domestic service and crime, especially prostitution. The social survey commissioners had engaged in elaborate sophistry to explain away the obvious connection between this form of employment and women's engagement in prostitution. The low wages and acknowledged lack of personal freedoms that typically characterized domestic service were swept aside by declarative statements that, because domestic servants received room and board, as well as familial surroundings, any woman who left domestic employment to enter the sex trade (either professionally or occasionally) had a personal pathology that defied simple causal explanations.[80] Indeed, like Patterson's vagrant woman, most women incarcerated at the Mercer were paroled to domestic service positions on the reasoning that this would help restore them to respectability. This belief in the redeeming value of domestic service, however, meant that theft by domestics was further evidence of moral sickness.

Magda Fahrni's examination of the mistress-servant relationship in turn-of-the-century Ontario reveals that domestic service is best seen as "a unique spatial process that transgressed the physical separation of the classes ... In so doing, it strained an equally rigid ideological separation between the respectable and the disreputable."[81] These strains were evident when day servants Sarah and Mary appeared in the Women's Court for stealing leftover food from their domestic employer. The court reporter chose not to examine the low wages or working conditions under which Mary and Sarah laboured but, instead, found the (seemingly elusive) motive for their crime in their home life: "No one ever suspected Mary and Sarah of having any kind of life apart from the kitchen, but some of the detectives wanting to probe the motive for this apparently useless theft discovered that each had a husband, and these husbands have a strong objection to earning their own roasts and puddings. To them each night Sarah and Mary, like dutiful wives, carried home as much provender as they could successfully manoeuvre at a time."[82] Fahrni notes that cast-off clothing and surplus food had once been the perquisites of the job, but as employers moved away from this tradition in the twentieth century, "it is possible that servants' appropriation of their 'due' became, in the eyes of their mistresses, theft."[83] However, if Mary and Sarah were taking only what they believed they were owed, we would not learn of it from the press. To the contrary, their case was reported as a cautionary tale about masculinity and femininity. Men who failed to provide for their families were not only disreputable on their own merit but forced "their" women to dishonour themselves as well. Thus, an example of class inequality was transformed into a story of moral respectability. As Fahrni argues, as much as women employers hoped to impart middle-class values to their employees, the threat was ever-present that their employees would bring working-class vices – idleness, sexual licence, insobriety, and dishonesty – into the middle-class home. In charges of domestic employee theft, the Women's Court took its role of policing working-class respectability seriously.

Given general middle-class anxieties about "the servant problem," it is possible that the sentences for these crimes were meant to be exemplary ones. Magistrate Denison said as much when he convicted Minnie M. for stealing from her employer: "If they get it into their heads that for the first offence they get off, there will be no stopping this."[84] Ella L., "a maid in the house of the Government officials," received a reformatory sentence after being found guilty of "tak[ing] advantage of her opportunities to go through the pockets and handbags of guests."[85] Her crime might have unnerved Denison, who, given his position, may well have been one of these house guests. The usual routes to lenience – active contrition and evidence of otherwise respectable character – were less successful when domestic servants stole the personal property of their employers. Thus, even though hotel maid Kathleen O.'s employer spoke well of her and was "very kindly disposed toward [her]" and Kathleen herself "dropp[ed] her head on the arm that lay at right angles on the dock rail [and] sobbed violently" during her trial for theft from the hotel safe, she was sentenced to two months at the Concord jail farm.[86]

Although it was undifferentiated in the arrest records, it is clear that theft had variant forms and multiple meanings. Officially distinct from offences against morality, theft could prove to be yet another regulatory device for women whose public personae were troublesome to urban reformers. Clear differences also existed between those women whose offences were an affront to middle-class notions of female propriety and those women whose crimes affirmed their very femininity. The ideal-type kleptomaniac was characterized as "the wife of a respectable man and the mother of children"[87] who had weaknesses that could, at least, be understood, if not always condoned. The more that women called on their familial belonging and deference, the more likely they were to be released or given a light sentence. Meanwhile, women who stole from their employers seldom received lenient treatment. Domestic service was meant to redeem, and its violation through petty larceny was an affront not only to the putative victim but also to middle-class values and feelings of security in general. To the extent that the mistress-servant relationship was imbued with maternalist ideals, the existence of thieves in its midst was unsettling evidence that the relationship "fell short of the ideal of maternal benevolence and daughterly deference."[88] The Women's Court offered a form of restitution for this effrontery. Overall, different aspects of gender ideology were played out repeatedly in theft cases, and these cases offered up varying bases of legitimacy for the Women's Court. From time to time, these cases also show us female offenders in their daily lives, workplaces, and public arenas such as department stores and hotels – places in which their petty crimes were lent significance by the very existence of the Women's Court itself.

Conclusion

The central concern of maternal feminists in the Women's Court was the sexual safety and propriety of their metaphorical daughters, and vagrancy was the criminal charge that most directly regulated the public behaviour of young urban women. Yet, even their attention to vagrancy was organized by limitations and imaginative conventions. Because it was a broad, vague, and flexible status offence, vagrancy had many meanings and different implications for the large number of women who were criminalized for their publicly "deviant" behaviours. Women who worked as prostitutes were distinguished from those who had temporarily lost their moral compass, and this distinction was a core feature in the very legitimation of the court itself. Yet, both types of vagrant women could find themselves incarcerated, in one case to punish and in the other to "protect." It is unlikely that the convicted women themselves saw much distinction between these ends.

Thieving was another common route into the Women's Court, and it was another potentially redeemable offence, depending on the type of "girl" the detainee could present herself as. Drawing on available tropes of femininity, including befuddled matronhood, daughterly deference, and maternal desperation, and demonstrating active contrition through visible confusion, bowed heads, and tears, some women were able to navigate their way through a court appearance to relative safety. In large part the evidence presented here confirms other feminist empirical research into women's criminal case outcomes that challenge the chivalry thesis, that is, the idea that judges are unlikely to be punitive to women out of a sense of chivalric protection. As scholars such as Helen Boritch have pointed out, this hypothesis has no foundation; rather, those women who most closely fit with idealized versions of femininity were those most likely to be granted leniency.[89] By contrast, women who strayed too far from the normative centre of "good womanhood" were more likely to receive harsh sentences for less serious offences than men. But a close examination of women who stole reveals that the meanings attributed to women's petty theft were even more layered. Street theft was distinguishable from kleptomania and theft from employers. The very location and type of theft was itself a marker of character and gave stealing a variety of meanings that were carried into the courtroom.

Together, vagrancy and theft charges grant us insights into the ways that young and mostly one-time offenders were treated in the Women's Court. Women charged with vagrancy and theft often embodied the friendless girls who were originally imagined as the principal beneficiaries of a separate court for women, and their trials were, therefore, the most publicized in the minutes of the women's organizations and the most likely to be broadcast in the local newspapers. Although both charges could mean different things to different women and, therefore, should not be too broadly characterized, they are nevertheless distinct from the other two main categories of crime violated by Toronto women: bawdy house and alcohol-related offences. Most notably, the charge of drunkenness brought in far more women far more often than either vagrancy or theft, yet it was rarely spoken of at all, by either the TLCW or the press. But taken together, the charges of drunkenness and those related to bawdy houses reveal a very different picture of female criminality than that offered by the TLCW. Here, the recidivist population is most evident, and it is here that the Women's Court's legitimacy was most sorely tested. The next chapter turns to these offences to examine how the Women's Court functioned less as a site of (potential) redemption for wayward women and more like a police court that dispensed routine justice.

"Up again, Jenny?"
Repeat Offenders in the Women's Court

The cases of vagrants and thieves might have been most amenable to reformers' narratives, but the most likely reason for an arrest and appearance in the Women's Court was public drunkenness. Of the 4,781 entries collected about women's cases from the jail registers, 1,088, or nearly one in four (23 percent), were for drunkenness.[1] The rates at which women were arrested for drunkenness tended to mirror their overall arrest rates in general. For example, in 1913, when women constituted 6 percent of all arrests, they also represented 6 percent of all drunkenness charges.[2] Moreover, these were often the same women. Women charged with drunkenness were the women most likely to be repeat offenders: 65 percent of all drunk charges are attributable to recidivists, and recidivists charged with drunkenness constitute a full 15 percent of all women charged with an offence that resulted in at least one night in the city jail.

This chapter explores the world of repeat offenders to the extent that their lives were made visible by their journeys through the Toronto Women's Court. Unfortunately, this view is a limited one. Most women charged with drunkenness were not sent to the reformatory, and, in the absence of case files, it is difficult to get information about the circumstances that led to most of these arrests. Police reporters did not write up women's drinking cases very often either, presumably because they represented such an ordinary and, as I will argue below, unwomanly offence. When they did, their "manner of telling the truth"[3] tended to construct drunk women, like drunk men, as victims of their own inner demons and a general lack of self-discipline.[4] Capturing the essence of both the humour and the inevitability of such indulgence, a reporter from the *(Toronto) Star* related the following about one Women's Court habitué:

> "Up again, Jenny?" queried the magistrate, looking into the wheedling face which hadn't a forty-year-old brain behind it for nothing.
>
> "Sure, now, and I'm working, an' I wasn't so drunk an' all but I could have go' home. I have a good place, your Honor, and if somebody hadn't give me a glass ..."
>
> Upon confirmation of the working part of it by the matron, Jenny was discharged to go her voluble way until next time a friend should spend a dime on her.[5]

Although an object of some amusement, "voluble" Jenny, in court neither for the first nor, we are assured, the last time, did not fit within reform discourse about the potentially therapeutic value of a separate court for women.

The records from the Toronto Women's Court help to flesh out the story of petty criminality by women whose routine encounters with the criminal justice system stemmed largely, albeit not exclusively, from their drinking patterns. As was already indicated, these repeat offenders were demographically distinguishable from the young women adrift whose plight captured the imagination of the Toronto Local Council of Women (TLCW). Seventy-nine percent of women charged with drunkenness were over the age of thirty; they were overwhelmingly Roman Catholic; and they tended to be itinerant. They moved in and out of the formal labour market as domestic workers, and many of them worked as prostitutes from time to time. They were as likely to be arrested in bawdy and disorderly houses as on the streets. They were charged under the local bylaw prohibiting public drunkenness[6] and under *Criminal Code* charges for vagrancy and frequenting or keeping houses of ill fame. Their lives were entangled with one another's, and they were often arrested, convicted, and incarcerated together. Some were repentant and promised to abstain from intoxicating substances, while others were defiant and determined to lead their own lives. Importantly, through their repeated encounters with the criminal justice system, they gained a knowledge of the mechanisms of justice that allowed them to navigate the system in ways that could mitigate its severity. At the same time, because of their repeated offences, they came under an evolving network of surveillance coordinated through reformatories, parole officers, police, and courts that tells us something about how officials viewed the lives of street women.

In sharp contrast to the highly moralized protective justice offered to young women charged with vagrancy and petty theft, these women's appearances in the Women's Court elicited few secular sermons from the bench on the "right path" to restored femininity. Perhaps most illustrative of the ordinariness of these charges is the exchange between inveterate drinker and sometimes prostitute Daisy H. (1913-34) and temperance-supporting, anti-prostitution campaigner Magistrate Margaret Patterson. Arrested for public drunkenness on 18 June 1925 with Bridget D. (1913-28), Daisy H. had been ordered to the local jail to sober up for her appearance in court the next day:

> Daisy is one of the most cheerful "regulars" around the court. In addition she possesses a ready smile and a ready wit. She is Irish.
>
> "I'm out of work," she announced.
>
> "No need to be," flashed the bench. "Employers are trying to buy women to do work."
>
> "I wish," shot back Daisy, "somebody would buy me."
>
> The little verbal tilt put the court in high spirits and after the amusement subsided it was discovered Daisy had escaped with a lecture on the virtues of temperance and timely advice to hie herself to the employment bureaus.[7]

Bridget was also discharged, after promising (unrealistically) to "take the pledge." The presumed inevitability of drunkenness, the routine nature of prostitution, the confident bearing of court "regulars," the racialized explanations of disorderliness, and the clear familiarity between the bench, the press, and the women charged on these offences put to the test claims about the necessity of a distinct criminal venue for a distinct group of offenders. The co-appearance of two long-term recidivists is also noteworthy. Indeed, older street women were themselves part of a community. This community was not organized by gender alone, nor did it have much of a relationship to the imagined maternal authority and moral reform practices of Toronto's prominent women activists. Organized by class, ethnicity, urban geography, and a penchant for alcohol, street women in Toronto were not always distinguishable from the women of the brothels. Although this does not suggest that drunk charges were, in reality, prostitution charges, it does indicate fluidity in the criminality of Toronto's recidivist population. In combination, alcohol and bawdy house offences reveal a decidedly distinct community of criminalized women in Toronto whose material existence was not a part of the imaginings of crime put forward by white, middle-class maternal feminists.

"Her inordinate desire for liquor"

Despite a clear relationship between drinking and female criminality, little scholarship exists that examines the female world of alcohol consumption and its criminalization. One possible reason for this is suggested, respectively, by Mary Anne Poutanen and M. Elizabeth Langdon, both of whom argue that the nineteenth-century equation of female criminality with prostitution remained remarkably stable throughout the twentieth century.[8] As a result most studies of female crime focus on vagrancy, and within these studies, "contemporary researchers often uncritically reproduce the opinion of nineteenth-century social reformers that all women vagrants were street prostitutes."[9] However, empirical research demonstrates that female crime is not only, or even predominantly, prostitution-related. Poutanen's research, for example, suggests that although most researchers count drunk and disorderly arrests as thinly veiled forms of the regulation of prostitutes,[10] the relationship between these charges is more complex. Her analysis of women arrested for vagrancy from 1810 to 1842 in Montreal indicates that the converse is at least equally accurate: vagrancy charges were often laid against women who were publicly drunk and disorderly. Similarly, Judith Fingard concludes from her survey of ninety-two Halifax "jailbirds," forty-three of whom were women, that "few of [their] crimes ... were unconnected with drunkenness."[11]

Perhaps the most determining factor in the relative lack of attention to the relationship between alcohol and female criminality is that drinking has been seen (and, arguably, continues to be seen) as a feature of a rough-and-ready working-class male culture.[12] Cheryl Warsh suggests that the equation of men with drinking is akin to the equation of women with prostitution: both conceptual frameworks emanate from nineteenth-century criminological theory and from the middle-class reformers' politics of the double moral standard.[13] The rise of the medical profession in the late nineteenth century and the activism of the temperance movement led to social changes in perceptions of alcohol consumption. Whereas in the earlier decades of the nineteenth century drinking by women for medicinal or social reasons was acceptable, by the latter decades abstinence from alcohol became a part of the definition of respectability for women.[14] Moreover, the women's temperance movement engaged in a stinging critique of the male subculture of drinking, especially the saloon: "The temperance movement vilified the saloon as a den of iniquity that sent forth drunkards to impoverish, injure and perhaps murder their families, and drinking establishments of any type were portrayed as the enemies of all women. Women who frequented such places were assumed to be ... gin-shop derelicts."[15] Mariana Valverde adds that this was also a racialized politics: the feminist attack on drinking was, simultaneously, an attack on specifically European masculine vices and a statement on "civilization." White male temperance became the hallmark of the ability to rule an empire.[16] Given the racialized masculinization of the drinking culture, women who drank or who participated in the saloon culture were de-womanized and seen, instead, as exhibiting features of a "bastardized masculinity."[17] As the flip side of the coin to hypersexualized prostitutes, "deviant women, like the alcoholic ... transgressed sexual boundaries," albeit in different ways.[18]

Despite historians' relative inattention to women's drinking cultures, drunk charges, like vagrancy offences, were a potent regulatory device. Renisa Mawani has argued for a different context that "[a]mong other things, the regulation of liquor was about space – who could drink, where, and with whom."[19] A similar claim can be made about early twentieth-century Toronto: drunkenness charges were another way to patrol racialized and sexualized borders. Some women charged with drunkenness were clearly in violation of imagined racial boundaries. White women's relationships with black men were especially suspect. In 1916 (the same) Daisy H. (1913-34) was committed to the Mercer after evidence was presented that "she was drinking and living with a colored man to whom she is not married (she is a white woman) ... I believe she is better given the protection which this institution affords."[20] In 1927 Fannie H. (1917-31), another white woman, was also afforded institutional "protection" after her husband reported that she had "stayed out all Saturday night at 313 Adelaide Street West (with bunch of niggers), and she was drunk when he brought her home on Sunday, and that she would not stay but returned to the Adelaide Street address."[21] Fannie was also sentenced to the Mercer.

Most women convicted of drunkenness, however, served their time at the Concord Industrial Farm for Women. Police court magistrates tended to treat drunkenness as a routine, but not acute, problem that was easily answered by a short sentence. Overall, 585 of a total 1,088 (54 percent) drunk charges noted in the jail registers resulted in conviction. Thus, drunkenness had a higher conviction rate than the overall rate of conviction experienced by women detained in the local jail cells. One in five women convicted for drunkenness (116) were able to pay their fines, usually from jail, although 6 percent (35) had enough money in pocket when they were arrested to pay their fine of ten to fifty dollars (plus costs) in court. Only 4 percent (25) of those convicted for drunkenness were sent to the Mercer, and in 1919, 1922, 1925, 1931, and 1934, no woman convicted of being drunk was sent from the city cells to the reformatory. Thirty-nine percent (229) served their sentences, usually of thirty days or less, in the city jail, and another 30 percent (176) were sentenced, typically for three to six months, to the Concord. These relatively short prison sentences were often referred to by the press as "taking the rest cure."

As the term *rest cure* indicates, the reform ideals for these women were limited to a vaguely therapeutic notion of time spent at a jail, where productive labour involved minor agricultural work. In other words physical outdoor labour and compulsory abstinence was as much "reform" as chronically drunk women could expect. Some of the drunken women evidently also believed in the benefits of forced abstinence for themselves. Helen G. (1916-19), arrested for drunkenness seven times between May and October 1914 alone, was assessed by the reformatory doctor, John King, as "a woman of unusually bright intellect, and possessed of good general knowledge; but unfortunately has been a slave to ardent spirits, and when indulging in their use, gets into trouble through an ungovernable temper and is ready for a wordy explosion, or physical disturbance." At her latest arrest, on 23 October 1914, she herself asked the court to sentence her to six months at the Mercer, "hoping," wrote the doctor, "by having that long period of abstinence to withstand any further temptation." After serving an indeterminate sentence as an exemplary inmate, Helen was released in July 1916. Unfortunately for Helen, however, the temptations of the outside world were too much. She was back in the Women's Court and sentenced to the jail farm for public drunkenness by December of that year.[22]

In the main, the files of those few women who were sent to the Mercer Reformatory from the Women's Court on drunkenness charges indicate, more than anything, how little the officials at the reformatory wanted them there. For example, long-time offender Susan W. (1913-34) was convicted for her "20th to 30th time" on 19 May 1921 for drunkenness and sentenced to six months at the women's farm, but she found herself transferred, instead, to the Mercer (the reasons for this transfer are not stated in the file). Superintendent Emma O'Sullivan wrote immediately to Provincial Secretary Dunlop to request that Susan be transferred back to the farm: "This woman was an inmate of the Reformatory the first year of my superintendence [1901], was then, and is now, a victim of Drunkenness. She has degenerated until she seems scarcely responsible for her actions ... and is very difficult to manage among the many young girls, who now constitute the largest portion of our population ... Do you not think she would be better at the Industrial Farm at Concord?"[23] Similarly, Annie B. (1913-17), another woman regularly convicted for drunkenness, found herself serving her December 1916 sentence for drunkenness at the Mercer. Annie's case worker characterized her as "a confirmed alcoholic, forty years of age, [who] gives no promise of ever being much better" and recommended that she be transferred to the Concord: "She is of the type of heavy drinkers for whom the farm life would appear to be especially suitable ... I believe that if there is a chance for her anywhere, it is more likely to be at the Farm than in an institution where the life is as confining as it is here."[24] Clearly, reformatory officials were not entirely unsympathetic to these older, alcoholic women. But nor did they see them as appropriate charges for whom a program of reformation into a more respectable form of womanhood was either suitable or possible.

In part as a response to the undeniable connection between alcohol and arrest rates, the *Ontario Temperance Act (OTA)* was proclaimed on 6 September 1916.[25] Originally passed as a war-time measure, the *OTA* became a permanent piece of legislation after a province-wide referendum in 1919, and it remained in effect until 1926, when it was replaced by the *Liquor Control Act*. Newspapers heralded the salubrious relationship between a dry province and general well-being, especially as measured by crime rates.[26] The *OTA* prohibited the sale, keeping, and distribution of liquor and beer, except in a private dwelling or by those approved by the newly established Licensing Commission.[27] The penalty for a breach of the *OTA* was, on the first offence, a fine of no less than two hundred dollars and no more than one thousand dollars or imprisonment for no less than three months. For a second offence, the penalty was imprisonment for no less than six and no more than twelve months, with no option of a fine. An amendment in 1920 increased the maximum fine to two thousand dollars. The effects of the *OTA* on crime rates were immediate and two-fold: the number of women (and men) arrested dropped dramatically, especially for drunkenness, but a whole new group of women, with no observable history of conflict with the law, was criminalized for breach of the *OTA* (BOTA charges).

In 1913 a total of 15,116 men and women were arrested by the Toronto police for drunkenness: 924 were women. In 1916 the police made a total of 9,639 arrests for drunkenness, and women accounted for 492 of them. But by 1919 the numbers had dropped staggeringly: there were only 3,925 arrests for drunkenness, and only 222 of these arrests involved female offenders.[28] The number of women who spent at least one night in jail on a drunk charge dropped from 361 in 1913 to 105 in 1916 to a mere 20 in 1919. Fourteen of the latter were recidivists. Clearly, most women were no longer able to get themselves inebriated enough to catch the attention of police, although some women never stopped drinking, and many of them continued to get caught while under the influence.

The determination of some to carry on their inebriate ways must have come as a shock to criminal justice officials. So convinced were they that stemming the flow of alcohol would be sufficient to cure women of their vices that several women, all with long histories of drunkenness, were released from the Mercer in the days immediately following the passage of the *OTA*. A memo from Letitia Scott, field officer for the Mercer, dated 4 October 1916 demonstrates the cautious optimism with which the *OTA* was passed:

> *Re confirmed alcoholics:* Annie B., Ethel S. and Helen H., who have all served several terms for intoxication and are confirmed alcoholics, are very anxious to be given a trial on parole as soon as possible now that prohibition is in force. While I do not consider any one of them to be particularly hopeful, at the same time they ... might do much better now than formerly ... I am in favour of giving them a chance to make good on parole – on condition that they are placed under the supervision of the Field Officer and ... abstain from intoxicating liquors.[29]

At least eight other "confirmed alcoholics" were released on the day, or in the days shortly after, the *OTA* came into force, and all had the same notation in their files: "[T]he principal trouble with [this inmate] is her inordinate desire for liquor."[30] As it turned out, Scott's misgivings were not wholly misplaced. Several of these women, including Ethel S. and Annie B., were soon returned to the Mercer for breaching their parole conditions by indulging in intoxicating liquors.

The continued appearance of repeat offenders for drunkenness can be explained not only by their "inordinate desire for liquor" but also by its availability. On 22 September 1916, just six days after the proclamation of the *OTA*, Pearl W. earned "the honor of being the first lady in Toronto to be crowned with a fine ... under the canopy of the Ontario Temperance Act."[31] By 1925 breaches of the *OTA* were the fourth most common offence among women that resulted in at least one night in jail. The *OTA* may have limited access to some social activities, but clearly it also created new opportunities for women to contribute to their household economies, particularly in the Ward. Thus, Rachel S., a Jewish woman, "being a bit of a philanthropist, and aware that a desert thirst is just as likely to attack a man with only ten cents to his name as one with the price of a case ... opened a liquor shop in her kitchen and did a thriving business in ten cent 'hips' until arrested by police."[32] Similarly, Esther R., another Jewish woman from the Ward, was sentenced to the Concord after selling liquor from her home on Walton Street. Esther was a thirty-two-year-old Austrian immigrant who had been living in Canada for ten years, a mother to four young Canadian-born children, and a woman whose "housekeeping might be preserved in the Museum to be exhibited to Domestic Science students as a fearful example." Her husband taught Hebrew school in the winter and was a peddler in the summer. Esther, officially listed as a housewife, sold illegal alcohol to expand her household's income.[33]

Rachel S. and Esther R. are, in many ways, representative of the women criminalized by the *OTA*. Women charged with breaching the *OTA* – by having, selling, or distributing liquor without a licence – tended to share certain demographic characteristics that distinguished them from other criminalized women. Notably, whereas less than half of all women in my records were born outside of Canada (46 percent), a staggering 71 percent of those arrested on BOTA charges were non-Canadian born. Overwhelmingly, these women were of eastern European (mostly Russian, Polish, and Austrian) descent. Similarly, while only 4 percent of all cases against women surveyed in the jail registers are listed as Jewish, 27 percent of the women arrested on BOTA charges were Jews.[34] Kelly Pineault's survey of Concord inmates between 1915 and 1935 reveals that 90 percent of all women sentenced there for BOTA offences were Jews and Catholics.[35] Additionally, women charged with BOTA offences tended to be married, with housewife listed as their occupation, and, with very few exceptions, they were over thirty years of age, with many of them over the age of forty. Nor were these women recent postwar (or, in the case of Russians, post-revolution) immigrants: almost to a woman, they had been living in Canada for ten to twenty-five years. In other words these women had been living relatively peacefully, at least according to official records, in Toronto for a decade or more, and they were criminalized by the *OTA*. The vast majority (84 percent) were one-time offenders. If they were convicted and were unable to pay the fines, they were most likely sentenced to the Concord Industrial Farm for Women. Remarkably, and perhaps as evidence of the lucrativeness of the trade, 21 percent of the women paid the hefty fee of two hundred to one thousand dollars levied by the courts on conviction.

Although they never again approximated pre-*OTA* levels, charges for drunkenness once again began to dominate the court dockets after the repeal of the Act in 1926. In 1928, 163 women spent at least one night in the local cells because they had been charged with drunkenness. No doubt driven by their "inordinate desire for liquor," nearly half – 48 percent – were repeat offenders. In 1934, 107 women spent at least one night in the city jail because of an arrest for drunkenness, and 51 percent of them were repeat offenders. And women continued to supplement their household economies through the unlicensed sale of alcohol. In 1928, breach of the *Liquor Control Act* was the most common charge for women that led to the city jail, and it was the third and the second most common charge in 1931 and 1934, respectively. Regardless of various liquor regulations, the consumption and sale of alcohol continued to be important parts of women's community life throughout the period under examination.

"A segregated and despised class"

Although repeat offenders were most likely to be arrested for drunkenness, almost half of them had at least one bawdy house offence on their record, and a great deal can be learned about their offending patterns by locating them in their urban environment. Indeed, when the social survey commissioners lamented the diffusion of "immorality" beyond a commercialized locale defined by "a segregated and despised class," they were, in effect, acknowledging the existence of a boundary that determined where prostitution should, and should not, occur. As the records from the Women's Court show, this moral cartography was, largely, realized.

The "out and out prostitute" was sometimes arrested for vagrancy, but more often she was charged for being a member of a house of ill fame. Between 1913 and 1934, 554 women were arrested and detained as keepers, and 431 women were detained as inmates, frequenters, or those found in houses of ill fame. Conviction rates were higher for keepers than for inmates. Overall, 52 percent of keepers were convicted, compared to 48 percent of inmates. However, "keeping" stands out in the arrest records because it was one of the few charges (along with abortion and fortune-telling) for which women consistently outnumbered men in arrest rates. Although being an inmate was a feminized offence, in the sense that the proportion of women arrested for this offence consistently exceeded women's general arrest rates, more men than women were arrested for being found in a house of ill fame.[36] My records show that 85 men were detained and tried in the Women's Court for being keepers, while 106 were charged for frequenting or being found in a house of ill fame or disorderly house.[37] As will be discussed below, many of the men charged with keeping were the business partners or husbands of female co-defendants.

Calculating these charges based on local jail entries is an uncertain task, because legal definitions and arrest records could differ in important ways. Technically, the *Criminal Code* grouped together all common bawdy, gaming, betting, gambling, and opium houses as disorderly houses. Thus, a bawdy house charge was a subsection of the broader range of offences that fell under the umbrella of "disorderly houses." The arrest records tended to distinguish between those charged with keeping or being found in a house of ill fame and those charged with the same offences in disorderly houses. However, existing case records indicate that it would be an oversight to dismiss those charges that do not specify a bawdy house offence. In particular, women who used their homes to welcome men could be charged with either keeping or being found in a disorderly house. For example, in 1925 thirty-six-year-old Sarah F. was sentenced to an indeterminate sentence at the Mercer for being a keeper of a disorderly house, because "she admitted that she had brought men into her [rented room in a] home for immoral purposes but stated that no other women had ever been there with her."[38] Similarly, nineteen-year-old Marie L. was sentenced to the Mercer in 1932 for keeping a disorderly house, because she "was constantly sitting at the window [of her sister's house] waving at boys going past. She and her sister invited two into the house and I [Patterson] understand that these boys each gave her two dollars."[39] A private home or rented room used too indiscriminately could easily become a "disorderly house" in court.

A statement given to the police by sometime prostitute Ruby L. offers further insight into the multiple uses of certain addresses as well as the multiple offences with which women were charged. Ruby, thirty years old and with one previous BOTA charge on her record, was arrested for receiving stolen goods in 1924. Although she was initially given a suspended sentence by Judge Emerson Coatsworth of the County Court Judges' Criminal Court, Ruby did find herself serving an indeterminate sentence at the Mercer because she was arrested as a vagrant while on this suspended sentence. Her case file includes her statement to the police about her activities preceding this second arrest:

> I went to live with Mrs. W. at 38 Grange Ave about 6 months ago while I was living with her I brought men to the house for imoral [sic] purposes[.] I used to charge them $5.00 to let them have intercourse with me[.] I kept this up till I left her house that was about a month ago paying Mrs. W. $1.00 for every man I would take to her house[.] [S]he knew what I was taking the men there for[.] I have bought whiskey and alcohol from Mrs. W. and she kept a bootleggers joint while I was living with her ... The money I made for imoral purposes I spent in whiskey in Mrs. W's house.[40]

That illegal liquor and sexual services were combined at 38 Grange may be why some houses were labelled as disorderly rather than as common bawdy houses. I have, therefore, included the more broad disorderly house charges within my calculations for keepers and inmates.[41]

Additionally, the aggregate statistics for disorderly and bawdy house offences must be treated with caution. Although keeping a bawdy house and being an inmate of a bawdy house were the fourth and fifth most common charges overall among women that led to at least one night in jail, there is an enormous fluctuation in the rate of these charges in different years. For example, in 1925, 141 charges of keeping a bawdy house and 129 charges of being found in a bawdy house were laid against women, resulting in their detention in the local jail; in 1919, however, only 18 charges for keeping and 28 charges for being found in a bawdy house are recorded. In 1928, 1931, and 1934, charges for being found in a bawdy house drop out of the top five offences leading to at least one night in jail. In an attempt to explain the nearly 50 percent drop in bawdy house arrests from 1916 to 1917 (from 165 to 91), the chief of police borrowed the logic of the social survey commissioners, concluding that the decrease in prosecutions "does not necessarily indicate that the morality of the City has improved, but merely that sexual intercourse is indulged in in other ways and places beyond the reach of the Police."[42] Another possibility, however, is that the actual number of bawdy houses did not differ substantially over the years, and the statistics may tell us more about policing practices than they do about brothels.

Indeed, this was the conclusion drawn by Toronto's moral reformers, including members of the TLCW. Adamant that police should act to suppress, rather than tolerate, houses of prostitution, Toronto reformers were ever vigilant regarding the practices of the local police. The necessity of this vigilance was articulated by the social survey commissioners, who argued that "[i]f the traffic in vice is tolerated ... it must be in direct violation of the law. And no community can afford to deliberately adopt a policy which sets before all its citizens an example of lawlessness."[43] In response the Toronto police assured the public that "[h]ouses of ill-fame and frequenters thereof ... receive close attention, the law being applied when a conviction was probable ... The allegations made in some quarters that the Police were inclined to be tolerant with sexual vice, are as fantastic as they are untrue."[44] The TLCW was not wholly convinced of this. As is argued in Chapter 2, members continually challenged the (male) police and the (masculine) courts for what they saw as their self-interested disinclination to eliminate houses of prostitution.

The various *Criminal Code* amendments that more sharply delineated the laws surrounding bawdy houses, including crimes specific to men as profiteers and the duty to prosecute by the courts, are indicative of the success moral reformers enjoyed in convincing legislators that the brothel was a pressing social problem.[45] These successive amendments, however, also render a simple count of charges a difficult task. Prior to September 1913, procuring, living on the avails of prostitution, and keeping, being an inmate of, and frequenting a bawdy house were summary conviction offences under the broader vagrancy provisions of the *Criminal Code,* although keeping a bawdy house was also an indictable criminal offence. In 1913, in response to pressure from moral reformers, a new offence, being found in a bawdy house, replaced the vagrancy offence of frequenting a bawdy house. The intent of this amendment was to remove the legal requirement of proving habitual visitations to bawdy houses that was being read into the term *frequenter.*[46] In 1915 keeping and being an inmate of a bawdy house were removed from the vagrancy provisions and made indictable offences.[47] Further amendments in later years increased the penalties for these various offences. Comparing different years of arrests and dispositions, then, can be something like comparing apples and oranges.

More importantly, the general statistics tend to belie the interconnected nature of the lives of many of the repeat offenders, which comes into sharper focus only through a more textured examination of bawdy house offences. Moving away from the aggregate statistics and looking instead at who was arrested, and where, offers a different picture of Toronto's brothel life than that which was constructed by the politically charged meanings attached to brothels by reformers and the police. Indeed, the addresses of those arrested for these offences, the addresses of the houses in which prostitution was alleged to be taking place, and the addresses of repeat offenders between 1913 and 1934 reveal a clear geographical pattern that is highly suggestive of a community of women (and men) who depended on one another for resources, companionship, and support in ways that were invisible to reformers. More importantly, rather than being a segregated and despised class, these offenders were often the same women with whom criminal justice officials were already familiar through their repeated arrests for drunkenness and other disorderly behaviours.

Certain streets and certain houses appear in the records with striking regularity. Terauley Street and St. Patrick Square, Elm Street and Walnut Street, Adelaide and Gerrard streets, and McCaul and Grange avenues, these and neighbouring streets are listed time and again on warrants of commitments that specify the location of common bawdy houses in which women were arrested. Furthermore, these are the streets on which other repeat offenders lived, even if their offence was drunkenness, vagrancy, or theft. Recall, for example, Lizzie C.: of her twenty-four recorded arrests, twenty-two were for drunkenness but one was for keeping a house of ill fame. This disorderly house was located at 54 Beverley Street. Twelve other repeat offenders gave a Beverley Street address, and two women lived next door at no. 52 (in 1916 and 1928, respectively). Another house of ill fame was located at no. 133, and a woman arrested twice for vagrancy (both times in 1925) lived at no. 135. This is the story of only one street.[48]

In addition to the clustered nature of the distribution of addresses among repeat offenders, it is equally clear that there was a significant amount of interchange among the residents of these disorderly houses. Repeat offenders with long records of drunkenness and vagrancy could also be found in houses kept by repeat offenders with similar records, demonstrating "the permeability and improvisational nature of public and private spheres, as well as the blurred divisions between everyday life and the criminal underworld."[49] These women's stories begin to intersect in complex ways when the places where they were arrested are examined. To follow only one route of cross-associations, "inordinate" drinkers Annie B. (1913-17) and Ethel S. (1913-17) were both sent to the

Mercer in 1917 because they "did frequent a certain disorderly house situate and known as number 16 Hagerman Street."[50] This address was provided by Bridget D. (1913-28) and her partner, Frank M., who were convicted on opening day in the Women's Court of keeping a bawdy house at the same address.[51] Ethel's sister, Sarah, was arrested at the Hagerman Street address for being an inmate in 1916. Meanwhile, Ethel herself had been arrested in 1915 as a keeper of a house of ill fame located at 172 Adelaide Street.[52] Daisy H. (1913-34) gave that same address in 1925 when she was arrested – with Bridget D. – for drunkenness. Across time, but not space, an interwoven pattern emerges that indicates something of an institutional connection among Toronto's most criminalized women.

Nor was this only a community of women. Contrary to the argument put forward by the TLCW that only women could provide support and friendship to other women, men were an important (if sometimes problematic) part of street women's lives.[53] Men and women often arrived in the Women's Court as co-accused charged with keeping a bawdy house. Often, these men and women were partners in the trade, although it is not always clear that they were husbands and wives. For example, in 1916 Margaret J. was convicted for keeping a "bad home," while Edwin H. was fined thirty dollars or thirty days because he "took a commercial interest in the business."[54] A similar commercial relationship is evident between Lottie W. (1913-15) and Robert Y. Although the two were charged together in 1915 for keeping a bawdy house, it appears that Robert was a front for Lottie's business. Mercer officials characterized Lottie as "a notorious keeper of a house of ill fame and one very difficult in the past to convict."[55] Lottie's elusiveness likely stems from the careful administration of her business affairs, which have left traces in written records only because Robert launched an appeal of his conviction and the court deposed Lottie in the case. Her statement is revealing: "I got deft [defendant] to rent this house 81 Marlboro Street. He did not live there but was there in and out. He knew I wanted him to rent it for me. I knew deft about a month before I got this house. He brought friends to the house. I gave the rent to [Robert] and he paid it to [the landlord]." Robert's appeal failed.[56] This case also shows that women were not always the victims of men: in this instance, Lottie was clearly in charge of the relationship.

Nonetheless, husbands and wives did appear with sufficient regularity to suggest that this was a relatively normalized part of the trade. Peter and Bella Hanson, for instance, were both sentenced to three months for keeping an "unsavoury home."[57] Beatrice and Frederick Sullivan were likewise convicted, but whereas Frederick received a ninety-day prison term, Beatrice was offered the option of a thirty dollar fine, which she paid.[58] These conjugal arrangements were not always harmonious. In 1914 George Daly was arrested for keeping a disorderly house and assaulting his wife, Margaret. Margaret, who had been "severely kicked and beaten," was George's co-accused on the disorderly house charge. George received a fine of thirty dollars or sixty days in prison on the common assault charge and a sixty-day prison sentence for keeping a disorderly house. Margaret was also convicted of keeping a disorderly house but, perhaps because of her circumstances, she was only charged a fine of one dollar (or thirty days).[59] Despite marital violence, the Dalys continued to operate, and get arrested for keeping, their disorderly house on Nelson Street.[60] It is possible that co-operation between men and women was a useful part of the trade. For example, when Rose J. (1913-15) was convicted and sent to the Mercer for keeping "a certain house of ill fame situate and known as number 163 Chestnut street" in early April 1915, she left the running of her brothel to her husband, Fred. He, however, was no more successful in eluding the law than she had been: two months later he was also convicted for keeping a bawdy house at the same address. Even more interesting, Emma S. (1913-16) stood as Fred's co-accused on this charge. Emma had three previous convictions as an inmate, but this was her first charge for keeping a bawdy house. Emma seems to have been promoted in Rose's absence to help Fred manage the establishment.[61]

Other instances of arrest indicate that men were not necessarily part of the "family" relations of brothels. In one terrible instance, a mother and daughter who worked together in a bawdy house run by the mother came to the attention of officials when the daughter, Amy, died in jail "of diseases resulting from immoral living." Her mother, Johanna, was subsequently charged with keeping a house of ill fame.[62] The *Telegram*'s police court reporter could hardly refrain from open contempt when he wrote about Annie A., who faced a charge of keeping a bawdy house with her "twin babies [lying] on [her] spacious bosom ... and two other kiddies, aged 6 and 7, [clinging] to her skirts."[63] Anna M., "with assurance that could not have been surpassed by the most hardened ... protested her innocence of the charges against her, that of keeping a house of ill-repute. She was convicted on the same charge not long ago." Despite these protestations, Anna was convicted and fined ten dollars and costs or thirty days in prison. However, the fine was "promptly paid by the woman's daughter."[64] Unlike Annie Allison's rush to defence of her mother (see Chapter 4), this example of mother-daughter solidarity was not sentimentally proclaimed to be a "beautiful thing."

The considerable horror in which middle-class maternal feminists held brothels may be attributable to this female and familial quality. Houses of ill fame were anathema to the sexual-moral universe of female criminality constructed by the reforming classes. White, middle-class women may have hoped that the Women's Court would act as an arena for redemption and salvation, but their use of terms such as *petticoated fiends, human vulture,* and *vile being* to refer to madams and procuresses betrayed their real views.[65] Women who were perceived as making their living by enticing men into their homes, thereby corrupting the moral fibre of the city, were typically held to be beyond redemption. Meanwhile, the use of the legal term *inmate* to refer to the women who worked in houses of ill fame is telling in itself. The term suggests imprisonment, and it positions the keeper of the house as a warden. Women incarcerated for this offence thus went from being an inmate in one type of (bad) female home to being an inmate in another (good) one. It is far from certain that the women who were regularly arrested for various breaches of good order would have made the same kinds of moral assessments.

Experience, Resistance, and the Criminalization of Women

One thing that becomes clear in a reading of the recidivist population's criminal justice experiences is that an increasingly coordinated network of surveillance emerged throughout the 1910s and 1920s that permitted reformers to monitor the lives of recidivists in greater detail. A growing array of officials, empowered by an expanding network of legal mechanisms for surveillance, permitted reformers to enter into the lives of offenders and to offer extended judgements about their more general life choices. Although some criminal women responded positively to these interventions, other women clearly resented these intrusions and, instead, made use of their own knowledge of criminal justice mechanisms to navigate the tightening net in which they were entangled. The exercise of this kind of agency was often met with sheer bafflement by criminal justice officials, who viewed it not as the product of knowledge but as the behaviour of recalcitrant, troublesome individuals. Evidence of this kind of resistance can help to further illustrate the limitations of a system of feminized justice that proclaimed a woman-centred version of justice as its central goal and means.

The most significant surveillance technique to emerge in this time period was the system of parole. Parole was the next logical step after the implementation of indeterminate sentencing, and only those on indeterminate sentences were eligible for early release. Together, these criminal justice reforms performed two simultaneous functions. First, they were intended as the carrot to what reformers saw as the self-evidently flawed stick of incarceration: indeterminate sentences were translated into early release on the basis of good behaviour by the inmate, thereby making the prisoner an agent in the determination of her own sentence. If a prisoner proved herself worthy – through self-discipline, good work habits, conformity with institution rules, and some form of visible penitence – her time would be reduced accordingly. If, however, she was ill-behaved during her incarceration, she could serve the entire maximum term specified in the indeterminate sentence. This is what happened to Jennie L.: having "carr[ied] on an obscene conversation, and being disorderly in her Corridor," Mercer staff decided that "she is not ready for Parole [and] her conduct does not justify one in believing that she will lead a better and more respectable life after leaving the Institution."[66] In this example, we see, too, the second function of parole, which was to allow for the continued monitoring of convicted women. This function was also welcomed by officials. As Mercer Superintendent O'Sullivan wrote: "[I]t is much better to release a girl under supervision than to wait until the end of her term and let her go without anyone being responsible for looking after her."[67] Parole, therefore, helped to control women's behaviour inside carceral institutions while also extending the reach of the criminal justice system well beyond the courtroom and the prison.

Prior to the formal existence of the Parole Board, prisoners serving provincial sentences had access to early release through the more limited, but similarly spirited, 1906 *Ticket-of-Leave Act*. The ticket of leave was granted by the federal government. It contained no criteria for early release or the revocation of a licence, and it only required an offender to notify local police of an address and, usually, to report to the police once a month. Licensed offenders were to abide by four general conditions, including not using intoxicating liquors and staying away from "bad associates." Breaches could be brought to a magistrate, who could sentence the prisoner back to the institution to serve out the remainder of her sentence, not including any time on release.[68] Mercer officials began to employ field officers to follow up on women conditionally released from the reformatory on a ticket of leave. Margaret Howe was field officer from 1915 to 1918, and she was joined by Letitia Scott, a former bailiff at the Toronto Jail and who would later succeed Emma O'Sullivan as superintendent at the Mercer, in 1927.

The position of Mercer field officer was phased out when the Ontario Parole Board became operational after 1917. The Ontario Parole Board had informally existed since 1915 and was given statutory powers through 1916 amendments to the federal *Prisons and Reformatories Act*.[69] Former prisons inspector J.T. Gilmour was the first chief parole officer, but after his death two years later, Alfred Lavell was appointed to head up the Ontario Parole Board, and he retained this position until 1930. The Ontario Parole Board had jurisdiction over all provincially sentenced inmates serving indeterminate sentences. At the insistence of the TLCW, one woman, Mrs. Kate Luella Brodie, was appointed to the board in 1920, although she only attended women's parole cases at the Mercer and the Concord. In 1922 Edna Haskayne was hired as Ontario's first female parole officer, and she had jurisdiction over all paroled women in the province. Following a scandal involving her former boss, Provincial Secretary Dunlop, Haskayne was fired in 1925, and her caseload was transferred to a male Salvation Army captain working for the Parole Board.[70]

An overview of the few cases in which parole was relevant to repeat offenders helps to illustrate its role in the regulation of criminalized women. Sometimes, the extended supervision could work to some women's advantage. For example, regular drinker and prostitute Sadie S. (1913-34), sentenced to the Mercer on an indeterminate sentence for vagrancy in 1914, was not only defended by Mercer officials, they also challenged police and the courts on her behalf for what appeared to them to be specious arrests. In this case something of a friendship appears to have existed between Sadie and Field Officer Letitia Scott. Sadie, then twenty-nine years old, was granted release on a ticket of leave in August 1915. In October the Mercer received a report from the police matron, Miss Carmichael, that Sadie had appeared in the Women's Court for drunkenness, thereby breaching the conditions of her leave. She was returned to the Mercer and released once more on a ticket of leave in November 1916, after the passage of the *Ontario Temperance Act*. In February 1917 her ticket-of-leave licence was found in the possession of a man convicted in the courts for vagrancy, and the chief constable of Toronto cancelled Sadie's licence and issued a warrant for her arrest.

It was at this point that Scott, to whom Sadie was assigned to report fortnightly, weighed in on Sadie's behalf. As she explained in her correspondence with O'Sullivan, Sadie had given her licence to the man in question to hold for her because she had no privacy in the room where she lodged and was afraid that others would find out she was a paroled prisoner: "Of course she should not have done this but as you know these unfortunate women are very ignorant and in their struggle to keep straight, with the past records looming up at every turn, they do many foolish things and I confess I had great sympathy for her, she in particular, had much to fight down." This appeal seemed to convince O'Sullivan that Sadie may have been unfairly targeted by the police; she promptly appealed to Dominion Police Chief Archibald, who was in charge of ticket of leaves, to give Sadie another chance: "Sadie has been numerous times in the hands of the police, though still a young woman. It would be quite possible for a police officer to judge her present conduct by what is publicly known of her past, and to confuse the past with the present ... I shall hold your warrant and the magistrate's commitment until I hear again from you." Sadie's licence was renewed.[71]

Sadie's case offers a paradigmatic example of feminized justice, by which women justice officials challenged male authorities, particularly to warn them against the tendency to permanently characterize female offenders as "fallen" women. For her part Sadie also seemed to find her relationship with these women officials useful: she maintained contact with Scott and was able to receive her trust and support. But Sadie's behaviour was also interpreted through the filter of reform tropes: her decision to "live down" her former life, her willingness to not only report regularly to Scott but also to keep her consistently abreast of her movements, and her good work habits suggest a woman who was a willing participant in her own reform and, thus, a woman for whom infelicitous circumstances could be chalked up to a desperate "ignorance" and "foolishness." This was not a relationship that was extended to all inmates, and not all released women were as willing as Sadie to try to create a new life for themselves.

In many women's files, we find that the increased knowledge that parole and supervision allowed created an opportunity for criminal justice officials to make wider and generally disparaging judgements about a broader array of life choices. The case of Millie S. (1919-27) offers an example. Millie was found guilty of the rather pedestrian theft of "a number of Lady's [sic] dresses and other articles the property of the T. Eaton Co. Ltd," but she was sentenced to an indeterminate period at the Mercer because her other known behaviours alarmed Magistrate Patterson.[72] Millie had a long record. As a youth she had been examined by Dr. Clarke, the renowned Toronto psychiatrist, deemed by him a "moral degenerate," and sent to an industrial refuge.[73] Millie escaped from the refuge by setting a fire and running out "in the excitement." After serving a sentence for "incendiarism," she spent the next several years in and out of jail for bawdy house offences, and she once gave evidence against a man who was ultimately convicted for living on the avails of prostitution. At the time of the theft charge in 1925, Millie was cohabiting with a man whom Patterson, Parole Officer Edna Haskayne, and the Mercer officials assumed to be her pimp, although Millie and the man in question maintained that they had a common law relationship and that he intended to marry her. Ultimately, then, Patterson took advantage of Millie's arrest for shoplifting to enforce incarceration as a long-term solution to the broader problem Millie posed. Simply put, Patterson decided that Millie "was not a fit person to be at liberty." Haskayne agreed with this assessment. When Millie's impugned male friend called upon Haskayne to request Millie's parole, Haskayne wrote that his "sordidness ... disgusted me but I decided that it would be better to treat him civilly and thereby keep in touch with him and perhaps protect the girl from him later on." Millie never was paroled and served her full sentence, which was technically for theft but clearly because criminal justice officials thought it best to separate her from a man they deemed indecent.[74]

Nor was the subjective assessment of women's fitness for liberty based only on normative gender expectations. Racial propriety was also clearly a factor, as is evident in those case files in which white women engaged in interracial relations. For example, Mattie B. was returned to the Mercer after only one month on a ticket of leave "because she had become associated with undesireable [sic] colored people in Toronto."[75] White woman Doris M. was denied early release on her indeterminate sentence for receiving stolen goods when she insisted to officials that "she is very fond of colored people and has been friendly with them for some time."[76] That respectability, whiteness, and supervised release were interconnected is even more clear in the case files of those offenders who were themselves not white. Quan K. was not granted parole after his conviction in the Women's Court for keeping a disorderly house because, the members of the Parole Board explained, they would "rarely, if ever, recommend a Permit for Chinamen or Japanese, or other Orientals as this act is too likely to be interpreted by them as condoning the offence. They have not the basic grasp of our methods and principles."[77] That Quan had been deemed to have a sufficient grasp on the law to be held criminally responsible for the state of his home seemed not to bother these officials. Black inmate Hazel W. was also denied parole, not only because it was decided that "she will probably never make a desirable citizen anywhere and gives no promise of improvement" but also because her entire family was considered disreputable. Hazel's case also demonstrates how well-coordinated the system of supervision was becoming. Originally from the United States, Hazel had requested that she be paroled to her sister's care in Philadelphia. The Mercer field officer, who was dubious, made inquiries through Philadelphia's Charity Organization Society, which sent out its own inspectors and the police to investigate the living conditions of Hazel's family. What they discovered was that the sister's address was located in "one of the worst neighbourhoods in the city, and that everyone connected with these houses was very degraded morally." Upon receiving this report, the field officer denied Hazel her parole: "If the place and people to whom she wished to go had been respectable I would have recommended her parole for the good of this country ... but in view of the above information I consider that she is better remaining here for the present."[78] As these cases suggest, respectability, morality, and the good of the country were highly racialized concepts that were policed with increasing administrative efficiency.

Not surprisingly, some women actively resisted the intrusive surveillance over their lives that parole allowed, and this resistance could sometimes take the form of open defiance. Cecilia D. – who appeared several times in the Women's Court for bawdy house offences, vagrancy, and drunkenness – received a suspended sentence for keeping a house of ill fame in September 1925 on condition that she leave Toronto and return to her husband in Listowel, Ontario. In October she was back in the Women's Court, having broken both conditions and displaying a stubbornness that clearly confounded Magistrate Patterson: "Her council [sic] Mr. Horkins asked her in the Witness Box if she would return to her husband if she were given a chance and she replied that she would *not*, that they did not get along and she would never live with him again. That she would *not* leave Toronto and I could not make her." Cecilia's flat rejection of both wifely devotion and deference to maternal authority led Patterson to the conclusion that she "is one of the worst characters I have had before me [and] I cannot understand why any clemency should be shown [to her]."[79]

Resistance could come in other forms as well, and there were women who did not necessarily lash out at authorities but who found ways to stump them, nonetheless. One strategy was simply to refuse to co-operate with officials as they tried to gather information about them. Mary J., who insisted that she had been wrongly convicted of keeping a bawdy house on Bay Street (she said she was employed as a house cleaner and "did not have anything to do with the girls coming there"), would neither give Mercer officials any information about her relatives nor disclose the name of the father of her child (born while she was in the Mercer).[80] Mercer officials concluded that this tendency to be "unrespon-sive" meant that she was a "mental defective," but other women were similarly unenthusiastic about helping criminal justice officials to enter any further into their lives. Indeed, a clearly rational decision was made by Daisy H. (1913-34), whose regular appearances in court and in various prisons gave her enough experience to know the advantage of keeping to herself. Convicted (again) of drunkenness and sentenced to a six months' definite and an additional six months' indeterminate sentence at the Concord in May 1926, Daisy met with the Parole Board in February 1927. The board was prepared to parole her, but Daisy "said she would not accept a parole with any strings on it and that she would prefer to serve the balance of her time and be a free woman when she went out."[81] Clearly aware of the surveillance powers allowed to officials who supervised prisoners on conditional release, Daisy made a choice that preserved her own sense of integrity. It was also a decision that flew in the face of the re-habilitative reform logic that underlay the feminists' approach to criminal justice. In response to reformers' efforts to render more aspects of criminalized women's lives intelligible and governable, the more experienced offenders drew upon their own knowledge to thwart their efforts. These small but important acts of resist-ance to the ever-expanding criminal justice net put feminized justice to the test.

Conclusion

Despite the obvious significance of alcohol to the day-to-day business of the Women's Court, liquor offences did not figure proportionately in the universe of good and evil constructed by the maternal feminists. The best that reformers seemed able to offer to repeatedly drunk and otherwise disorderly women was a rest cure and the *Ontario Temperance Act*. For most offenders these were, at best, a palliative that did little to radically transform their lives, even assuming they were interested in self-reformation. Indeed, it is clear that outside of the middle-class imaginings of female-specific criminal problems, there existed in Toronto a women's community of confirmed alcoholics and illicit liquor ped-dlers for whom a culture of drinking was a central feature of their lives, and of their criminality. Moreover, these were the same women who often found themselves in Women's Court as keepers and inmates of disorderly houses. Rather than reclamation, these women were treated with pity, at best, and some received only enmity. Their own disorderliness was an ongoing challenge to the very legitimacy of a special court for women.

Importantly, these women's revolving door relationship to criminal justice networks gave them insights into the workings of that system and knowledge about their keepers, even as those keepers attempted to develop knowledge about them. Clearly, repeat offenders understood the grinding routine of police court justice and "the commonplaceness of discharge, remand, and commitment."[82] To the best of their abilities, they used this knowledge to navigate their regular journeys through the system. Yet their very experience with courts and prison networks was precisely what was troublesome about them. Intransigently disruptive, these women were not easily ordered into credible salvation narratives that gave meaning to a distinct court for women. Unlike their middle-class counterparts, these women were not able to map their own meanings onto the criminal justice system. For the most part, they were simply written out of the middle-class rendering of the story of the Women's Court. Perhaps not surprisingly, one result of this has been their relative marginality to histories of women's crime.

By contrast, the interpretations of female-centred justice put forward by reform-minded women, as well as the politicized nature of their experiences as women, was precisely what granted middle-class feminists the authority to intervene in the criminal justice system in the first place. In the case of the Toronto Women's Court, the person who stood at the centre of this political reform was Margaret Patterson, instigator of the Women's Court and, not surprisingly, its first – and, as it would turn out, its only – female magistrate. The next chapter looks specifically at Patterson's tenure in the court. As magistrate, Patterson tried to bring together her fervent belief in the necessity of law reform as a means to women's equality, her religious commitments, her equally deep commitment to science and medicine, and her place as a woman in a masculine world of law. Putting these philosophies into practice was no easy task, and it was made more complicated by the fact that the daily case load in the Women's Court did not follow the simple lines that the maternalist reformers believed that it did. Toward the end of her tenure, Patterson faced increasing pressures from without, including declining public support both for her tenure and for the court itself. Perhaps as a reflection of this, she also faced conflict in the court. Her battles with criminalized women became a matter of public interest and reveal a great deal about tensions between women as they struggled, albeit from different subject positions, with the law.

"Can her justice be just?"
Margaret Patterson, Male Critics, and Female Criminals, 1922-34

> Margaret Patterson, who presides over the Women's Court, is a clever woman. Her popularity with the Bar is therefore debatable. With a number of Women's Organizations, it is beyond all doubt and peradventure. Her sternest critics call her a vivisectionist. Certainly she X-rays her own sex with professional skill. Not being a lawyer, her decisions are sometimes attacked. It is not unlikely that the lady would rather be attacked than ignored.
> – Harry M. Wodson, "The Woman Who Gavest"[1]

While previous chapters have focused on each side of the Women's Court equation separately, this chapter brings the reformers and the offenders together to examine their dynamic relationship to each another as this relationship was structured by the court. The interactive relationship between women's criminality and the feminists' sexual interpretation of crime was nowhere in better evidence than during the tenure of Margaret Patterson. It was her appointment, after all, that was the culmination of the Toronto Local Council of Women's (TLCW) efforts in regard to local law reform. Patterson herself proclaimed that her magistracy "fulfilled the promise for which the Women's Court was established, namely to give to the woman or girl ... the privilege of giving their evidence to a woman magistrate."[2] Her career as a magistrate brought to the foreground the complex and interrelated trajectories of the Toronto Women's Court. Under her magistracy the Women's Court was both an institutionalized feminist challenge to male-stream legal administration and a site for reproducing unequal social relations through the implementation of feminized justice.

In this chapter I explore the complex nature of the authority exercised by Margaret Patterson over criminalized women. What was the debate about the appointment of women to positions of judicial authority, and how did various actors with an interest in the Toronto Women's Court understand this authority? On what terms did different groups – maternal feminists, criminalized women, local court watchers, lawyers, journalists, and government officials – evaluate the appointment of a laywoman with a history of "energetic welfare work [and] a keen insight into the social and moral complexities of modern life" to a court mandated expressly to implement feminized justice?[3] Most importantly, in what ways did the Women's Court function as the meeting place between these diverse groups, and in what ways did these varying interests enter into conversation with one another? It is this conversation that fundamentally shaped the Women's Court and Margaret Patterson's tenure as Ontario's first and only female magistrate.

In itself Margaret Patterson's own self-characterization as one who bestowed a privilege speaks to the one-way relationship that maternal feminists imagined themselves in with respect to the women they sought to help. At the same time, Patterson and her supporters had to face challenges to their ability to lay claim to this authority in the first place. The relatively unique power that Patterson was able to obtain as a magistrate put her under a much more intense scrutiny than other, male, magistrates had to endure. As a result she was often forced into a defensive position to maintain her role as the organized women's community representative and voice. But Patterson's appointment was not structured by gender alone. Even as she faced male opposition to her role as a female magistrate, she was also able to act with considerable latitude – as the term *privilege* implies – as an official of the state empowered to regulate the ordinary moral standards of the community. The way in which she navigated between the external limitations placed on her as a woman and the power she was enabled to exercise over other women as a magistrate illustrates the complex bases of authority within which her magistracy was situated.

I argue in this chapter that Patterson was not accountable, nor did she always see herself as accountable, to the organized women's community alone. Rather, she also saw herself, and was celebrated by her women peers, as working in the interests of the nation. Within this nation the "women's community" invoked by Patterson and her supporters was not a community of equals. In her philosophies and her practices, Patterson demonstrated that the women's community to which she was committed was characterized by authoritarian relations *between* women that were based on class and race. It was this commitment that situated Patterson as a legitimate disciplining power over other women.

But the criminalized women over whom Patterson had such disciplinary power also had something to say about the feminized authority being practised on their behalf. Although their voices are muted – by the historical records themselves and by the active processes that inhered in their marginalized status as criminalized women – from time to time they are palpable presences whose competing visions of justice raise the very questions I seek to address in this chapter. In whose name did Patterson speak as a female magistrate? Were a girl's chances improved by virtue of appearing before a woman in a courtroom designed to give weight to her story *as* a woman? What was the privilege for women of giving their evidence to a female magistrate whose authority was staked in their names? And what was the price of that opportunity? To address these questions, the concluding section of this chapter explores two cases in the Women's Court in which criminal women raised these issues. Both cases generated further debate among Torontonians about the capacities of Ontario's female magistrate and her implementation of feminized justice. In the first case – that of Myrtle Cook – Patterson would receive the support of the (male) legal establishment; in the second, that of Cecile Gereau, she would not. The relative material and discursive positions of Cook, a black woman, and Gereau, a white woman and bereaved mother, made a palpable difference to the broader reactions to Patterson's judgments. Contrasting these two cases and the debates that ensued demonstrates the multiplicity of communities to which Patterson was accountable and their sometimes complementary and sometimes conflicting interests. In the context of this highly structured and profoundly unequal dynamic among disparate groups, the contours of Patterson's authority are rendered visible. To the degree that her work "in service to the state" harmonized with her own views on the necessity of gender-specific legal reform, Patterson was supported as a woman magistrate in a Women's Court.[4] However, when these two projects collided, Patterson had to defend her feminist goals against more mainstream interpretations of justice to which she set herself in opposition. These variables and their interplay with one another show how, and to what end, the feminized justice articulated by Margaret Patterson could, and could not, be practised.

"The anomaly is plain": The Debate about Women Magistrates

> The *Edmonton Journal* says: "Toronto has a woman's court, but a man sits on the bench." The anomaly is plain. The wisest of women might find it difficult to judge always in the best and fairest way in a "man's court," but reverse this and we know that the "wisest of men" will continually be nonplussed to judge in the "best and fairest way" when the delicate intricacies, the many-sided reasons, the complex causes of the crimes of women are being "tried" – in fact, when someone is trying to lay them before the man.
>
> – "A Long Stride toward Adjustment," *Woman's Century*[5]

Were a girl's chances improved by virtue of being tried before a female magistrate? The maternal feminists certainly thought they were. The organized women's movement answered the question by taking a long view. Patterson and her supporters preferred to confront the problems of immorality through the implementation of corrective justice tailored to individual circumstances, rather than through the hasty and narrow judgements typical in overcrowded courts. Through this approach Patterson hoped that one appearance in the Women's Court would suffice: "For example, a girl who gets two years less one day at the Mercer for a first offence soon finds – and not unnaturally – that the conditions there are not altogether to her liking."[6] Punishment and protection were enmeshed together in this feminist approach to women's criminality.

The authoritarian relationship that feminists envisioned themselves as having over the women ostensibly in need of their intervention was repeated endlessly by the feminists. Indeed, Margaret Patterson explained that the Women's Court was necessary because "girls" released from jail were being met by men "who taking advantage of their lonely, often friendless and penniless condition, induced them to go into immorality."[7] Having identified the problem of female crime in this way – that is, as a product of female loneliness and vulnerability – a Women's Court appeared to be a viable solution. To quote Patterson again, the clear advantage of a court in which the audience was composed only of "ladies [who] are interested in the welfare of women and girls" was that it "gives to the accused woman the moral support of a good woman's presence, and very often one has the opportunity of befriending the unfortunate."[8] Presentations of the problem and its solution such as this – as well as the gendered terms by which Patterson's supporters, and critics, evaluated her tenure – make it clear that the community of women was not a community of equals. Rather, this was a community of metaphorical mothers and daughters. Accused women are presented as being notably distinct from "good women" and in need of the friendship and guidance that Patterson was uniquely positioned to grant.

But despite the feminists' confidence in their project, the rise of Patterson to the Women's Court bench was contested. In addition to jurisdictional struggles over her appointment (see Chapter 1), legal professionals, "motivated partly by self-interest related to an over-abundance of lawyers and partly by a more altruistic concern about the growing lack of due process in the administration of lower-court justice," were opposed to Patterson's appointment.[9] At the sixteenth annual meeting of the Ontario Bar Association, held in March 1922, only two months after Patterson's appointment and within weeks of her taking the bench, Patterson's appointment was strongly condemned: "Your committee [on law reform] regrets to note the appointment of a lady who has had no legal training to the position of Police Magistrate in the city of Toronto. It seems incomprehensible that a matter involving the collection of a debt of, say, $5 must be submitted to a Judge with legal training, when the liberty of the subject can be disposed of by a person without any legal knowledge and without any idea of the rules of evidence."[10] As Dorothy Chunn notes, this disapproval of Patterson's appointment was consistent with the legal profession's overall position that laypersons should not hold legal office. Within that context, however, "the appointment of someone who was not only a non-lawyer but also a woman to the Bench of the Toronto Women's Court" was "the worst blow."[11]

Nor was it simply Patterson's appointment that was viewed as a blow to male prerogatives. More generally, early women adjudicators were subjected to a variety of male antipathies as some men grouched about female trespasses onto male preserves. For example, the biography of Helen Gregory MacGill, assistant judge in the Vancouver Juvenile Court (for Girls), is peppered with accounts of how she tactically manoeuvred around male hostilities. Her daughter recounted the challenges MacGill faced from "certain little anti-feminists [who] cavilled at a woman 'doing a man's job'":[12]

> Backstage at Court and City Hall political and personal enemies plagued her with petty tyrannies. The official amenities were withheld or delayed – the streetcar pass that came with the appointment, the use on occasion of an official car, the invitations to public receptions and banquets, the civic courtesies. Because of chance, because of inadvertence, because she was an outsider, because she was a

woman the tendency to overlook her or treat her less favourably than her [male] colleague [Judge Shaw] amounted almost to a conspiracy.[13]

Early female magistrates and judges had to contend with unsuppressed masculine disapproval of their perceived transgressions into an arena formerly monopolized by men.

Male wariness about a female magistrate would lead Margaret Patterson into "storms of controversy" twice in the course of her tenure.[14] In 1928 Patterson handed down a three-year sentence to a man she convicted of living on the avails of prostitution and procuring. The sentence was quashed on appeal by Chief Justice Mulock, who determined that the sentence was "an astounding verdict" that was unsupported by the evidence.[15] Although being overturned on appeal was no novelty for any magistrate (including Denison and Patterson), this case was turned into something of a spectacle, and for a three-month period after the appeal decision no male defendants were brought to Patterson's court.[16] This action was received – probably correctly – by the organized women's community as a direct blow to Patterson's feminist intentions. As one contemporary commentator observed: "This move, although it does not end, considerably halts and cripples one of the most effective experiments in morality-enforcement which the country has known. Social workers are agreed that the purveyors of vice more greatly fear coming before Toronto's woman police magistrate, than facing a month of ordinary sessions."[17]

By the time the dust settled and the Women's Court's docket included men again, the damage to Patterson had extended beyond mere embarrassment or chastisement. This incident was directly responsible for her inability to secure the judgeship in the Domestic Relations Court, the establishment of which had been announced in the midst of this lawyers' strike against her (see Chapter 1).[18] Patterson would suffer another public humiliation several years later. In 1932 she found herself again at the centre of a public scandal, this time for her decision to sentence a man to jail on a charge of non-payment of a debt of $1.50. Her sentence was ruled to be disproportionate to the severity of the crime, and Patterson received a formal censure in the form of a "verbal dressing down" by the attorney general, Colonel Price.[19] Although Loraine Gordon is correct to suggest that "it is now impossible to even guess at what was on her mind when she passed [this] sentence," this incident also makes apparent the degree to which her femaleness was itself seen as somewhat scandalous by some observers.[20] In yet another example of sensationalist and blatantly sexist reporting, the *Telegram* reported the formal censure of Patterson under the headline: "Magistrate M. Patterson Is Given Verbal Lashing, Renfrew Officer Warned." Yet, only two paragraphs of this two-page story gave an account of the official admonition of Patterson. The remainder of the column was about the much more serious allegation of a misappropriation of funds by the Renfrew magistrate. As these largely media-orchestrated scandals illustrate, just as women were uncomfortable with men's ability to sit in judgement of women, so too were men, on occasion, visibly uneasy with the ability of a woman to judge men's cases.

But Patterson's decisions regarding men were not always viewed with suspicion. No eyebrows were raised when Patterson had a man – a "foreigner" – arrested for vagrancy because he was waiting for his friend, Catharine M., who was answering to the charge of being a keeper of a bawdy house in the Women's Court.[21] Indeed, this case was feminized justice in action. Upon noticing Marat S. "loitering in a public place, the city hall," Patterson instructed the morality officer in her court to "[a]rrest that man and put him in the cells. We want to stop this sort of thing." Marat admitted that he was waiting for Catharine, an answer that translated as "being unable to give a satisfactory account of himself." He was taken into custody. Catherine had originally been given a suspended sentence for keeping a resort but, as a result of Marat's arrest, became, instead, a material witness against him. Patterson's actions transformed her from a criminal to a victim. One clear message from this example is that women in conflict with the law were to find "friendship" only with other women. The other clear message is that some men, notably those considered foreign, were more vulnerable to the dictates of feminized justice than others.

But Patterson did not simply do battle with men to assert her authority, and anti-feminist voices were not the only ones arrayed against her. Criminalized women also voiced their resistance to her magistracy. Of course, it is not surprising to find that women sentenced by the court were visibly angry at the fact. This was hardly a reaction unique to Patterson's tenure. Women sentenced by Denison could, and did, give vent to frustrations or anger. Recall Bridget D. (1913-28), convicted on opening day of keeping a house of ill fame, who "denied everything, upbraided the judge, questioned the witnesses, and when she was led away by the matron, muttered vindictively her opinion of the law that would send folks away for nothing."[22] Similarly, Becky G., upon learning of her conviction (by Denison) for being an inmate of a bawdy house, "put up a tremendous protest against going down stairs [to the local cells], and it required the combined efforts of P.C. Miss Leavitt and P.C. Bart Childs to take the lady below."[23] And after another series of convictions of women for bawdy house offences in 1915, the remainder of the police court's business had to be put on hold when "a fair imitation of the wails of the lost came up from the cells below. Shrieks and cries of the women who had been sentenced went on during the latter part of the court and for half an hour afterward."[24] These few examples indicate that criminalized women did not always accept their convictions with passive humility. These snippets of protesting voices remind us of the "current of resistance often forgotten in the history of women and crime."[25]

These protesting voices take on a slightly different tenor, however, when, under Patterson's tenure, female offenders used the very rhetoric of the Women's Court to express anger, frustration, or contempt for their treatment. In 1925 Myrtle Cook angrily announced that she hated Patterson. The assertion was a direct rebuff to the "friendship" a woman magistrate was meant to be able to offer.[26] In 1927 Cecile Gereau absolutely refused to be tried by Patterson, declaring that she would prefer to be tried in "any court but this."[27] In 1929 Susan W. (1913-34), upon being sentenced for three months for drunkenness, snapped at Patterson, "You're too hard, that's all. You should be off the bench."[28] Similar sentiments were expressed by Irene A. (1928-34). Convicted by Patterson of vagrancy for being drunk in a taxicab, Irene angrily cried out, "[Y]ou don't get a chance here," before being led away to jail.[29] Regardless of whether they were by design, these sentiments went directly to the heart of the foundational reasons for a Women's Court with a woman magistrate. Two of these cases, those of Myrtle Cook and Cecile Gereau, generated debate among Torontonians that caused them to further question the legitimacy of Patterson's implementation of feminized justice. Importantly, however, it is clear that at least some criminalized women were well aware of the politics of the "privilege" on offer to them, and from time to time they attempted to use those same politics to their advantage, albeit with unequal resources and, often, limited success.

There were, then, a variety of voices that weighed in on the question of a female magistrate. These voices emanated from diverse social locations and are indicative of disparate sets of interests and political allegiances. These contestations are useful to evaluating the nature of feminized justice. While most historians focus on the limitations and, often, failures of these experiments, I suggest that the points of collision and collusion between contemporary actors can also show us the contexts – and the costs – of the success of feminized justice and illuminate the extensive authority that some women were empowered to exercise.

Whose Women Magistrates? Feminism, the State, and the Law

On the surface the organized women's community celebrated women magistrates as their own, a point made nowhere more obviously than in an article that appeared in *Chatelaine* titled "Our Women Magistrates."[30] The author, Anne Anderson Perry, presented the value of female magistrates as a direct answer to criticisms emanating from male legal circles. Perry examined "our women magistrates" to pose "the whole question of women in the judiciary, and their special value, if any, in that capacity." At the time of publication, in July 1929, there had been six women appointed to the bench,[31] and Perry provided information on "the personalities, backgrounds, abilities and principles of our women magistrates" to show how "these ladies, having come to their work on the bench well prepared for it through experience, character and life, now show in their judgments and in their expressed opinions a common reaction toward many of the problems which they are obliged to face" that differentiated them from "the average male Solon."

Perry's overall point – and a direct salvo to male critics – was that lack of formal legal training and knowledge was itself one of the greatest assets possessed by Canada's earliest women magistrates.[32] Each of the women magistrates was asked to comment on her relationship to the technicalities of law. Each woman gave a similar answer. Alice Jamieson, the first woman appointee, to the Calgary Juvenile Court in 1914, answered: "I had very little knowledge of the law, but I had looked very carefully into the disabilities under which women laboured at that time, and had often attended the Police Court when women or girls were being tried. I have found that what I need is not only the letter of the law, but its spirit. One requires exactly those qualities that go to make a successful mother: patience, sympathy and just dealing." This sentiment was echoed by Emily Murphy, the second woman appointee, who was well known to Canadians for her many achievements, including as magistrate of the Edmonton Women's and Juvenile courts.[33] Murphy responded to the question about her capacity with respect to the law with her usual wit, eloquence, and vigour:

> I had a feeling of woeful ignorance when my first case was called in Police Court, but in a day or two it became clear to me that I had been a magistrate for a long time. Every mother is or ought to be. In training children, we have to deal with false pretenses, incitements to breach of the peace, assaults, cruelty to animals, obstructions of justice, trespass, idle and disorderly persons, false evidence, etc.,

these offenses being in the family, as in the state, of an anti-social nature. I would say that women ought to make, for these reasons and because they are more concerned with building character than with punishment of wrong doing, the very best of magistrates.

What "our women magistrates" shared was an understanding of their roles not as legal experts but as nation-builders. That the nation was to be created in their own image seemed to go without saying. More explicitly, it was their specifically gendered background in motherly compassion that was the crux of this unique commitment to justice and, thus, to the nation. This view of women's acumen *as* (white and middle-class) women was evident in the tenures of American women adjudicators as well. On her first day in the Los Angeles Women's Court, Georgia Bullock, who was a lawyer, made clear her understanding of her role as a woman judge in a way that was remarkably similar to that expressed by her Canadian peers: "Bullock explained ... that she had a social worker orientation toward the female defendants and expected to help rather than punish them."[34] Similarly, Miriam Van Waters, who was a referee in the Los Angeles Juvenile Court for Girls in the 1920s and, like her Canadian counterparts, not trained in law, "tried to play down the judicial nature of these hearings [and to] emphasize mediation and diagnosis, rather than judgment."[35] When charged by critics for being overly parental in her judgements, Van Waters responded: "[T]he thing is impossible; we have not been parental enough."[36]

This shared maternal view among early women adjudicators is entirely consistent with the politics of the equal moral standard. To paraphrase Estelle Freedman, in the world view of these women activists, it was (man-made) law that appeared to be criminal, rather than the women who were arrested because of it.[37] It hardly made sense for activist women to become the carriers of the very same legal rules that they more broadly impugned. As Elsie Gregory Mac-Gill wrote, "[I]t is the moral duty of a judge to do justice but if the law by which she must judge be unjust, can her 'justice' be just?"[38] Early women magistrates took it upon themselves to effect a new, and explicitly gendered, view of justice.

Margaret Patterson was, thus, in good company when she brought a thoroughly feminized vision of justice to the bench. She similarly distinguished herself as a woman magistrate by framing her qualifications as being (beneficially) different from men's. For example, it is unlikely that the concerns of the Bar Association were assuaged, or were meant to be assuaged, when Patterson, immediately on hearing the news of her appointment to the Women's Court bench, gave an interview to the *Star* in which she admitted to having little legal knowledge. When asked by the reporter whether she "was worrying about that," Patterson replied, "Well, I am going to study it as carefully as possible of course ... But I rather believe that it is part of the duty of the crown attorney to furnish the law, and I'll rely on him."[39] Some months later Patterson declared that she had "found all the court officials very kindly disposed and helpful in every way" and that legal processes, "while rather terrifying at first, do not appear so formidable now."[40] Having so quickly mastered the law, Patterson added, likely to the horror of most Toronto lawyers, that, as far as she was concerned, "the work on the Bench is the least important of all."[41] At least of equal importance were her organized "conferences with every social agency and with the editors of the newspapers, for co-operation, help and suggestions."[42] Seven years of experience as a Women's Court magistrate did little to change her views. As she told Perry in 1929: "While it is absolutely necessary that every accused person be tried strictly according to the rules of evidence, the individual as well as his crime should be carefully studied before sentence is pronounced. I do not believe that anyone can deal out even approximate justice, based only on testimony developed in open court. The ramifications of the actual cause of any so-called crime are too intricate to reduce to a legal formula."[43] Unlike the members of the Bar Association, Patterson clearly did not see law and due process as the only, or even the most important, areas of concern for an incoming female magistrate. It was precisely this that made her appointment political, and it was this that she shared with her female colleagues.

But Patterson also set herself apart from her peers, in part through the dual nature of her jurisdiction (see Chapter 1), but also, and significantly, through her staunch insistence on viewing crime through a medical model. This was not a view unique to her, but she was the only Canadian woman magistrate with a professional background in (missionary) medicine, and it was Patterson who was the most articulate in advancing this alternative approach to the law. At the 1914 Social Service Congress, she combined her evangelical Christianity with her medical training to offer the following analysis of the problems with the court system:

> In the 8th Chapter of St. John's Gospel, we are given a sample case, and we see how the greatest Judge of all treated it ... He did not consider the case hastily. He studied the patient, and did not rely solely on the evidence given. He purified her surroundings and removed her accusers, forgave the sin, and sent her out, not to

be a danger to society, but a useful Christian woman. There is no reason why we cannot do the same to-day ... When will we have a proper system of treating ... men and women, and a moral hospital [jail farm] to which they will all be sent on indeterminate sentence? When will these people be regarded as patients, and treated in a way that will lead to their moral recovery? [44]

Upon her appointment to the Women's Court, Patterson reiterated this point of view. As she told the *Star:* "Like diseases, the cause of the malady, crime or otherwise, must be ascertained and, if possible, removed. I should not want to sentence anyone until the fullest consideration of every factor of the case had been carefully given." [45] In another of many medical references to crime and social work, Patterson joked that it was not a doctor, like herself, that was needed in the court, but a chiropractor, "because the work is largely one of making adjustments." [46]

Mariana Valverde has written about Margaret Patterson's "ominous" combination of law-and-order aims, science, and religion. Valverde concludes that "the combination of religion, medicine, and criminology was in this case a great deal more coercive than any of the three elements taken separately; to describe it as science marred by moralism would be to miss the point." [47] Certainly, the notion of excising the cause of crime through the use of a "moral" institution that could treat criminals in the way that a hospital cured patients is indicative of the coercive inclinations that characterized this experiment. As a medically trained woman with legal authority over the lives of women charged with a criminal offence, Margaret Patterson saw it as her duty – to the nation, to womankind, and to the individual women before her – to provide "institutional protection" to those she considered a cancer to a productive and moral society. As she chillingly put it, those women "who display vicious habits and have established loose companionship" and, thus, those who have demonstrated that they are incapable of "normal" living, were "really at war with society. War always means hardship, destruction and sorrow." [48] Her role in the ensuing battle, she told the members of the Women's Institutes, offered her a unique "opportunity to serve 'Home and Country.'" [49]

Through her varied experiences as a missionary doctor, war volunteer, and active social service worker, including with the Councils of Women at the national and local levels (see Chapter 1), Patterson established her credentials as a leading authority on the moral conditions affecting women's lives. Her various activities also reveal a clear and continuous commitment to a broad political platform. In her career as a medical missionary in India, she learned many of the social and political skills that would make her "the right sort of woman" for the magisterial post.[50] Her work with camp followers in India aligned her with the concerns of an imperial army that viewed sexually active women as a moral and physical danger. This experience probably helped her significantly when she later presided over a court that had jurisdiction over the enforcement of vagrancy provisions and infractions of *An Act for the Prevention of Venereal Disease*. Similarly, her work in the Seward Medical Hospital consisted of providing "several separated rooms ... with private entrance and separate cooking places, so that women who had to observe the caste system were able to do so."[51] Surely, the existence of a distinct location for the treatment of female patients in India informed her belief that women's legal cases should be heard separately, and within a medical model, in Toronto. Patterson's commitment to missionary work in general likely put her in good stead as both a Toronto moral reformer and magistrate: after all, what was moral reform if not aimed "to civilize the urban jungle"?[52] Her concrete aid to the imperial government in India was not unlike her volunteer activities as one of Toronto's most "energetic welfare workers."[53]

Yet Patterson was no mere puppet of formal state interests. One of the things that unifies all of her diverse reform activities is a clear and unequivocal commitment to women. As an early "lady doctor," an intern at the Detroit Women's Hospital, a member of the American Presbyterian Women's Missionary Society, and a worker for and with women, both in India and in Toronto, Margaret Patterson's priorities are evident.[54] She was dedicated to improving – as she saw fit – the lives of women. That her definition of *improvement* fit with the needs of empire and nation meant that, like other prominent white, middle-class women activists of her day, she put forward a politics that was both oppositional, in its strong articulation of women's need for justice, and conformist, in its adherence to a model of moral citizenship that was organized through a politics of nation, race, and class. It was this politics that she brought to the Women's Court bench and these beliefs and experiences that informed her implementation of feminized justice.

Magistrate Margaret Patterson was positioned – by herself, her supporters, and her critics – as a woman "with ideas."[55] Her approach to the adjudication of women's criminal cases was, and was meant to be, different from that of male magistrates. As an expert member of "the new school of moral medicine,"[56] and as an activist with a "keen insight into the moral complexities of modern life,"

Patterson was vested with what Beverly Blair Cook calls "moral authority."[57] In her medicalization of crime, her critique of the androcentric criminal justice system, and her belief that a more moral society was possible, Patterson deliberately distanced herself from the "male Solons" and the narrow confines of legal formulae. In her world view, the overlapping problems of crime, disease, and immorality could be met with the overlapping solutions of punishment, treatment, and feminized justice. In this world view, Patterson made no distinction between treatment and confinement or between protection and punishment. At one and the same time, she could boast that her practices as a magistrate prioritized "tak[ing] every case and before forming any opinion, inquir[ing] into all the circumstances that led to the misdemeanor ... for without thorough investigation we can never do our best for our patients"[58] and argue that "[s]ome cases ... must always be punished, and I believe that when punishment is given it should be stiff."[59]

It was because women adjudicators emphasized that these qualitative differences set them apart from their male counterparts that Perry could write of women magistrates as if they were magistrates who belonged to the women's community and, therefore, who carried into the criminal terrain an oppositional, and better, approach to women and crime. Perry concluded her article with full praise for these women's exemplary moral and maternal qualities: "It must be apparent that in no instance were they weak, emotional creatures who approached their judgeships as sentimental neophytes. On the contrary, the majority of them are strong-hearted, brainy mothers of families, mellowed by time and enriched by years of constructive struggle in both public and private life; the others are women, who as doctors or teachers have been also well seasoned, trained, and broken in to do valuable service for the state." But through this celebration of "our women magistrates," Perry inadvertently identified the key contradiction that underlay the tenures of early women adjudicators. At the same time that early women magistrates, such as Margaret Patterson, held to the idea that, as women, they had something special to contribute to the administration of justice, they also saw these contributions as a service to the state. To the extent that their capacities were uncontested as a service to the state, their magistracies as women were a welcomed intervention in the adjudication of morals crimes. However, when there was a discrepancy between the feminist and the masculinist interpretation of "state interests," feminists had to navigate a path that pitted their interpretation of justice against the status quo.

In these contests, the feminists' identity as women came to the foreground as the basis of their capacities and deliberations.

Feminized Justice in Action: Margaret Patterson and Criminalized Women

Margaret Patterson v. Myrtle Cook

The "privilege" of giving evidence to a wise woman, rather than a wise man, came at a price. To receive this privilege, it was necessary to meet silent, but palpable, criteria as a deserving beneficiary. As a result women's ability to speak of the "delicate intricacies, the many-sided reasons, and the complex causes of [their] crimes" was predicated on a formula that required them to act in particular ways. When women failed, or appeared to have failed, to conform to their role as victims in need of the friendship ostensibly on offer, their stories were treated, by a female magistrate, with contempt. The trial of Myrtle Cook is a case in point.

On Thursday 11 June 1925, Magistrate Margaret Patterson began what appeared to be a typical day in court.[60] She first released on bail a woman charged with writing a threatening letter to her neighbour, a reckless action that was attributed to the woman's having read too many pulp novels. Next, Patterson heard the case of a "striking spinster arrested in an intoxicated condition." This woman was ordered to return to Buffalo. Patterson also ordered a shoplifter's husband to put up a $200 surety for his wife's release and remanded the accused to his care. The last case reported by the *Star* also appeared to be nothing out of the ordinary. Twenty-two-year-old Myrtle Cook, a black woman, was up on a vagrancy charge. Cook had just been released the previous Friday from the Mercer Reformatory, where she had served a one-year sentence for possession of drugs. On the arresting police officer's testimony that Cook had been found wandering the streets late at night, unable to give a satisfactory account of herself and with no visible means of support, Patterson registered a conviction for vagrancy and ordered Cook back to the reformatory on an indeterminate sentence of one year less a day.

The difference between Cook and the other three accused was her demeanour. The first three women, all of them white, not only accepted the magistrate's verdict but also, at least according to the *Star* reporter, showed visible signs of deference in the court. Betty Pecalis, the writer of the threatening letter, looked humbly down at her shoes as Patterson questioned her, exercised her right not to speak, and allowed her male defence counsel to present her case to the court. Rose Paul, the intoxicated spinster from Buffalo, promised to speedily return home and thanked the court for its lenience. Carrie Pednoit, the married shoplifter, cried, "trembled," and promised to obey her husband if she was allowed to go home with him. But Cook showed no such deference. Instead, according to the *Star*, "her cries shattered the usual stillness of the court room." In other words, Cook tried to argue that the charge against her was baseless. Not only was she unsuccessful in making her case; in the end she would be severely punished for the attempt.

The arresting officer claimed, in a storyline that should by now be familiar, that he had found Cook on her way home from a dance late at night. She had stopped several men in the street and appeared to be intoxicated. But Cook had a different version of events. She had been at a dance, she said, but she had not been drunk at all. Moreover, she explained, she had not been soliciting men on the streets. Instead, she had been asking them for matches: "I had no money to buy them as I hadn't been able to get work." Here, then, was the penniless and lonely woman identified by Patterson as the raison d'être of the Women's Court. Yet, on this day, Patterson was less predisposed to see this as the kind of victimization that warranted the special privileges she was positioned to bestow. To the contrary, she asked Cook, "Surely you weren't looking for work last night?" There was nothing in Cook's record to suggest she had ever been involved in the sex trade, a point Cook tried to make when she replied, "Certainly not." Perhaps seeing where this was going, Cook also repeated, for good measure, "And the officer is telling stories when he says I was drinking."

Regardless of whether it was intentional, Cook had put the legitimacy of the Women's Court on trial. It was now her word against that of a male police officer in a venue that had been created to listen to women's voices precisely because of the biases that inhered in masculine interpretations of law. And yet, for reasons that were not recorded, Patterson chose to believe the policeman's version of events. Cook's lawyer then spoke and asked for leniency because, he told the court, Cook was friendless. This request evoked the very foundations of the Women's Court, yet, once again, it found no foothold: "Friendless nothing," Patterson replied, "[a]pparently she had some friends last night." Thus denying Cook's testimony, Patterson convicted her and sentenced her to one year at the reformatory. Upon hearing her sentence, a frustrated Cook cried out: "I don't want to listen to the magistrate. She can do what she likes with me. I hate her and I don't care if I get ten years." In response, and apparently because she was "astonished" at this outburst, Patterson added another year to Cook's sentence. Cook was led away from court, "cursing justice and all connected thereto."

The clearly punitive reaction of Magistrate Patterson was sufficiently egregious to warrant reactions from concerned citizens. A Mrs. M.L. Morris felt quite indignant over a sentence that seemed, to her, to be "severe and unjust."[61] One Mr. Llon Penhall Rees was even more condemnatory. He submitted a letter to the editor of the *Star* that questioned the very authority and "poise and judgment" of Magistrate Patterson: "Now, sir, while the dignity of the court must be maintained, the more important prerogative must never be forgotten, and that is mercy. While both ladies were lacking in control, as I see it, the magistrate deserves more censure than the unlucky prisoner. I consider the action of Magistrate Patterson a stain on our civic honor."[62]

These individual concerns were handled (for reasons that are unclear) by Alfred Lavell, chief parole officer for Ontario, who undertook to respond to each personally. In his initial responses, Lavell attempted to dismiss the complaints through obfuscation. Rather than respond directly to the critiques of Patterson, he commended the writers for their interest in Cook's case, which he assumed from their letters meant they were "acquainted with the circumstances of the girl," and asked "if [they] know any good home or position that could be given her."[63] Neither Mr. Rees, a music teacher, nor Mrs. Morris, a housewife from Riverdale, was in a position to provide a suggestion, and the implicit chastisement brought an end to Mrs. Morris's interest in the case. Mr. Rees, however, insisted on having his concerns answered, replying to Lavell's letter that "nothing has appeared, to my knowledge, which throws any other light on this monstrous miscarriage of Justice ... Until officially informed to the contrary, the general public must believe that this unlucky girl is serving one year for daring to talk back to a Magistrate." He further suggested that "the best interest of the community would be served if Magistrate Patterson was removed from Office."[64]

Rather than request Patterson's resignation, or even inquire further into the matter, Lavell voiced his unequivocal support for the magistrate. He now took the time to explain to Rees not only that Patterson had acted in a "most just and kindly" way but also that the sentence was "in the interests not only of the public but of the girl herself": "Sentences are not usually given in these days so much for punishment as for control and guidance, and if any one needed control and guidance this girl does ... In our experience one of the most unfortunate courses which can be taken in the cases of girls like these is to give either a fine or a short sentence. It seems kindly but in reality it is a most certain way of assisting them to go to the devil."[65] Lavell's response reveals that the language of protective surveillance was not the preserve of the women's community alone. Officials did not think that Patterson had stepped beyond her bounds when she punished Cook for her defiance. To the contrary, Patterson was praised for doing the very job she was expected to do as a woman magistrate.

The case of Myrtle Cook reveals the contours of the moral authority enjoyed by Patterson. Cook was – in the view of Lavell, legitimately – denied the status of being friendless and turned into an agent of her own decline; therefore, her story could not be heard. Cook's defiance, and her open contempt for the magistrate whose very authority was staked in her name, was taken as proof of her waywardness, which justified a stern response. Cook's insistence that she might have some legitimate claims to being out on the streets at night talking to men placed her outside the realm of victimized womanhood and put her at odds with the aims of the Women's Court. It thus became just and kindly to sentence her in her own interests.

This same theme was echoed five years later when Judge Denton upheld the vagrancy conviction of Violet Davis (discussed in Chapter 4) as being in the interests of the ordinary moral standards of the community.[66] It is significant, then, that both cases involved non-white subjects. As a black woman, Myrtle Cook was discursively situated outside the idealized image of womanhood that was both the foundation, and the goal, of the Toronto Women's Court. Violet Davis, meanwhile, had been found to be in violation of the community's moral standards because, although a white woman, she chose to cohabit with a "colored" man. In Davis's case, Judge Denton explicitly noted that because Patterson was a woman magistrate, she "[knew] quite as much, if not more, than a man what is the best to be done" for Davis. Indeed, Denton went so far as to call Patterson "our woman magistrate."

Denton's use of the phrase *our woman magistrate*, like Lavell's use of the language of protective surveillance in the "interests" of Myrtle Cook, reveals that Margaret Patterson's authority was legitimate not only because she was female. Clearly, Denton was not referring, as Anne Anderson Perry was, to an "us" made up of women when he called Patterson "our woman magistrate." Rather, his invocation of the term signals a broader community, perhaps the province of Ontario or the community of judges and magistrates or, most probably, a community of well-positioned persons with an active interest in achieving a more moral society. Denton's and Lavell's defence of Patterson reveals that the community that authorized Patterson's tenure extended beyond support for her role as a "first woman" to include her actions as a member of a white, professional, middle-class elite. To the extent that Patterson was able to use her womanhood to achieve these simultaneous purposes, she was broadly accepted as "our woman magistrate."

The case of Myrtle Cook indicates that Patterson's authority was legitimated when her constituents could make scant claims to their own legitimate inclusion within a respectable community of women. This exclusion might be because of their race or national origin, their "immoral" choices, their insistence on autonomy, or any combination thereof. As a magistrate, Patterson was empowered to patrol the borders of that female community, a task that conformed with both the goals of feminized justice and the interests of the broader state, of which she was an agent. However, when Patterson exercised her power over women with much stronger claims to an idealized womanhood, this authority became increasingly questionable, and her capacities as a woman became central to the debates about her ability to render effective service to that same state. In the case of Cecile Gereau, Patterson's critics found ample cause for concern.

Margaret Patterson v. Cecile Gereau

On 25 August 1927, two stories from the Women's Court appeared side by side in the pages of the *(Toronto) Evening Telegram*. The first, titled "Closed Court Edict Meets with Criticism," related the frustrations of the newspaper's court reporter on being barred from the preliminary proceedings of an abortion case.[67] Consistent with her long-standing belief that the press should not report salacious details from the court, and because she was convinced that public accounts of this particular case (which was ordered over to a jury trial) would bias a jury and prevent a fair trial, Patterson refused to allow the press access to her court. Although some reporters accepted this ban on their access to proceedings, the *Telegram* reporter did not.[68] Seeking support for the right to attend court, the reporter interviewed Senior Magistrate Coatsworth (Patterson's boss), city councillors, and lawyers, and he consulted the *Criminal Code*. Ultimately, however, the *Telegram* reporter was not satisfied: no authority would directly condemn Patterson for her actions.

Perhaps because it was bitter about being "deprived ... of a potentially juicy story" by Margaret Patterson,[69] the *Telegram* took full advantage of the critical elements of the second story, that of Cecile Gereau, to turn Patterson's court into a public relations spectacle. Gereau's story opened with her vocalizing her distaste for the Women's Court and its female magistrate: "Cecile Gereau, charged with escaping from custody, was remanded a week. Cecile was sentenced to two years' imprisonment on a conviction for receiving, and evidently held such strong opinion as to the justice of her sentence that though Magistrate Patterson promised T.J. O'Connor, her counsel, that she would not add to the sentence imposed, she refused absolutely to be tried by Magistrate Patterson. 'Any other court but this,' she said, which amounted to an election to be tried by jury."[70] Perhaps sensing the good copy that would follow, reporters from both the *Telegram* and the *Star* were present two weeks later, on 7 September, when Gereau appeared before Judge Denton in the County Court Judges' Criminal Court for her trial. For the next two weeks, the *Telegram* would doggedly report "the story of pathos and pity," producing four full-length articles about the case. Some of the more detailed information about Gereau's background is contradictory, but the underlying message to be learned about her was not. Gereau's experiences offered a (possibly angry) *Telegram* reporter the opportunity to show that Margaret Patterson – who was conveniently away from Toronto on vacation when the story became headline news – was unfit to adjudicate criminal cases.[71]

Gereau's story was compelling. She was remanded on 7 September for one week while court workers investigated her reasons for escaping from custody. What was uncovered was a sensational story of motherly love and cruel punishment. And unlike Myrtle Cook, Cecile Gereau was found to be credible: all those involved in the case, including Judge Denton, declared that Gereau's story was "absolutely true."[72] Twenty-three-year-old Gereau was white, of French-Canadian origin, and "of a fairly good family."[73] But she was not spotless. She had been deserted by either a husband or a lover and was raising a two-year-old daughter alone. She had been in the Women's Court before, under a different name (Lucille LaRue), for bawdy house offences. Importantly, on her last appearance, in March 1927, she had been fined one hundred dollars by Patterson, who also told her, "If you come back again I'll give you two years less a day." In June, Gereau was charged with receiving a stolen coat and again appeared before Patterson, who made good on her earlier threat or warning (the difference between the two would be a central consideration in the dispute that would follow) and sentenced Gereau to an indeterminate sentence not to exceed two years less a day. This sentence was to be served at the Home of the Good

Shepherd, a Catholic institution managed by nuns and designated (by *An Act Respecting Industrial Refuges for Females*) in 1919 as a custodial institution.[74]

In July, Gereau escaped from the sisters after telling them repeatedly that she was going to do just that. She offered two reasons for her escape: "[F]irst, that she had been given a sentence which was not justifiable, and secondly, she wanted to see her sick baby."[75] Her two-year-old daughter, Viola, was then in the care of the Isolation Hospital, where she was being treated for diphtheria. Presumably tipped off by the nuns, police stationed themselves at the hospital on the assumption that Gereau would show up.[76] She stayed away for as long as she could and found work in a cloak factory on Spadina Avenue. Finally, on 4 August, after learning of her daughter's worsening health, Gereau attempted to gain entry into the hospital. She was arrested for escaping lawful custody and held in jail. While Gereau was in custody awaiting trial – during which time she appeared before, and refused to be tried by, Patterson – Viola died.

The *Telegram* easily massaged these events into a dramatic narrative. Gereau was painted as a tribute to motherhood, one whose love for her daughter had caused her to act with noble self-sacrifice. Gereau also had articulate, law-abiding, and respectable friends, who not only spoke endlessly of her good character but raised money so that a lawyer could be retained. Letters of support poured in from people all around Toronto as people offered to help (and some even offered to marry) Gereau. Gereau's plight was contrasted with what was characterized as the severe, punitive, and uncaring attitude of Toronto's only woman magistrate. As the *Telegram* reporter put it: "Tragedy, in the form of a two years less a day sentence at the hands of Dr. Margaret Patterson in Women's Court, for 'receiving' a stolen coat, last June had torn a mother's care from a sick child."[77] The designation of good and bad protagonists could not have been made clearer.

The words that Patterson spoke to Gereau when the latter appeared before her in March on a bawdy house offence were particularly damaging. Unnamed friends of Gereau insisted that the words amounted to a threat: "I question the right of any judge or magistrate to threaten anyone like that, much less to carry out the threat," one friend told the *Telegram*.[78] Legal experts, solicited by the newspaper, concurred. In the opinion of A.R. Hassard, LLB, Toronto barrister, "The fact that Magistrate Patterson threatened the girl with two years less one day regardless of the offence with which she was charged were she to become a defendant in that court again, is not what I would call altogether ethical":

I know very well that it is the practice of some magistrates, in suspending sentence, to warn the accused that if they return things will go badly with them. These threats are usually made in the interests of the accused, to keep them from slipping anew from the paths of virtue. Nevertheless I am of the opinion that a magistrate should confine himself to warnings, and not threats. It is most certainly not in the interest of justice and humanity to send a defendant from court trembling with fear of being discriminated against in the event of another appearance.[79]

Even the attorney general, Colonel Price, stepped into the fray, saying that he had asked Patterson to submit a "full report on the case" and agreeing that it "appear[ed], under all the circumstances, that the magistrate imposed a pretty severe sentence."[80]

For her part Cecile Gereau never wavered in her defence of her escape from the Home of the Good Shepherd. She claimed not only that she had forewarned the nuns at the home that she would take "French leave" but also that she felt justified in so doing, not only because of her desire to see to her child but also because Patterson "gave me a sentence I didn't deserve."[81] At her trial she told Denton that her sentence was quite severe and that "if I only had the money I would fight this thing."[82] She further claimed that she had attempted to plead for mercy on the basis of her child's illness at the time of her appearance before Patterson for receiving stolen goods, although this was denied by the Crown attorney.[83] Clearly, however, when Gereau was recaptured and brought before Patterson on the charge of escaping from lawful custody, her sense that she would not receive justice was based on her own experiences. Her adamant insistence that she be tried in "any court but this" makes abundant sense in light of her sense of the injustice of Margaret Patterson's rulings.

Ultimately, Judge Denton did sentence Gereau to a three-month sentence for escaping, to be served concurrently with her existing sentence for receiving stolen goods. This result was the same as that promised by Patterson when Gereau appeared before her. But it was not the result that mattered. That Gereau's background, dying child, penniless condition, and noble character had to be discovered by the county court judge only further undermined Patterson's claims to authority. It was she, after all, who insisted that hasty judgements without thorough investigations were tantamount to "criminal negligence."[84] And yet, to all appearances, she handed down an "exemplary sentence" without consideration of the factors behind Gereau's crime.[85] Patterson's refusal to do so was characterized as merciless, severe, uninformed, and in contravention of ethical principles. Indeed, the *Telegram* blamed Patterson for the fact that Gereau had been unable even to say goodbye to her dying child: "In fear of the bench that had already given her 'two years less a day,' Cecilia [sic] Gereau awaited in Toronto jail her plight before a judge, where she thought justice would be more tempered with mercy." In other words, if Patterson had been more disposed to listen rather than punish, and if she had been inclined to show mercy in the name of motherhood rather than discipline, Gereau may well have been able to see her daughter. Because Patterson had treated the poor mother so severely, Gereau had seen no other option but to exercise her right to a different venue and, thus, miss the opportunity "to hold the hand of her little babe in its dying moment."[86] Patterson had missed the key point: "That maternal love which [Gereau] displayed is evidence enough of the fact that there is something in the girl worth saving."[87] Patterson was the only one who failed to grasp this.

Ultimately, Patterson could not win against a mother with a dead child whose sentimental plight was so moving – and exploitable. Central to Patterson's faults was her ease with disproportionate sentencing. Although wholly consistent with her own views on how to repair a girl's chances, this tendency to use punishment as a tool – or weapon – to achieve a more moral society was disquieting to many observers. Another "authority vested in court matters" responded to the *Telegram*'s request for expert opinion on Patterson's decision in the Gereau case with a more encompassing critique of her tenure: "[Gereau] was one of many young girls who receive sentences in Women's Court that are entirely unbalanced in proportion to the crime. We have cases every day before magistrate Patterson in which the court deals entirely too severely with the accused when all phases of their case are taken into consideration. Bank bandits, gun-men and robbers are let off with comparatively light sentences while an unfortunate girl with no one to fight for her falls before a bench with little mercy."[88] This "authority" was, in all likelihood, one of those legal professionals with no love of either Patterson or lay magistrates in general who was able to use this case to make a useful political point. Nonetheless, this critique also cut to the quick of the arguments for feminized justice. The similarity between the argument for women judges and that against Patterson is noteworthy. Women interested in overturning the double standard of morality looked at comparable crimes committed by men to show how friendless women were unfairly situated before the law. The causes of women's crime, therefore, needed to be put before a woman magistrate who would know how to hear them and what to do about them. Now it appeared that Patterson had done the very same thing that she and the women's community had long argued male judges had done to a fault.

Nor was this view confined to legal and male critics. One court watcher with a background in "reforming" former prostitutes wrote a letter to the editor of the *Telegram* (which she signed only as "Help the Weak") to condemn the practices of Toronto's woman magistrate.[89] She praised the efforts of the *Telegram* for "prominently bringing to notice the undue hardship of an unfortunate woman," and she hoped "that it may lead to an investigation that will cause officials and well-disposed persons to interest themselves, not only in the case in question, but in others of a similar nature, to save and assist to reform wayward females, instead of driving them to desperation by undue persecution and cruel punishment." In other words this woman shared with the organized women's community a sense of outrage that the criminal justice system itself was part of the problem of, rather than the solution to, women's criminality. But, now, the female magistrate whose tenure was meant to be the answer to this problem was implicated in this very injustice. For this letter writer, the case of Cecile Gereau also brought to mind the circumstances of Myrtle Cook. The double critique is worth citing at length:

> How lightly the magistrate of the Women's Court thinks of a year's sentence on [luckless girls] may be judged by the case of the young woman who, after serving a year's sentence for vagrancy, was tracked by the police and arrested for addressing a man in the street. When sentenced by the same magistrate for another year for so doing, the girl in her agony exclaimed: "I don't want to be tried by that — — woman" (using an opprobrious term). For the use of such words the sentence was altered to two years. Two years ... as in the case of Cecilia Gereau – two years the life of a white slave – wash! wash! wash! morning and afternoon without pay and without variation ... and then to be turned adrift at the end of the term a penniless outcast, without home or friends, only to be looked after by police, but temptation is awaiting, so is it a wonder that they again fall ... to lower depth?[90]

By her own actions, Margaret Patterson was condemned for becoming part of the problem that she was expressly committed to resolve. That the letter writer above equated institutional protection with white slavery and the perpetuation of women's victimization can only be read as a stinging indictment of all that Patterson held dear. A similar critique of Patterson would surface two years later, when she sentenced Lucy Ratcliffe to the women's jail farm after

Ratcliffe had presented herself for "protection" (see Chapter 3). In that case, again, Ratcliffe's penniless and friendless condition was contrasted to Patterson's severe and unjust rulings. Concerned and angry citizens wrote letters to the newspaper offering to help where Patterson had failed. The (same) attorney general was asked to look into the situation and to reprimand Patterson. Once again the woman charged with a criminal offence became the sympathetic victim and Patterson the merciless foe. The implementation of feminized justice contained its own internal dilemmas and was, indeed, "accompanied by setbacks."[91] Importantly, these setbacks were not initiated only by "little anti-feminist men." Criminalized women's complaints could spark broad debate about the relationship between feminized justice and women's service for the state.

Conclusion

> It cannot, I think, be fairly said that [women's] admission has had any marked effect upon the Bar or the practice of law; their influence on legislation for the protection of women and children is considerable, but not more than that of an equal number of women who have not joined the profession – what influence there is has been, I think, uniformly good.[92]
> – William Rednick William, "Women as Practitioners of Law"

In his 1918 essay addressed specifically to the question of women as lawyers, Ontario Supreme Court Justice William Riddell assured his contemporaries that women's entry into the profession of law was not worrisome. He told his colleagues that practising women lawyers – who, at the time of his writing, numbered only "perhaps a dozen in all" in Canada – "are not 'wild women'; they are earnest, well-educated women who ask no favours but are quite willing to do their share of the world's work on the same conditions as men." They did not, Riddell vouched from experience, "trade upon [their] sex," and, if anything, their impact on the profession had been negligible. The woman lawyer, he announced with certainty and, perhaps, some relief, exhibited the same "sound sense as her masculine *confrère*."

It was, in part, with this same expectation that she act with "sound sense" in accordance with the rules laid out by men that Margaret Patterson was appointed to the bench. That is, in some way, she was expected to act as her male colleagues did: as a magistrate, it fell to her to regulate the ordinary moral standards of the community. At the same time, her female supporters, and her male critics, expected her to act as a woman. Her appointment to the bench met with both the enthusiastic support of women's and moral reform groups and condemnation and concern by the almost all-male legal profession. Importantly, both of these groups responded to the same characteristic that Patterson represented, namely, her status not only as a woman but as a laywoman without specific legal expertise. To the women's community, this was her chief asset as a female magistrate; to the legal community, it was her chief fault.

For twelve years Patterson was largely able to defend her particular brand of feminist expertise against masculine disapproval of her tenure in the Toronto Women's Court. At the end of her career, she continued to espouse the same principles that had led to her ascending to the bench in the first place. Reflecting on her tenure in 1935, she explained to the readers of *Chatelaine* the importance of her magistracy: "The lesson I have learned from twelve years of intensive work with girls is that it requires the personal touch. You must gain their confidence, make them feel that you care, and that you will be disappointed if they do not make a real effort to do better. To do this effectively, you must care tremendously and realize the value of the girl to her country."[93]

In these terms Patterson's approach to justice – in its very intensiveness, its ethic of caring, and its emphasis on individualized and personalized treatment – was distinct from that of men. To themselves and to their male colleagues, women magistrates presented their work as sufficiently different to warrant its characterization as (courageously) oppositional.[94] At the same time, Patterson's vision of justice had grander purposes as well: the interests of the country and a girl's responsibility to those interests were central to her interpretation of "doing better." For Patterson these two goals were of a piece. For her detractors they were often at odds, and their conflicting nature could sometimes be usefully exploited.

Meanwhile, the protesting voices of criminalized women like Myrtle Cook and Cecile Gereau serve as important reminders that the debate about the tenure of a female magistrate did not simply interest prominent men and prominent women. Of course, the cases of Myrtle Cook and Cecile Gereau are, in some ways, atypical of criminalized women's appearances before a woman magistrate. It was not usual for criminalized women's protesting voices to gain currency within debates about law and justice in general and feminized justice in particular. As ultimately happened to Cook, accused women's frustrations, anger, or contempt for the criminal justice system was typically, and easily, waved away by authorities and reporters as proof of the women's amorality and, thus, need for correction by those who knew better. Margaret Patterson herself was of this view, as she (prophetically) explained to the members of the National Council of Women in 1915: "We must not expect the offenders to thank us for our efforts ... for the longing for spurious freedom that has been their undoing is still strong and they resent the treatment until the moral uplift of wholesome surroundings asserts itself."[95] In this top-down approach to the needs of women in conflict with the law, it was assumed that there was only one legitimate type of freedom. That freedom was secured by complying with the specific definition of womanhood invoked by the organized women's community.

But for many criminalized women, that price was too high. Including their voices within the debates about the legitimacy of Margaret Patterson's tenure serves to undermine the dichotomous language of women versus men that was the most common public presentation of the values of a morals court for women. Through this lens, the Toronto Women's Court emerges as a multifaceted institution. During, and because of, Patterson's tenure, the court did mark a significant shift in some women's status: Margaret Patterson was the only woman in Ontario empowered to exercise legal authority over both women and men, and her institutionalization of an informal domestic mediations court provided a place in which poor, married women could bring their complaints against bad husbands. And this feminist-inspired institution did raise the hackles of certain "little anti-feminist" men who were alarmed, for a variety of reasons, by its very existence and, all the more so, by its presiding female magistrate. At the same time, however, the Toronto Women's Court brought Margaret Patterson into direct conflict with other Torontonian women whose insistence on their own "freedom," spurious or otherwise, belied Patterson's invocation of a unified community of women arrayed consistently against men. Indeed, Patterson's own actions show that she did not believe in this ideal either. Rather, in the name of womanhood, she was determined to divide good women from bad through the authority vested in her as a woman, and she did so as much in the interests of her vision of a moral society as for the benefit of the individual women appearing before her. In this goal, she aligned herself once more, just as she had as a medical missionary, with the interests of the nation in her role as an agent of the state. Often enough, she would receive the support of other male state agents as "our woman magistrate."

Clearly, different actors answered the question, what are a girl's chances? differently. Broadly speaking, three distinct groups offered diverse opinions on this foundational question that the Women's Court was meant to answer. Lawyers and male detractors pinpointed due process and legal rights as key elements of justice and faulted Patterson for her often cavalier attitude toward these principles. Feminists responded by critiquing the "narrow confines of legal formulae" as being insensitive to women's plight and as anathema to justice, and offered themselves, and their alternative insights into "treatment," in lieu of male legal authorities and unjust laws. Criminalized women had a more immediate concern: meeting the requirements for the benefits of the "privilege" on offer to them was no easy task, and it was often a frustrating process. Their contempt for Patterson's Women's Court brought these varying viewpoints into sharper focus and raised the possibility that feminized justice was unjust. This, too, shaped the tenure of Margaret Patterson in the Toronto Women's Court. Although, on their own, neither Cook nor Gereau, nor any individual woman in conflict with the law, unseated Patterson from the court, their combined struggles as women against a woman reveal the very tenuous grounds on which her authority was staked. In all likelihood neither Cook nor Gereau grieved at the final foreclosure on feminized justice, when Patterson was forced off the bench in 1934 and the "great achievement" of the Toronto Women's Court came to an end.

Conclusion

In 1935 Margaret Patterson, then a private citizen, wrote an article titled "Bad Girl" for Canada's national feminist magazine, *Chatelaine*. In it Patterson offered her experiential sense of the causes of women's crime. Her express aim in writing this article was to dislodge popular conceptions of criminalized women as truly bad, by which she meant ruthless destroyers of happy family life. While conceding that some women did fit this description, Patterson argued that most of the women who had come before her in her twelve years on the bench lacked either the mental or the moral resources to be as good as they should be. But, she continued, "not all our sex delinquents are of low mentality":

> In a separate group come the unfortunate, unhappy and underprivileged. This was the most varied group of all, and from their number came some of the greatest disappointments but also the encouragements of one's work. Here we have the girl who was unfortunate in her choice of companions. Perhaps her mother had devoted too much time to giving her daughter material comforts to have the energy or time to devote to her in a way that introduced her to the fields of creative adventure or character training in helpfulness and in thoughtfulness of others; had never realized the importance of being chums and keeping her confidence. So the girl ... is quite unguided by older and wiser friends, and ... is tempted by the

glowing accounts of the adventure and romance of "hitch-hiking" and night life, to venture forth. Mothers do not realize just how common this has become or how disastrous it may be.

Maternal neglect, then, was the second leading cause of crime among women. The solution to this problem was evident: where biological mothers failed, the country's women's organizations, "made up of the mothers and women of the community," "should consider it their first duty ... to make [each girl] feel that they are there to help her and that the organization needs her." Patterson implored the women readers of *Chatelaine* to carry on the important rescue work that she had attempted in the Women's Court and to extend themselves as social mothers to reverse the slide of girls who were not so much bad as they were neglected daughters in need of moral guidance and character training.[1]

Patterson's emphasis on the role of social rather than biological mothers is consistent with the claim made in this book that maternalism transformed social relations into statements on authority. These authority relations, naturalized through familial references, helped to constitute white, middle-class women as members of a class and as a political constituency that made important contributions to the making of the nation. Women – mothers – who devoted too much energy to material comforts and who, therefore, failed to offer friendship to their daughters were juxtaposed, without any consideration of differing material conditions among women, with the organized women of "the community," whose knowledge of the real needs of the nation could be put to altruistic purposes. Within this moral discourse, we can also see the tendrils of imperialist projects and notions of racialized, gendered citizenship. The invocation of rescue and protection, of duty and nation, is suggestive of the multivalent implicationsof the phrase *mother of the race,* whereby white women positioned themselves as uniquely qualified to engage in the necessary uplift of their less fortunate "sisters." Women's organizations, nation, friendship, comfort, wisdom, moral guidance, character training, and motherhood were elided into a single framework and presented as an answer to the question of the female "sex delinquent." The Toronto Women's Court was the institutional "solution" to this feminized view of the "problem" of female crime.

As I have argued throughout this book, the Toronto Women's Court resulted from the maternal feminists' belief that moral typologies could be mapped onto criminal law enforcement with relative ease. That is, they made little distinction between morality and the law and saw the latter as a tool to achieve the former.

The relationship between the work of the Committee for an Equal Moral Standard, moral regulation, and criminological reform as undertaken by maternal feminists indicates that the desire for a more moral society was inseparable from imaginings of a more just legal system. Women reformers, therefore, challenged the mainstream view of the moral and, thus, legal dilemmas faced by women in conflict with the law. Turning the language of causality around, women activists argued that men with base interests promoted a legal system that protected these interests, thereby failing to anticipate and acknowledge women's experiences. The Women's Court was, thus, an active intervention by which to reverse these tendencies and place women's circumstances *as women* at the centre of legal adjudication. All the better, they argued, if that same Women's Court was presided over by a female magistrate who could carry this philosophy and empathy into the courtroom in practical ways.

But it has also been shown that women's criminality did not fit easily into moral categories. That is, it was not always readily apparent that women's legal wrongs were equivalent to, or explainable within, moral discourses. Indeed, in many instances the morality tales woven through the fabric of feminist legal reform projects were a key contributing factor to women's criminalization in the first place, for they translated (some) women's agency into a script for (other) women's intervention, ostensibly for their own good. In their narrative devices, the women reformers, aided greatly by court reporters, had to either refashion or simply erase the existence of some women and their crimes to maintain the Women's Court as a relevant and viable institution. In this way the very existence of the Women's Court fuelled the imaginative conventions that had led to its creation, despite the complexities represented by women's patterns of criminality.

Indeed, from the perspective of female criminals, the Women's Court "solution" was often *their* problem. It is clear that some women were aware of the requirements of feminized justice and were simply unable, or unwilling, to meet them. Seventeen-year-old Georgina R., sentenced by Patterson to the Mercer Reformatory in 1925 for vagrancy, attempted to write a letter to her boyfriend to explain her dilemma:

> Well Joe I have five months done of my time and am not going to do my two years ... [W]e can try Parole if we're good. I can't be good here so I'll never get Parole. I promised [the assistant superintendent] Mrs. Scott that I would be good as long as I'm here but I can't[,] it is too hard. I've tried my best for two weeks and that's

the longest I can be good. I don't like to give Mrs. Scott any trouble because I like her but if they don't send me [out] I will give them so much trouble here that they will get sick of me and send me.[2]

Importantly, the personalized nature of woman-centred correction was accepted by Georgina. She liked Mrs. Scott and did not "want to give [her] any trouble." But, for Georgina, confinement itself was the problem, and motherly guidance toward a more moral life was not, in itself, an answer. True to her word, Georgina did give her warders a great deal of trouble: she was disciplined seven times between November 1925 and July 1926, including one incident in which her behaviour was considered "insubordinate beyond endurance" and the Mercer officials requested permission from the provincial secretary to use the strap.[3] In September 1926 Georgina was transferred to the Queen Street Asylum. Georgina recognized that being good meant being deferent. She also paid the price for her refusal to show daughterly subordination.

The gap between the maternal moral reformers and their targeted populations was made even more clear in a letter by Clara M., who was serving an indeterminate sentence at the Mercer Reformatory after being convicted of vagrancy in the Women's Court (see Chapter 3). Clara was a particularly unhappy inmate. She had been disciplined many times, including being sent to the isolation cells, for breaking the reformatory rules. Her warders thought her a "complete misfit" whose stubborn and unreasonable behaviour proved her "complete lack of reasoning power."[4] Clara eventually escaped from the Mercer and, contrary to her keepers' opinions, demonstrated her rationality by penning an apologetic letter for Superintendent Emma O'Sullivan to find. In explaining to O'Sullivan why she felt it necessary to take "French leave," Clara posed a question that, in all likelihood, many similarly situated women would have liked answered: "I wonder if you could realize the following?":

The first time I was in the dungeon I lay on the stone floor for a long time crying[.] [N]o tears came out but it seemed as though I were choking "(for I sobbed so hard)" with anger, shame, and grief and defiance[.] [A]fter when I had exhausted myself I fell asleep ... [A] long time seemed to have past [sic] when I found myself in an underground place with stone walls and floor and iron gratings; I stood up, looked around, wondered if I were dreaming, how I had got there or if I was sick and had mental delusions and several minutes elapsed before I realized I was in the dungeon downstairs. I did not cry again but it seemed as though something cold, hard and heavy was inside of me, that I was stunned some way or another and often since it seems as though some day I will wake up and find it all a horrible dream.

I do not know why I have written all this but I wish I could make you understand how I cannot stay here.[5]

Far from being a mysteriously recalcitrant woman who wilfully defied all benevolent attempts to rescue her, Clara knew herself to be a woman to whom an injustice had been done. It was the reform project itself that had damaged her, not the activities that had brought her to the attention of reformers. Her repeated requests that O'Sullivan try to understand her on her own terms speak volumes about the relationship between middle-class women reformers and the women targeted for their reform projects. Personalized justice and intensive caring institutions were not what Clara wanted: she was searching for a dialogue among equals. That she had to escape tells us that this one thing was denied to her. It was not, in the end, what the woman-centred reform goals were about.

These contrasting views of women's criminality return us to the central question of this book. How could feminized justice be understood as a great achievement by some women and as a source of contempt or injustice by others? In light of these highly polarized understandings of feminized justice, what can be concluded about its implementation through, and as, the Toronto Women's Court? This feminized police court operated through a language of gender, specifically, a language of woman-specific familialism, while perpetuating, and legitimating, inequalities between women as a matter of legal routine. Its politicization as an explicitly feminist intervention into the masculinist biases of the criminal justice system was, at the same time, an authorization of some women's power over others and a site of the coercive punishment of "bad" women in the name of "womanhood."

The differing routes by which women entered into the legal arena are instructive in contextualizing the complex meanings of women's justice. Although the Toronto Local Council of Women (TLCW) spoke of women as subjects who were sufficiently distinct from men to warrant legal specificity, it is clear that in their imaginings of the world of female criminality and in the Women's Court itself they tended to differentiate between women in a way that mattered a great deal. Young, one-time offenders arrested for vagrancy because they had been caught in some public indiscretion and married women who shoplifted underwear or dresses from department stores experienced the Women's Court in substantively different ways than did the chronic alcoholics or the "human vultures" of the Ward. Certainly, they were meant to have different experiences, and different messages about gender were routinely read into different types of crimes and, perhaps even more importantly, different types of women. Women who were contrite, women who had respectable familial belonging, and women who were young and perceived to be endangered were distinguished from women who lacked any or all of these qualities. The existence of the Women's Court may have separated women from men, but the visible practices of the court proved that its work did not end there. It was equally important for the court to separate the erring from the hardened, the daughters from the daughters of the night, and the women in need of protection from the women from whom the city needed protection.

This, of course, is not to say that young women and first-time offenders, who were most visible in the records for vagrancy and theft, did not experience the coercive power of the law. As the example of Jean G., who faced Magistrate Patterson on a charge of vagrancy because she went to the house of a "Chinaman," demonstrates, women who seemed to be making poor judgment calls could receive long sentences in order to get "a proper perspective on life."[6] Indeed, as the accounts of vagrancy cases indicate, a chilling pattern of "protective" custody was a normalized part of the Women's Court practices. Organized more through extra-legal concerns for "the girl adrift" than by legal considerations of proportionality, young women were particularly vulnerable to a brand of feminized justice that punished them for experimentation in the urban youth culture. It is, of course, an open question as to whether these same young women experienced the Women's Court as a legal boon or as a great achievement.

Theft was another criminal category that tended to capture more first-time than repeat offenders. The broader conduct of women who stole was no less subject to scrutiny than that of women vagrants. Usually counted separately from offences against public morals, property offences offer another glimpse into the mechanisms by which the Women's Court was an arena for sexual-moral surveillance. If family was seen as an important absence in the lives of many young, vagrant women – one that could be filled by the familial organization and practices of the Women's Court – familialism was a palpable presence in the adjudication of women's theft cases. Demonstrable family belonging, along with feminine demonstrations of contrition – bewilderment, tears, and self-sacrifice – could go a long way to making amends for the affront of petty theft. Women shoplifters in particular could mitigate their crimes by "reinforc[ing] the common assumption that the female was often unstable, ruled by her nervous system and her emotions."[7] Pronounced to be a condition of feminine weakness by medical experts, kleptomania was a regrettable transgression that strengthened prevailing gender beliefs. The appearance of a husband or (needy) child in court only enhanced the accused's feminine status. By contrast, women whose thieving was an affront to this construction – domestic employees, pickpockets, and those whose broader life circumstances did not fit within the familial code – could expect far less sympathy, even, or perhaps especially, in the Women's Court.

But despite the media's and the reformers' constructions of female crime – which were perpetually reinforced through a selective narrative of the Women's Court and the business of the court itself – the bulk of the court's work was taken up by confirmed alcoholics who appeared time and again and for whom little was expected in terms of reform. Routinely sentenced but rarely spoken of, these women have, to date, been largely absent from accounts of female crime. They seldom appear in the case files studied by historians, and the specific circumstances of their arrests are hard to come by. Their family circumstances were rarely considered relevant enough to talk about. But they were there, on almost every day of the court, arrested in pairs, in small groups, with men, or alone. That they knew each other, had bonds with one another, and lived a life outside the imaginings of middle-class reformers is clear. Whether a separate court for women meant anything to them is not. They provided material for humour, revulsion and, sometimes, pity, but their lives, their struggles, and their joys were of little interest to commentators on women's criminality. Sentenced regularly for relatively short "rest cures," their frequent appearances remain largely a numerical fact that deserves greater attention.

These same women are also visible in the bawdy house charges that did animate reformers. That these were often the same women is also not typically commented upon, either by historians or early twentieth-century reformers.[8] Indeed, the differential discursive constructions of the *same* women, depending on whether they appeared as keepers or inmates of bawdy houses or drunks, suggests a wilful disregard on the part of reformers of the ways that these offences were linked in the lived experiences of many Toronto women. This deliberate act of ignorance tells us more about law than it does about crime: the official distinctions between being a member of a brothel household and a confirmed alcoholic obscures rather than illuminates the exigencies of criminalized women's lives in Toronto.

In these ways the history of the Toronto Women's Court also has something to offer to historical debates about experience, agency, and resistance. The central question in these debates is, "How do we interpret the experiences, strategies, and perceptions of those women, men, and children who did not leave behind their own written record and who appear in the historical record only fleetingly and usually as the objects or targets of more powerful others?"[9] In the Toronto Women's Court, this historical power differential came to be embedded within the extant records of the institution. Our knowledge of those women who were paraded through the court for a variety of criminal offences is skewed by the very sources that document their presence in the first place. Case files from the Mercer Reformatory, newspaper reports that often sound a great deal like reformers' tracts, and select anecdotes told by the members of the TLCW to one another to congratulate themselves on their own good works within the court all tell us much more about the project of the Women's Court than they do about its practices and its target populations. These sources only hint at, and typically reconfigure, the actual women hidden beneath the reproductions. Some historians argue that, in such a context, the search for an authentic historical experience is a misdirected pursuit and that the discursive meaning-making constitutions of categories of experience must foreground any analysis. For other historians, however, there are dangers to levelling the hierarchies in which people's lives are constituted into a series of examinable discourses. These scholars warn against "the death of the subject and her resurrection as an isolated locale of contingent experiential understanding."[10]

The example of the Toronto Women's Court as a feminist law reform project that was initiated by some women but that subjugated others foregrounds these same questions. Were there "real" women "criminals" whose experiences of the court can be unearthed as evidence of its success or failure? Alternately, was the court a discursive arena that constituted "criminal women" as a meaningful category that could then be regulated and can now be understood through its strategic and ordering narratives? The foregoing analysis suggests that the answer lies somewhere between these two possibilities. Generally speaking, it is clear that women charged with a criminal offence did have "experiences" that alarmed, unsettled, or perhaps threatened white, middle-class women and that often led to their criminalization in the first place. In this way these women were the material context upon which feminized justice was founded. At the same time, the significance attributed to those experiences by maternal feminists did not necessarily reflect them but, nonetheless, had palpable effects on the outcomes of many trials. In this sense both the discursive interpretations of criminalized women's experiences and the evidence of differing kinds of experiences among poor, itinerant, and marginalized women are equally important concerns for an analysis of the Women's Court.

Additionally, the example of the Toronto Women's Court suggests that it is important to historicize the epistemological concept of experience in social history. Not only did differently situated women have (necessarily) different experiences of the court, but experience itself was a crucial element that structured the possibility of a separate venue for women in the first place. As I argue in Chapter 6, it was the specific experiences of white, middle-class women, such as Margaret Patterson, that enabled them to lay claim to their authority over other women. Patterson and her magisterial peers across North America celebrated their particular *experiential* backgrounds as mothers, as social workers, and as effective activists for women. As women "well seasoned, trained, and broken in to do valuable service for the state," they saw themselves as having, and were seen by many contemporaries to have, the qualifications necessary for the work they were expressly mandated to do: resolve "morals" cases involving women in specialized venues. Margaret Patterson, Alice Jamieson, Emily Murphy, and Helen Gregory MacGill could also boast of their expertise in criminal matters because they had sat in on police court proceedings prior to their respective appointments to the bench and, thus, had sufficient experience of court processes to enable them to make a difference. Their experiences earned them the "privilege" of their legal authority.

But criminalized women, and especially repeat offenders, also had experiences with the criminal justice system. Although their opinions were either not solicited or not recorded, repeat offenders arguably had knowledge of the workings of the criminal justice system, by simple virtue of their repeated movements through it, that was at least equal to that of any middle-class observer. In and out of police stations, court houses, and jails with a remarkable frequency, these women surely understood the machinations of the law and the processes of criminal justice as well as anyone in the city. Thus, Meg H. was able to navigate her way through the system in order to stage her own dignified death. Lucy Ratcliffe anticipated that the police and the courts would offer "protection" to a woman in need and was outraged when her prediction proved wrong. Daisy H. refused parole to free herself from the surveillance that it allowed. Cecile Gereau knew enough about the court system and its personnel to waive a summary conviction trial, despite the personal costs. None of these examples of experienced decision making, however, were what the members of the TLCW meant when they spoke of the beneficial experiences that women could bring to bear on "justice." To the contrary, in the Women's Court it was these women's knowledge of, and experiences with, the criminal justice system that constituted the "badness" the TLCW was trying to prevent.

The Toronto Women's Court, thus, also offers a lens to view the multiple meanings of agency and resistance. For the members of the TLCW, the court was, in and of itself, a form of resistance to a particular masculine order and an important example of their agency with respect to criminal law reform. However, by asserting this anti-patriarchal stance, and by exerting their agency as white, middle-class women, the members of the TLCW also constrained the agency of women in conflict with the law. Indeed, as Edith Chapman predicted, Margaret Patterson's appointment as magistrate in the Women's Court was as much about denying some women's voices as it was about listening to others: "We doubt if the cleverest professional offender will 'put much over' in the new women's court ... [Patterson] has protected more than one lonely girl stranded away from her family and has made herself a real terror in certain quarters."[11] Drawing on the ability of (some) women to protect lonely girls and the state's power to produce terror in others, the Toronto Women's Court regulated Toronto women whose exercise of their own agency was at the heart of the necessity for feminized justice.

As a police court designed by and for women, the Toronto Women's Court reflected, and structured, relationships among very differently situated women in Toronto. For women charged with a criminal offence, the court was often the site of their criminal sanctions and an unwelcome intervention into their lives. For the white, middle-class women who called it "our court," the Women's Court was a new and innovative institution that legitimated their role as the arbiters of women's justice. For those charged, the Women's Court could appear to be unjust; for the members of the TLCW, it was their own articulation of justice and "one of [their] great achievements." It is precisely these multiple tendencies that make the Toronto Women's Court a significant historical example of maternalist moral feminism in action. There can be no doubt that the desire, on the part of the TLCW and its supporters, to graft feminist principles onto the criminal justice system itself sprang from a comprehensive and critical assessment of the law as a masculinist institution that systematically discriminated against women and denied them justice. Nor can there be any doubt that this political insight, when translated into practical reform, ultimately made those same feminist critics complicit in the perpetuation of injustices faced by women in conflict with the law. In the end, the laudable political goal of feminized justice proved to be the largest obstacle to its achievement.

Notes

Introduction

1 Ethel M. Chapman, "How 'Bob's Maggie' Grew into Her Job," *Maclean's* (1 February 1922), 52-53.
2 A.E. Popple, "Police Court Systems," *Canadian Law Times* 41 (1921): 523.
3 Harry S. Wodson, *The Whirlpool: Scenes from Toronto Police Court* (Toronto: n.p., 1917), 15, 17.
4 Chris Burr, "'Roping in the Wretched, the Reckless, and the Wronged': Narratives of the Late Nineteenth-Century Toronto Police Court," *Left History* 3, 1 (1995): 83-108; Paul Craven, "Law and Ideology: The Toronto Police Court, 1850-80," in David Flaherty, ed., *Essays in the History of Canadian Law*, Vol. 2 (Toronto: Osgoode Society for Canadian Legal History/University of Toronto Press, 1983), 248-307.
5 Chapman, *supra* note 1, 52-53. Until indicated otherwise, all quotes that follow are from this article.
6 "Police Commissioners Will Not Revoke Star Licence," *(Toronto) Daily Star* (5 February 1913), 7 (hereafter *Star*).
7 "'Booze' and 'Dope' Are Four Women's Curse," *Star* (12 February 1913), 2.
8 "The Toronto Local Council of Women," in May Covington, ed., *Toronto Women's Directory* (Toronto: n.p., 1919).
9 The achievements and reforms initiated by the TLCW are too many to mention. For a historical overview, see Toronto Local Council of Women, *Nothing New Under the Sun: A History of the Toronto Local Council of Women, 1893-1978* (Scarborough: Reg Wilson Printing Co., 1978).
10 Robson Black, "A Dollar and Costs," *Canada Monthly* 14, 4 (1913): 8.
11 Dorothy Chunn, *From Punishment to Doing Good: Family Courts and Socialized Justice in Ontario* (Toronto: University of Toronto Press, 1992), 53.
12 For a description of the court structure and hierarchy at this time, see Margaret Banks, "The Evolution of the Ontario Courts, 1788-1981," in David Flaherty, ed., *supra* note 4 at 492-572.
13 Chunn, *supra* note 11 at 54.
14 Popple, *supra* note 2.
15 See, for example, Karen Dubinsky, *Improper Advances: Rape and Heterosexual Conflict in Ontario, 1880-1929* (Chicago: University of Chicago Press, 1993); Constance Backhouse, *Petticoats and Prejudice: Women and Law in Nineteenth-Century Canada* (Toronto: Osgoode Society for Canadian Legal History/Women's Press, 1991); Linda Gordon, *Heroes of Their Own Lives: The Politics and History of Family Violence* (New York: Viking Penguin Books, 1988). For general discussion about the possibilities of criminal case files for social history, see Carolyn Strange, "Stories of Their Lives: The Historian and the Capital Case File," in Franca Iacovetta and Wendy Mitchinson, eds., *On the Case: Explorations in Social History* (Toronto: University of Toronto Press, 1998), 25-48; Steven Maynard, "Sex, Court Records, and Labour History," *Labour/Le Travail* 33 (Spring 1994): 187-93.
16 On the Toronto Police Court as an example of low law, see Craven, *supra* note 4.
17 Douglas Hay, "Time, Inequality and Law's Violence," in Austin Sarat and Thomas R. Kearns, eds., *Law's Violence* (Ann Arbor: University of Michigan Press, 1992), 141-73. On the Toronto Women's Court as an example of low justice, see Amanda Glasbeek, "Maternalism Meets the Criminal Law: The Case of the Toronto Women's Court," *Canadian Journal of Women and the Law* 10, 2 (1998): 480-502.
18 Hay, *ibid.* at 171.

19 Judith Fingard, *The Dark Side of Life in Victorian Halifax* (Porter's Lake, NS: Pottersfield Press, 1989), 35.

20 There are few analyses of courts and trials that do not draw, in some way, on theatre metaphors or analogies. Karen Dubinsky (*supra* note 15) observes that, at the turn of the century, the relationship between theatre and courtrooms was mutually informing: court stories were reported in theatrical modes, while populist plays often used the courtroom as their central setting. See, too, Wodson, *supra* note 3. As the subtitle "Scenes from a Police Court" suggests, this book is set up like a play, in which each chapter is a scene. Similarly, Wodson describes himself and fellow court reporters as an audience to a play: "[T]he reporters, the silent, busy men ... watch, day after day, the tragedies and dramas, and occasional comedies, staged in a Police Court" (29).

21 "No Crowd, Male Hangers On," *(Toronto) Evening Telegram* (10 February 1913), 21 (hereafter *Telegram*).

22 Given that the Women's Court was predicated on removing men from women's trial proceedings, it was also a source of some pride that no male police court reporters were in attendance on the first day in the court. However, newspaper stories from the 1910s to the 1930s, especially police court reports, did not include bylines, and I am unable to tell if this practice was continued throughout the twenty-one years under examination here (although I suspect it was not).

23 "Three Girls Appear in Women's Court," *Star* (10 February 1913), 10.

24 *The Criminal Code*, R.S.C. 1906, c. 146, s. 238. The multiple meanings and applications of the vagrancy provisions will be discussed throughout the book and in detail in Chapter 4.

25 "No Crowd," *supra* note 21.

26 *Ibid.*

27 *Ibid.*

28 *Ibid.*

29 "Three Girls Appear," *supra* note 23.

30 *Ibid.* Patterson was wrong: Bridget was sentenced to thirty, not sixty, days. Accuracy would have made her point even stronger.

31 *Ibid.*

32 Angus McLaren, *Our Own Master Race: Eugenics in Canada, 1885-1945* (Toronto: McClelland and Stewart, 1990); Jennifer Stephen, "The 'Incorrigible,' the 'Bad,' and the 'Immoral': Toronto's 'Factory Girls' and the Work of the Toronto Psychiatric Clinic," in Louis Knafla and Susan W.S. Binnie, eds., *Law, Society, and the State: Essays in Modern Legal History* (Toronto: University of Toronto Press, 1995), 405-39.

33 Toronto's reformers were enormously vigilant about, and relatively successful in, ensuring that police and the courts pursued a policy of suppression, rather than toleration, of houses of prostitution. This argument is taken up in detail in Chapter 5.

34 "No Crowd," *supra* note 21.

35 "Three Girls Appear," *supra* note 23.

36 "First Court for Women in Canada," *(Toronto) Daily News* (10 February 1913), 1, 3.

37 "No Crowd," *supra* note 21.

38 "Three Girls Appear," *supra* note 23.

39 "First Court for Women," *supra* note 36.

40 "Three Girls Appear," *supra* note 23.

41 "No Crowd," *supra* note 21. The other newspapers reported a similar exchange. The *Daily News* recorded Denison as saying, "Remember, little girl, you will never find a better friend than your mother. Now go home with her in the future." The *Star* version was: "If I let you go back to your mother, will you behave yourself?"

42 "No Crowd," *supra* note 21.

43   "Three Girls Appear," *supra* note 23.

44   "Separate Courts for Women," *Jack Canuck* (15 February 1913), 6.

45   Carolyn Strange and Tina Loo, "The Moral of the Story: Gender and Murder in Canadian True Crime Magazines of the 1940s," in Margaret Thornton, ed., *Romancing the Tomes: Popular Culture, Law and Feminism* (London: Cavendish Publishing, 2002), 221-40.

46   On the politics of Progressive-era court reform, see Michael Willrich, *City of Courts: Socializing Justice in Progressive Era Chicago* (Cambridge: Cambridge University Press, 2003); Chunn, *supra* note 11; James G. Snell, "Courts of Domestic Relations: A Study of Early Twentieth-Century Judicial Reform in Canada," *Windsor Yearbook of Access to Justice* 6 (1986): 36-60. For contemporary accounts and enthusiasm, see, for example, "Courts of Domestic Relations," *Social Welfare* 5 (February 1923): 106; "Courts of Domestic Relations – A Step in the Evolution of Justice," *Social Welfare* 1 (October 1929): 19.

47   Willrich, *ibid*.; William N. Gemmill, "Chicago Courts of Domestic Relations," *Annals of the American Academy of Political and Social Sciences* 52 (1914): 115-23.

48   Beverly Blair Cook, "Moral Authority and Gender Difference: Georgia Bullock and the Los Angeles Women's Court," *Judicature* 77, 3 (1993): 144-55.

49   Mary Paddon , "The Inferior Criminal Courts of New York City," *Journal of Criminal Law and Criminology* 11, 1 (1920): 8-20; Frederick H. Whitin, "The Women's Night Court in New York City," *Annals of the American Academy of Political and Social Sciences* 52 (1914): 181-87; Freda Solomon, "Progressive Era Justice: The New York City Women's Court" (paper presented at the Seventh Berkshire Conference on the History of Women, Wellesley, Massachusetts, 19-21 June 1987).

50   See Emerson Coatsworth, *Report on the Administration of Criminal Justice Treatment of Prisoners in New York, Chicago, Detroit and Toronto* (Toronto: King's Printer, 1920). Coatsworth's research (and subsequent report) was conducted to help Ontario, and especially Toronto, in the reform of its lower court structure.

51   John McLaren, "Maternal Feminism in Action: Emily Murphy, Police Magistrate," *Windsor Yearbook of Access to Justice* 8 (1988): 234-51. Vancouver and Montreal would shortly follow suit. See National Council of Women of Canada *Yearbooks*.

52   See, for example, Tamara Myers, *Caught: Montreal's Modern Girls and the Law, 1869-1945* (Toronto: University of Toronto Press, 2006); Willrich, *supra* note 46; Joan Sangster, *Girl Trouble: Female Delinquency in English Canada* (Toronto: Between the Lines, 2002); Elizabeth Clapp, *Mothers of All Children: Women Reformers and the Rise of Juvenile Courts in Progressive Era America* (University Park: Pennsylvania State University Press, 1998); Mary Odem, *Delinquent Daughters: Protecting and Policing Adolescent Female Sexuality in the United States, 1885-1920* (Chapel Hill: University of North Carolina Press, 1995); Ruth Alexander, *The "Girl Problem": Female Sexual Delinquency in New York, 1900-1930* (Ithaca: Cornell University Press, 1995). A fuller discussion of other maternal justice projects that emerged in this time period appears in Chapter 1.

53   Estelle Freedman, *Their Sisters' Keepers: Women's Prison Reform in America, 1830-1930* (Ann Arbor: University of Michigan Press, 1981), 44.

54   Linda Gordon, *Pitied But Not Entitled: Single Mothers and the History of Welfare* (Cambridge, MA: Harvard University Press, 1994), 55.

55   John McLaren, "The Canadian Magistracy and the Anti-White Slavery Campaign 1900-1920," in Wesley Pue and Barry Wright, eds., *Canadian Perspectives on Law and Society: Issues in Legal History* (Ottawa: Carleton University Press, 1988), 348. For a similar argument about US courts, see Barbara Meil Hobson, *Uneasy Virtue: The Politics of Prostitution and the American Reform Tradition* (New York: Basic Books, 1987).

56   Cook, *supra* note 48 at 144.

57   Solomon, *supra* note 49.

58   *Ibid*.

59   Dorothy Chunn, "Maternal Feminism, Legal Professionalism, and Political Pragmatism: The Rise and Fall of Magistrate Margaret Patterson, 1922-1934," in Pue and Wright, eds., *supra* note 55 at 91-117.
60   *Ibid.* at 108.
61   *Ibid.* at 111.
62   Myers, *supra* note 52 at 99.
63   Mariana Valverde, "'When the Mother of the Race Is Free': Race, Reproduction, and Sexuality in First-Wave Feminism," in Franca Iacovetta and Mariana Valverde, eds., *Gender Conflicts: New Essays in Women's History* (Toronto: University of Toronto Press, 1992), 8. See, too, Linda Carty, "The Discourse of Empire and the Social Construction of Gender" (pp. 35-47), and Enakshi Dua, "Beyond Diversity: Exploring the Ways in Which the Discourse of Race Has Shaped the Institution of the Family" (pp. 237-59), both in Enakshi Dua and Angela Robertson, eds., *Scratching the Surface: Canadian Anti-Racist Feminist Thought* (Toronto: Women's Press, 1999).
64   Diana Pederson, "Keeping Our Good Girls Good: The YWCA and the 'Girl Problem,' 1870-1930," *Canadian Woman Studies* 7, 4 (1986): 20-24.
65   Carolyn Strange, *Toronto's Girl Problem: The Perils and Pleasures of the City, 1880-1930* (Toronto: University of Toronto Press, 1995). See, too, Alice Klein and Wayne Roberts, "Besieged Innocence: the 'Problem' and Problems of Working Women – Toronto, 1896-1914," in Janice Acton, ed., *Women at Work in Ontario, 1850-1930* (Toronto: Canadian Women's Educational Press, 1974), 211-60.
66   McLaren, *supra* note 51 at 249.
67   Estelle Freedman, *Maternal Justice: Miriam Van Waters and the Female Reform Tradition* (Chicago: University of Chicago Press, 1996).
68   *Ibid.* at 83.
69   Odem, *supra* note 52.
70   *Ibid.* at 109. The argument about maternal feminists' entry into the criminal justice system, especially as it pertained to adult justice, will be discussed extensively in Chapter 2.
71   See, too, Mary Odem, "Single Mothers, Delinquent Daughters, and the Juvenile Courts in Early Twentieth-Century Los Angeles," *Journal of Social History* 25, 1 (1991): 27-43; Myers, *supra* note 52.
72   Kelly Hannah-Moffat, *Punishment in Disguise: Penal Governance and Federal Imprisonment of Women in Canada* (Toronto: University of Toronto Press, 2001), 24. For nuanced distinctions between maternalist discourses, see Molly Ladd-Taylor, *Mother-Work: Women, Child Welfare and the State, 1890-1930* (Chicago: University of Illinois Press, 1993).
73   Hannah-Moffat, *ibid.* See, too, Jennifer Henderson, who prefers using the term *maternal authority* to get at the normative power of the expertise read into maternalism and at the normative power that allowed the women who used this framework to participate in a process of racialized nation-building: *Settler Feminism and Race Making in Canada* (Toronto: University of Toronto Press, 2003), 161.
74   Nicole Hahn Rafter, *Partial Justice: Women, Prisons and Social Control* (New Brunswick, NJ: Transaction Publishers, 1990).
75   Steven Schlossman and Stephanie Wallack, "The Crime of Precocious Sexuality: Female Juvenile Delinquency in the Progressive Era," *Harvard Educational Review* 48 (1978): 65-95.
76   "Woman Magistrate Scores Own Sex in Domestic Talk," *Star* (27 November 1929), 32.
77   Joan Scott, "The Evidence of Experience," *Critical Inquiry* 17, 4 (1991), 773-97.
78   *Ibid.* at 784.
79   *Ibid.* at 787.
80   Strange, *supra* note 15 at 25.
81   *Ibid.* at 43.
82   In itself, this is a much critiqued point. For debates arising from Scott's challenge to "experience," see, for example, Joan Hoff, "Gender as a Postmodern Category of Paralysis," *Women's History*

Review 3, 2 (1994): 149-68; Kathleen Canning, "Feminist History after the Linguistic Turn: Historicizing Discourse and Experience," *Signs* 19, 2 (1994): 368-404; Jane Roland Martin, "Methodological Essentialism, False Differences, and Other Dangerous Traps," *Signs* 19, 3 (1994): 630-57.

83 Steven Maynard, "On the Case of the Case: The Emergence of the Homosexual as a Case History in Early Twentieth-Century Ontario," in Iacovetta and Mitchinson, eds., *supra* note 15 at 83.

84 Archives of Ontario (AO), RG 20-100-1, series A, Toronto (York) Jail, Registers, 1910-35.

85 AO, RG 20-100-8, series D, Toronto (York) Jails, Description Books (males and females), 1911-35.

86 See, too, Ruth Roach Pierson, "Experience, Difference, Dominance, and Voice in the Writing of Canadian Women's History," in Karen Offen, Ruth Roach Pierson, and Jane Rendall, eds., *Writing Women's History: International Perspectives* (Bloomington: Indiana University Press), 79-106. Pierson argues that if, by "experience," feminist historians mean "the 'interiority' of human life, that is ... the phenomena of consciousness and subjectivity," then the usually available sources for these historians of women will inevitably leave "unanswered (and unanswerable) questions" (82-83).

87 I have used the *Star* and the *Telegram,* both of which had regular police court columns; the *(Toronto) Globe* was far less likely to report on crime news but from time to time carried a story about the Women's Court.

88 Paul Rutherford, in *The Making of the Canadian Media* (Toronto: McGraw-Hill Ryerson, 1978), notes that in this time period the modern media standard of "objectivity" was not yet a journalistic principle.

89 I do not suggest that newspaper reporters and the reformers were, by definition, one and the same. However, the relationship between these two groups was very close, and press reports often sounded much like reformers' tracts. For analyses of this relationship, see Richard Maltby, "The Social Evil, The Moral Order and the Melodramatic Imagination, 1890-1915," in Jacky Bratton, Jim Cook, and Christine Gledhill, eds., *Melodrama: Stage Picture Screen* (London: British Film Institute, 1994), 214-30; Joan Sangster, "'Pardon Tales' from Magistrate's Court: Women, Crime, and the Court in Peterborough County, 1920-50," *Canadian Historical Review* 74, 2 (1993): 161-97; Joel Best, "Looking Evil in the Face: Being an Examination of Vice and Respectability in St. Paul as Seen in the City Press, 1865-83," *Minnesota History* 50, 6 (1987): 241-51.

90 Wodson, *supra* note 3 at 149. Despite this slight on his female colleagues, Wodson himself had a strong tendency to weave imaginative and, often, maudlin narratives.

91 *An Act Respecting the Reformatory for Ontario,* S.O. 1913, c. 77 and *An Act Respecting the Andrew Mercer Ontario Reformatory for Females,* R.S.O. 1913, c. 78. The significance of the indeterminate sentence to women reformers is discussed in detail in Chapter 3.

92 This was particularly true, and the case files are more complete, during the brief tenure of Ontario's first female parole officer, Edna Haskayne, from 1922 to 1925. The relationship between parole and the regulatory powers of the Women's Court in particular, and feminized justice more generally, is discussed in Chapter 5.

93 Many of the sources I have used to uncover the practices and effects of the court are covered by a confidentiality agreement with Archives of Ontario. Accordingly, I have changed the names of most of the women in conflict with the law and refer to them by first name, which is an alias, and last initial. For consistency's sake, I therefore refer to other criminalized women in the same way, even if their cases come from public sources. Thus, I, too, contribute to a problem identified by Franca Iacovetta and Wendy Mitchinson: "[O]ur legal obligations as researchers to protect the privacy of individuals in the past can lead us to write the marginal into history by writing their names and faces out of it" ("Introduction: Social History and Case Files Research," in Iacovetta and Mitchinson, eds., *supra* note 15 at 6). By contrast, I refer to the women of the TLCW by their last names. Thus, this practice also contributes to the processes of infantalization of criminal women used by the members of the TLCW. When criminalized women's names are available in public sources and they openly challenged their trials, as in the cases of Lucy Ratcliffe and Violet

Davis discussed in Chapters 3 and 4 or Myrtle Cook and Cecile Gereau in Chapter 6, I refer to them by their last names, in the hope that this may help equalize their voices with those of the more consistently vocal and publicly active women reformers.

Chapter 1: The Toronto Women's Police Court as an Institution

1   The work of the juvenile courts has received extensive examination. For general discussion, see Tamara Myers, *Caught: Montreal's Modern Girls and the Law, 1869-1945* (Toronto: University of Toronto Press, 2006); Joan Sangster, *Girl Trouble: Female Delinquency in English Canada* (Toronto: Between the Lines, 2002); D. Owen Carrigan, *Juvenile Delinquency in Canada: A History* (Concord, ON: Irwin Publishing, 1998).

2   See Myers, *ibid.*; Mary Odem, *Delinquent Daughters: Protecting and Policing Adolescent Female Sexuality in the United States, 1885-1920* (Chapel Hill: University of North Carolina Press, 1995); Estelle Freedman, *Maternal Justice: Miriam Van Waters and the Female Reform Tradition* (Chicago: University of Chicago Press, 1996).

3   For contemporary accounts of US jurisdictions, see William N. Gemmill, "Chicago Court of Domestic Relations," *Annals of the American Academy of Political and Social Sciences* 52 (1914): 115-23; Frederick H. Whitin, "The Women's Night Court in New York City," *Annals of the American Academy of Political and Social Sciences* 52 (1914): 181-87; and Mary Paddon, "The Inferior Criminal Courts of New York City," *Journal of Criminal Law and Criminology* 11, 1 (1920): 8-20. For a summary, see Emerson Coatsworth, *Report on the Administration of Criminal Justice Treatment of Prisoners in New York, Chicago, Detroit and Toronto* (Toronto: King's Printer, 1920). For secondary literature on court specialization in Los Angeles, see Freedman, *ibid.*; Odem, *ibid.*; Beverly Blair Cook, "Moral Authority and Gender Difference: Georgia Bullock and the Los Angeles Women's Court," *Judicature* 77, 3 (1983): 144-55; in New York, see Freda Solomon, "Progressive Era Justice: The New York City Women's Court" (paper presented to the Seventh Berkshire Conference on the History of Women, Wellesley, Massachusetts, 19-21 June 1987); in Chicago, see Michael Willrich, *City of Courts: Socializing Justice in Progressive Era Chicago* (Cambridge: Cambridge University Press, 2003).

4   Willrich, *ibid.*; Dorothy Chunn, *From Punishment to Doing Good: Family Courts and Socialized Justice in Ontario, 1880-1940* (Toronto: University of Toronto Press, 1992).

5   Odem, *supra* note 2.

6   "Report of the Local Council of Women, Toronto," in National Council of Women of Canada, *Yearbook* (Ottawa: The Council, 1914).

7   City of Toronto Archives (CTA), RG 9, Reports, box 48, "Annual Report of the Chief Constable of the City of Toronto," 1913.

8   Robson Black , "A Dollar and Costs," *Canada Monthly* 14, 4 (1913): 8.

9   "Separate Courts for Women," *Jack Canuck* (15 February 1913), 6.

10 Harry Wodson, *The Whirlpool: Scenes from Toronto Police Court* (Toronto: n.p., 1917), 28.

11 Gene Howard Homel, "Denison's Law: Criminal Justice and the Police Court in Toronto, 1877-1921," *Ontario History* 73, 3 (1981): 171-86.

12 George Taylor Denison, *Recollections of a Police Magistrate* (Toronto: Musson Book Co., 1921), 23. The claim that the attorney general was entirely unaware of the Women's Court is somewhat dubious. The media reports of opening day were extensive and sensational, and it is unlikely that the attorney general did not read any of the *(Toronto) Daily News; (Toronto) Daily Star; (Toronto) Globe;* or *(Toronto) Evening Telegram* (hereafter *Daily News; Star; Globe; and Telegram*).

13 Library and Archives Canada (LAC), MG 29, E 29, Denison Papers (Diaries, 1850-1923; Scrapbooks, 1859-1925).

14 Wodson *supra* note 10 at 27.

15 Homel, *supra* note 11 at 171.

16 *Ibid.*

17 John McLaren, "The Canadian Magistracy and the Anti-White Slavery Campaign, 1900-1920," in Wesley Pue and Barry Wright, eds., *Canadian Perspectives on Law and Society: Issues in Legal History* (Ottawa: Carleton University Press, 1988), 340-41.

18 Chunn, *supra* note 4 at 54.

19 Homel, *supra* note 11 at 173.

20 *Ibid.* at 171.

21 "No Crowd, Male Hangers On," *Telegram* (10 February 1913), 21; see the Introduction for a discussion of Frank M. and Bridget D.'s case.

22 McLaren, *supra* note 17 at 343.

23 Homel, *supra* note 11 at 182.

24 "No Crowd," *supra* note 21.

25 "First Court for Women in Canada," *Daily News* (10 February 1913), 1, 3.

26 "At the Women's Court," *Globe* (12 February 1913), 5.

27 Mrs. Huestis, president of the TLCW, cited in "Women's Court to Remain," *Telegram* (9 February 1915), 18.

28 Willrich, *supra* note 3, especially Chapter 6, "'To protect her from the greed as well as the passions of man': The Morals Court."

29 Denison, *supra* note 12.

30 Willrich, *supra* note 3 at 176.

31 Archives of Ontario (AO), F 805-1, container 1, Toronto Local Council of Women, Minutes, 1903-38 (hereafter "TLCW minutes"), 21 May 1913.

32 Although they are not the same, I follow the TLCW's lead in using the terms *magistrate* and *judge* interchangeably in this chapter.

33 The comprehensive criminological platform envisioned and enacted by the members of the TLCW is explored in detail in the next chapter.

34 Chunn, *supra* note 4 at 55.

35 Cook, *supra* note 3 at 144.

36 Anne Anderson Perry, "Our Women Magistrates," *Chatelaine* (July 1929), 11. The degree to which this point was publicly debated is taken up in Chapter 6, which explores the tenuous authority exercised by Patterson during her tenure.

37 Cook, *supra* note 3.

38 Margaret Patterson, "The Care of Criminals," in Social Service Congress, *Annual Report of Addresses and Proceedings* (Ottawa: n.p., 1914), 226.

39 Cited in Solomon, *supra* note 3.

40 TLCW minutes, *supra* note 31, 20 January 1915.

41 "Woman Magistrate Likely," *Telegram* (25 November 1920), 8.

42 *The Police Magistrates' Amendment Act,* S.O. 1921, c. 4.

43 On Patterson's appointment, see "Dr. Patterson Chosen Woman Magistrate," *Star* (4 January 1922), 1; "Consecrated Common-Sense Is Quality New Magistrate Will Bring to Task on Bench," *Globe* (5 January 1922), 1; "Hopes to Make Women's Court Social Readjustment Bureau," *Star* (5 January 1922), 3; "Plenty of Work for Woman Magistrate," *Star* (6 January 1922), 27; "City Will Oppose New Appointment," *Globe* (6 January 1922), 6; "Must Pay the Salary of Woman Magistrate," *Star* (6 January 1922), 1; and "Did Not Seek Position," *Star* (6 January 1922), 10. More generally, see Dorothy Chunn, "Maternal Feminism, Legal Professionalism, and Political Pragmatism: The Rise and Fall of Magistrate Margaret Patterson, 1922-1934," in Wesley Pue and Barry Wright, eds., *Canadian Perspectives on Law and Society: Issues in Legal History* (Ottawa: Carleton University Press, 1988), 91-117; Loraine Gordon, "Doctor Margaret Norris Patterson: First Woman Police Magistrate in Eastern Canada – Toronto – January 1922 to November 1934," *Atlantis* 10, 1 (1984): 95-109.

44 "Must Pay the Salary," *ibid.*

45 "City Will Oppose," *supra* note 43.

46 Patterson received a lower salary than her male counterparts. When the City finally accepted her appointment, it declared her a junior magistrate, entitled to a salary of $3,500 per annum. Her colleague, Magistrate James Jones, earned $4,500 per annum. Twelve years later, at the end of her career, Patterson was earning the same salary; Magistrate Jones, promoted to senior police magistrate, was earning $6,000 per annum.

47 TLCW minutes, *supra* note 31, 19 October 1920; "Woman Magistrate Likely," *Telegram, supra* note 41.

48 One Mrs. Sinclair nominated herself for the magisterial position, but this was tabled, and ignored, by the TLCW. TLCW minutes, 13 December 1921.

49 Chunn, *supra* note 43.

50 Chunn, *supra* note 4 at 98. For discussion of the rural-urban relations that formed an essential part of the United Farmers of Ontario platform, as well as of the significance of women's participation in the UFO to its electoral success, see Kerry Badgley, *Ringing in the Common Love of Good: The United Farmers of Ontario, 1914-1926* (Montreal and Kingston: McGill-Queen's University Press, 2000).

51 Chunn, *supra* note 43 at 93.

52 Ibid.

53 "Hopes to Make," *supra* note 43.

54 AO, RG 62, A-1, Board of Health, Correspondence, box 362 (no file no.), R.R. McClenahan, Director, Division of Venereal Diseases, Board of Health, to Margaret Patterson, 7 January 1922.

55 Ethel M. Chapman, "How 'Bob's Maggie' Grew into Her Job," *Maclean's* (1 February 1922), 52 (emphasis in original).

56 *Ibid.*

57 The following description is drawn from a variety of sources that detail biographical information about Patterson, including Chapman, *supra* note 55; "Feminine Forces," *Globe* (15 April 1922), 18; Perry, *supra* note 36; and "First Woman in East Canada to Head Court: M. Patterson, Obituary," *Globe* (8 December 1962), 9. For secondary sources, see Chunn, *supra* note 43; Gordon, *supra* note 43; Jean Bannerman, *Leading Ladies, Canada* (Belleville: Mika Publishing, 1977). See, too, Toronto Public Library (TPL), Biographical Scrapbooks, vols. 15, 16, and 20.

58 "Consecrated Common-Sense," *supra* note 43. It is not clear whether these credentials are listed in order of importance.

59 Chapman, *supra* note 55.

60 Biographic Scrapbooks, *supra* note 57, reel 16, item 356, "Women Doctors to the Forefront Teaching and Practice of Medicine."

61 Chapman, *supra* note 55.

62 *Ibid.*

63 Gordon (*supra* note 43) could find no birth information on Patterson's son, Arthur, but Chapman (*ibid.*) writes that Arthur was thirteen when Patterson was appointed to the Women's Court in January 1922, which means that Arthur was likely born in 1909. John Patterson took up work with the Dominion Meteorological Service in Toronto upon their return.

64 Gordon, *supra* note 43 at 99.

65 Chapman, *supra* note 55.

66 "Report of the Local Council of Women, Toronto," *supra* note 6; see Introduction.

67 TLCW minutes, *supra* note 31, 13 November 1912.

68 The significance of the Committee for an Equal Moral Standard to the court and criminal justice reform work is taken up in Chapter 2.

69 On the Women's Institutes, see Margaret Kechnie, "Rural Women's Role in the 'Great National Work of Home-Building': The Women's Institutes in Early Twentieth-Century Ontario," *Canadian Woman Studies* 20, 2 (2000): 118-24; Linda Ambrose, *For Home and Country: The Centennial History of the Women's Institutes in Ontario* (Erin, ON: Boston Mills Press, 1996).

70 Gordon, *supra* note 43 at 8.

71 *Ibid.*

72 Patterson did sit sporadically in the Women's Court in March, but her name does not appear regularly in the jail registers (under "by what authority committed") until May. It became her usual practice thereafter to sit on the bench five days a week, including Saturdays. She took Wednesdays off.

73 AO, F 798-1, MU 2342, Provincial Council of Women, Minute Books, 1920-43 (hereafter "PCW minute books"), 1 June 1926.

74 TLCW minutes, *supra* note 31, 24 February 1927. For financial reasons, however, that luncheon was never held.

75 *Ibid.*, 23 September 1930.

76 AO, RG 4-32, Attorney General of Ontario, Central Registry Files, 1929, file 1917, "Re: Establishment of Domestic Relations Court."

77 Margaret Patterson, "The Women's Court of Toronto," *Social Welfare* 10 (July 1925): 188. As Chunn (*supra* note 4) notes, these cases had formerly been handled principally by the police.

78 "Did Not Seek Position," *supra* note 43.

79 "Re: Establishment of Domestic Relations Court," *supra* note 76.

80 See Chunn, *supra* note 4 and Chunn, *supra* note 43.

81 TLCW minutes, *supra* note 31, 16 May 1922.

82 "Courts of Domestic Relations," *Social Welfare* 5 (February 1923): 106-7.

83 "Courts of Domestic Relations: A Step in the Evolution of Justice," *Social Welfare* 1 (October 1929): 19. See, too, Judge D. B. Harkness, *Courts of Domestic Relations: Duties, Methods and Services of Such Courts – Are They Needed in Canada?* (Ottawa: Canadian Council on Child Welfare, 1924).

84 See, too, Dorothy Chunn, "Regulating the Poor in Ontario: From Police Courts to Family Courts," *Canadian Journal of Family Law* 6 (1987): 85-102.

85 Chunn, *supra* note 4 at 93.

86 The DRC was, in fact, explicitly modelled on the juvenile court structure. See *ibid.*; Harkness, *supra* note 83; James Snell, "Courts of Domestic Relations: A Study of Early Twentieth-Century Judicial Reform in Canada," *Windsor Yearbook of Access to Justice* 6 (1986): 36-60.

87 Patterson, "The Women's Court," *supra* note 77.

88 Margaret Patterson, "Some Needs of the Country as Seen in the Court," in "Report of the Women's Institutes," *Ontario Sessional Papers,* No. 41 (1923). At the time of this article, Patterson was the Ontario Women's Institutes' convenor of the Health and Child Welfare Committee.

89 TLCW minutes, *supra* note 31, 11 December 1928 (emphasis in original).

90 On protests, see "Ministers Protest against Changes in Women's Court," *Globe* (6 March 1929), 15; "Deputation Urges Cabinet Positions for Ontario Women," *Globe* (7 March 1929), 13; "Board Sends Protests to Attorney-General," *Star* (21 March 1929), 2. On the establishment of the Domestic Relations Court, see "Domestic Relations Court Established for the City," *Telegram* (15 June 1929), 1, 4; "Judge Hawley S. Mott to Head New Court of Domestic Relations," *Star* (15 June 1929), 1; "New Court Sworn for Family Spats," *Star* (19 June 1929), 1; "Family Court Opens to Mark Milestone of Justice in the City," *Globe* (20 June 1929), 14.

91 "Family Court Opens," *ibid.*

92 Gordon, *supra* note 43 at 102.

93 "Policeman Absent, Reconciliation Fails," *Star* (18 June 1925), 2.

94 On Patterson's removal from the bench, see "Cut Off 99 Magistrates, 10,000 JP's in Province," *Star* (17 August 1934), 5; "Police Court Changes Made Effective To-Day," *Telegram* (22 November 1923), 1; "Changes in Toronto Court Circles," *Globe* (22 November 1934), 5; "Case Re-Tried Due to Shuffle In Magistracy," *Telegram* (22 November 1934), 2; "Says Best Post Possible Given to Dr. Patterson," *Telegram* (23 November 1934), 1; "Liberal Group Air Question of Magistrate," *Globe* (23 November 1934), 8; "Magistrate Gets $6,000 Per Annum," *Telegram* (26 November 1934), 1;

"Mayor to Protest Paying Magistrate," *Telegram* (27 November 1934), 2; "Job as JP Is Rejected by Dr. Margaret Patterson," *Star* (7 December 1934), 27; "Woman Magistrate Asked for Toronto," *Star* (7 December 1934), 1.

95 Gordon, *supra* note 43 at 106.

96 Thomas O'Connor's name appeared often as a defence lawyer for charged women in the Women's Court. Dorothy Chunn argues that his appointment to the Women's Court bench is probably as much a result of the success of legal professionals asserting their exclusive place in courtrooms as it is a reflection on Margaret Patterson as a female magistrate. See Chunn, *supra* note 43. This argument is explored further in Chapter 6.

97 "Says Best Post Possible," *supra* note 94.

98 "Job as J.P. Is Rejected," *supra* note 94.

99 Anne Anderson Perry, "Is Women's Suffrage a Fizzle?" *Maclean's* (1 February 1928): 6.

100 "Liberal Group Air Question," *supra* note 94. Of course, a central dilemma for these partisan women was that it was their political party that had removed Patterson from the bench.

101 PCW minute books, *supra* note 73, 1935.

102 Chunn, *supra* note 4 at 112.

103 "Report of the Local Council of Women, Toronto," *supra* note 6, 1913.

Chapter 2: Feminism, Moral Equality, and the Criminal Law

1 Edith Lang, "The Canadian Criminal Code," *Woman's Century: Official Organ of the National Council of Women of Canada* 6 (Special Edition, 1918): 185 (hereafter *"Woman's Century"*).

2 The issue of the age of consent was one that arose often for the TLCW. See Archives of Ontario (AO), F 805-1, container 1, Toronto Local Council of Women, Minutes, 1903-38 (hereafter "TLCW minutes"), 20 March 1917, 17 April 1917, 16 October 1921. On the feminist campaigns to raise the age of consent more generally, see Mary Odem, *Delinquent Daughters: Protecting and Policing Adolescent Female Sexuality in the United States, 1885-1920* (Chapel Hill: University of North Carolina Press, 1995).

3 On adultery, see, too, AO, F 798-1, MU 2342, Provincial Council of Women, Minute Books, 1920-43 (hereafter "PCW minute books"), 16 March 1923, in which Margaret Patterson moved a resolution that adultery be re-included in the *Criminal Code*, reasoning, in part, that "it is a well known fact that Adultery, more than any other cause is destroying the homes of our country, and causing untold misery." See also AO, F 805-5, container 4, Toronto Local Council of Women, Annual Reports, 1926-66 (hereafter "TLCW annual reports"), 1925, in which making adultery a crime was included in an itemized list of priorities for the president of the council, Mrs. Henrietta Bundy.

4 Elizabeth Becker, "What Ontario Women Want: The Double Standard Shown in the Criminal Code," *Woman's Century* 6 (June 1918): 34 (emphasis in original).

5 See, for example, TLCW minutes, *supra* note 2, 21 May 1918, which record a discussion about petitioning the federal government for amendments to the age of consent sections of the *Criminal Code*: "A telegram was framed and sent to the Dom Gov't who were at that moment considering a section of *the moral code*" (emphasis mine).

6 Lucy Bland, *Banishing the Beast: Sexuality and the Early Feminists* (New York: New Press, 1995), xiii.

7 Ruth Rosen, *The Lost Sisterhood: Prostitution in America, 1900-1918* (Baltimore: Johns Hopkins University Press, 1982), 54. See also Lucy Bland, "Purity, Motherhood, Pleasure or Threat? Definitions of Female Sexuality, 1900-1970's," in Sue Cartledge and Joanne Ryan, eds., *Sex and Love: New Thoughts on Old Contradictions* (London: Women's Press, 1983), 8-29.

8 Sheila Jeffreys, *The Spinster and Her Enemies: Feminism and Sexuality, 1880-1930* (London: Pandora Press, 1985). Jeffreys argues that this early problematization of male sexual prerogatives was the forerunner of second-wave radical feminist critiques of male power.

9   Alan Hunt, *Governing Morals: A Social History of Moral Regulation* (Cambridge: Cambridge University Press, 1999).

10 "Equal Moral Standard," editorial, *Woman's Century* 6 (July 1918): 5.

11 See Barbara Meil Hobson, *Uneasy Virtue: The Politics of Prostitution and the American Reform Tradition* (New York: Basic Books, 1987); Rosen, *supra* note 7; Judith Walkowitz, *Prostitution and Victorian Society: Women, Class, and the State* (Cambridge: Cambridge University Press, 1980). For an analysis that locates these politics within the imperial context, see Philippa Levine, *Prostitution, Race and Politics: Policing Venereal Disease in the British Empire* (London: Routledge, 2003).

12 Philippa Levine, "Women and Prostitution: Metaphor, Reality, History," *Canadian Journal of History/Annales candiennes d'histoire* 28 (1993): 485.

13 *Ibid.* at 485.

14 In the United States, this question was not entirely rhetorical. In a great number of cities there was unequivocal evidence of corruption between municipal governments, local police forces, and houses of prostitution. See, for example, Hobson, *supra* note 11 and Rosen, *supra* note 7; for a contemporary account, see Josie Washburn, *The Underworld Sewer: A Prostitute Reflects on Life in the Trade, 1871-1909* (Lincoln: University of Nebraska Press, 1997 [1909]).

15 Estelle Freedman, *Their Sisters' Keepers: Women's Prison Reform in America, 1830-1930* (Ann Arbor: University of Michigan Press, 1981), 44.

16 *Ibid.* at 59.

17 See *An Act to Amend the Criminal Code*, S.C. 1913, c. 13; S.C. 1915, c. 12; S.C. 1917, c. 14; S.C. 1920, c. 43; and R.S.C. 1927, c. 36. More generally, see John McLaren and John Lowman, "Enforcing Canada's Prostitution Laws, 1892-1920: Rhetoric and Practice," in M.L. Friedland, ed., *Securing Compliance* (Toronto: University of Toronto Press, 1990), 21-87.

18 "New Laws for Protection of Women," *(Toronto) Daily Star* (6 September 1913), 1, 6 (hereafter *Star*). See, too, "Make Wife Desertion a Criminal Offence," *(Toronto) Globe* (8 February 1913), 9 (hereafter *Globe*); "Many Amendments to the Criminal Code," *Star* (16 May 1913), 1; "White Slave Law in Effect To-Day, Reformers Glad," *Star* (8 September 1913), 1, 4.

19 Lang, *supra* note 1.

20 Toronto Local Council of Women, (Grace G. MacGregor, Convenor), "Report of the Moral Standards Committee," in TLCW annual reports, *supra* note 3.

21 Joan Sangster, "Incarcerating 'Bad Girls': The Regulation of Sexuality through the Female Refuges Act in Ontario, 1920-1945," *Journal of the History of Sexuality* 7, 2 (1996): 241.

22 For a genealogy of moral regulation as a particularly Canadian and feminist brand of scholarship, see Amanda Glasbeek, ed., *Moral Regulation and Governance in Canada: History, Context, and Critical Issues* (Toronto: Canadian Scholars Press, 2006).

23 Mariana Valverde, *The Age of Light, Soap, and Water: Moral Reform in English Canada, 1885-1925* (Toronto: University of Toronto Press, 1991), 23. On the productive role of discourse more generally, see Michel Foucault, *The History of Sexuality, Volume 1: An Introduction,* trans. Robert Hurley (New York: Vintage Books, 1980).

24 Mary-Louise Adams, "In Sickness and in Health: State Formation, Moral Regulation, and Early V.D. Initiatives in Ontario," *Journal of Canadian Studies* 28, 4 (1993): 118.

25 Alan Hunt has argued that Foucault's analysis of law is his weakest point: "Foucault's Expulsion of Law: Toward a Retrieval," *Law and Social Inquiry* 17, 1 (1992): 1-48. For similar critiques, see, too, Carol Smart, *Feminism and the Power of Law* (London: Routledge, 1989); David Garland, *Punishment and Welfare: A History of Penal Strategies* (London: Gower, 1985). For a fuller attempt at a "retrieval," see Alan Hunt and Gary Wickham, *Foucault and Law: Towards a Sociology of Law as Governance* (London: Pluto Press, 1994).

26 Odem, *supra* note 2 at 108. See, too, Lucy Bland, whose analysis of early policewomen in England similarly argues that "a fair number of women police, many of whom were feminists, seem to have seen the more coercive actions of the policewomen as *legitimate*." Lucy Bland, "In the Name of

Protection: The Policing of Women in the First World War," in Carol Smart and Julia Brophy, eds., *Women-in-Law: Explorations in Law, Family, and Sexuality* (London: Routledge and Kegan Paul, 1985), 23-45.

27 Joan Sangster, *Regulating Girls and Women: Sexuality, Family, and the Law in Ontario, 1920-1960* (Toronto: Oxford University Press, 2001), 3 (emphasis in original). For a critical overview of moral regulation that emphasizes the importance of including an analysis of the state's powers of coercion, see Dorothy Chunn and Shelley Gavigan, "Welfare Law, Welfare Fraud, and the Moral Regulation of the 'Never Deserving' Poor," *Social and Legal Studies* 13, 2 (2004): 219-43.

28 Hunt, *supra* note 9 at 49.

29 See, for example, Carolyn Strange and Tina Loo, *Making Good: Law and Moral Regulation in Canada, 1867-1939* (Toronto: University of Toronto Press, 1997); Mariana Valverde and Lorna Weir, "The Struggles of the Immmoral: Preliminary Remarks on Moral Regulation," *Resources for Feminist Research* 17, 3 (1988): 31-34.

30 On the work of some of the other committees of the TLCW, especially those having to do with civic improvement, see Philip Gordon Mackintosh, "Scrutiny in the Modern City: The Domestic Public and the Toronto Local Council of Women at the Turn of the Twentieth Century," *Gender, Place and Culture* 12, 1 (2005): 29-48.

31 TLCW minutes, *supra* note 2, 16 December 1919.

32 A biographical sketch of Margaret Patterson, including her close connection to the work of the EMS Committee, is provided in Chapter 1.

33 Margaret Patterson, "Report of the Committee on Equal Moral Standard," in National Council of Women, *Yearbook* (Ottawa: The Council, 1915).

34 Nearly all studies of the sexual politics of the turn of the century discuss the white slave narratives and the Stead exposé. For particularly useful readings of this event, see Judith Walkowitz, *City of Dreadful Delight: Narratives of Sexual Danger in Late-Victorian London* (Chicago: University of Chicago Press, 1992); Carolyn Strange, *Toronto's Girl Problem: The Perils and Pleasures of the City, 1880-1930* (Toronto: University of Toronto Press, 1995); Valverde, *supra* note 23; Deborah Gorham, "The 'Maiden Tribute of Modern Babylon' Re-examined: Child Prostitution and the Idea of Childhood in Late-Victorian England," *Victorian Studies* 21 (1978): 353-79.

35 Valverde, "The White Slavery Panic," *supra* note 23 at 77-103; Strange, *ibid.* at 99-101.

36 TLCW minutes, *supra* note 2, 19 March 1913, cited in Strange, *supra* note 34 at 105.

37 National Council of Women of Canada, *Handbook* (1910), 54, cited in Strange, *supra* note 34 at 99.

38 More stringent penalties were also added to existing provisions, including the penalty of whipping for repeat offenders of procuring provisions. For contemporary analyses and celebrations of these amendments, see: "New Laws" and "White Slave Law," *supra* note 18.

39 For example, both Valverde (*supra* note 23) and Strange (*supra* note 34) refer to the EMS Committee as the "White Slave Committee" (at both the national and local levels). Although this title captures an important part of the early mandate of these committees, it does not reflect either the name shortening that occurred over the course of the 1910s or the broader and more continuous targetting of the criminal law to achieve related "moral" goals.

40 TLCW minutes, *supra* note 2, 13 March 1913.

41 *Ibid.*, 21 May 1913 and also 20 January 1915.

42 *Ibid.*, 21 March 1916 and 17 October 1916. Unfortunately, that report is not included in the minutes. But after the 17 October meeting, the special committee on the Women's Court was disbanded, because both Wood and Patterson were of the opinion that the Women's Court was functioning well enough, and with sufficient regular court volunteers, that the council no longer had to monitor it.

43 Janis Appier, "Preventive Justice: The Campaign for Women Police, 1910-1940," *Women and Criminal Justice* 4, 1 (1992): 3-36.

44   Bland, *supra* note 26. See, too, Tamara Myers, "Women Policing Women: A Patrol Woman in Montreal in the 1910s," *Journal of the Canadian Historical Association* 4 (1993): 229-45. For a contemporary account, see Helen D. Pigeon, "Policewomen in the United States," *Journal of Criminal Law and Criminology* 18 (1927): 372-77.

45   *Star* (11 February 1913), 8.

46   *Star* (20 March 1913), 5.

47   Appier, *supra* note 43.

48   See, for example, "Women Ask Place on Police Force," *Globe* (4 December 1911), 9; TLCW minutes, *supra* note 2, 12 April 1912 and 8 December 1912.

49   "The Police-Women More Like Matrons," *Star* (12 February 1913), 15; see also Mackintosh *supra* note 30 at 41.

50   City of Toronto Archives (CTA), RG 9, Reports, box 48, "Annual Report of the Chief Constable of the City of Toronto" (hereafter "ARCC"), 1914. In 1919 two more women officers were added to the force; their duties were similarly limited to those "cases in which females are intimately concerned" (ARCC, 1919).

51   TLCW minutes, *supra* note 2, 29 November 1913.

52   *Ibid.*, 17 December 1913.

53   *Ibid.*, 18 December 1917, 1 March 1918, 21 May 1918, 22 September 1931, and 31 January 1935.

54   *Ibid.*, 26 January 1928.

55   PCW minute books, *supra* note 3, 28 September 1920.

56   TLCW minutes, *supra* note 2, 14 February 1915. See Carolyn Strange, "Wounded Womanhood and Dead Men: Chivalry and the Trials of Clara Ford and Carrie Davies," in Franca Iacovetta and Mariana Valverde, eds., *Gender Conflicts: New Essays in Women's History* (Toronto: University of Toronto Press, 1992), 149-88.

57   TLCW minutes, supra note 2, 7 June 1911; 12 April, 8 May, 12 June, and 16 October 1912. See Karen Dubinsky and Franca Iacovetta, "Murder, Womanly Virtue, and Motherhood: The Case of Angelina Napolitano, 1911-1922," *Canadian Historical Review* 72, 4 (1991): 505-31. For other examples of active interest in women's criminal cases, see TLCW minutes, *supra* note 2, 13 November 1912 and 19 March 1913 (Madeleine LaLamonde); 16 April 1913 (no name given); 16 December 1919 (no name given); 3, 10, and 24 April 1928 (no name given); 29 April 1929 (Mrs. Minnegal); 25 March 1930 (no name given).

58   PCW minute books, *supra* note 3, 28 September 1920. For general (American) discussion, see Susan A. Lentz's two-part series, "Without Peers: A History of Women and Trial by Jury": "Part One – From the Women's Sphere to Suffrage," *Women and Criminal Justice* 11, 3 (2000): 83-106; "Part Two – The Law of Jury Service in the Twentieth Century," *Women and Criminal Justice* 11, 4 (2000): 81-101.

59   TLCW minutes, *supra* note 2, 18 January 1921; see, too, 13 April 1910, 8 March 1911, 16 December 1919, and 20 January 1920.

60   *Ibid.*, 21 March 1916.

61   Robson Black, "A Dollar and Costs," *Canada Monthly* 14, 4 (1913): 8.

62   Margaret Patterson, "The Care of Criminals," in Social Service Congress, *Annual Report of Addresses and Proceedings* (Ottawa: n.p., 1914): 226-30.

63   The short sentence, and its specific redress, is discussed in Chapter 3 in the context of the actual sentencing practices of the Women's Court.

64   Patterson, *supra* note 62 at 228.

65   *An Act Respecting the Reformatory for Ontario,* S.O. 1913, c. 77 and *An Act Respecting the Andrew Mercer Ontario Reformatory for Females,* S.O. 1913, c. 78. The introduction of the indeterminate sentencing was problematic in at least two ways. First, the use of provincial legislation to change sentencing – including for offences such as vagrancy, which was defined by federal law – is ques-

tionable at best. In 1916 the Parliament of Canada enacted a provision to allow, retroactively to 1913, for indeterminate sentencing (*An Act to Amend the Prisons and Reformatories Act*, S.C. 1916, c. 39). This provision was specific to Ontario. (My thanks to Shelley Gavigan for alerting me to this anomaly.) Second, the phrase "two years less a day" took some time to clarify. At first it was not clear to officials whether an indeterminate sentence was additional to the maximum definite term specified in the offence or whether two years less a day was the total maximum that could be given to any offender sentenced to a provincial institution. Eventually, it was determined that the latter was the appropriate action, but as a result of this uncertainty, some of the first women sentenced under this new legislation served up to thirty months (i.e., six months *and* an indeterminate sentence of two years less a day). Ultimately, Toronto magistrates got into the practice of giving *only* indeterminate sentences that ranged from six to twenty-four months less a day.

66 Patterson, cited in Edith M. Chapman, "How 'Bob's Maggie' Grew into Her Job," *Maclean's* (1 February 1922), 52.

67 *Ibid.*

68 Consistent with its view of the criminal justice system, the TLCW also lobbied (unsuccessfully) to have a woman appointed as chief probation officer (TLCW minutes, 16 December 1919 and 20 January 1920). The appointment ended up going to Judge Mott, formerly of the Juvenile Court. On probation, see *An Act to Provide for the Appointment of Probation Officers*, S.O. 1922, c. 103. For discussion and history, see Peter Oliver and Michael D. Whittingham, "Elitism, Localism, and the Emergence of Adult Probation Services in Ontario, 1893-1972," *Canadian Historical Review* 68, 2 (1987): 225-58.

69 On Canada, see Kelly Hannah-Moffat, *Punishment in Disguise: Penal Governance and Federal Imprisonment of Women in Canada* (Toronto: University of Toronto Press, 2001); Carolyn Strange, "'The Criminal and Fallen of their Sex': The Establishment of Canada's First Women's Prison, 1874-1901," *Canadian Journal of Women and the Law* 1 (1985): 79-82. On the United States, see Nicole Hahn Rafter, *Partial Justice: Women, Prisons and Social Control* (New Brunswick, NJ: Transaction Publishers, 1990); Freedman, *supra* note 15.

70 TLCW minutes, *supra* note 2, 21 October 1914, and, for other discussions of women and local jail conditions, see 1 March 1918, 19 October 1920, and 23 April 1930.

71 Strange, *supra* note 69 at 86.

72 The TLCW also followed through the stages of the criminal justice system to consider post-sentencing practices. The significance of parole to feminized justice is explored in Chapter 5.

73 Patterson, *supra* note 62.

74 See, for example, AO, RG 22-391, Criminal Assize Clerk Indictment Reports, York, box 141 and 142, 1908-22, and especially the Grand Jury presentments. The Grand Jury report from 1914 lamented that "Grand Juries have presented adverse conditions of [the Toronto jail] for years ... Overcrowding is everywhere evident, and this gives no proper chance for the separation and grading of prisoners. The first offender and the young ... are brought into close contact with the hardened criminal, thereby tending to lead them still lower, whereas, to reform should be the main aim."

75 Christine Stansell, *City of Women: Sex and Class in New York 1789-1860* (Chicago: University of Illinois Press, 1987), 194-95. See, too, Sarah Deutsch, *Women and the City: Gender, Power, and Space in Boston, 1870-1940* (New York: Oxford University Press, 2000).

76 Strange, *supra* note 34 at 107.

77 Patterson, *supra* note 62.

78 Chapman, *supra* note 66.

79 Stansell, *supra* note 75 at 66.

80 *Ibid.* See, in particular, Chapter 4, "Places of Vice: Views of the Neighborhood."

81 Rosen, *supra* note 7 at 54.

1   In *The Whirlpool: Scenes from Toronto Police Court* (Toronto: n.p., 1917), 145. It is not clear if this was written by Wodson himself or if it was a popular ditty that he was repeating.

2   D. Owen Carrigan, *Crime and Punishment in Canada: A History* (Toronto: McClelland and Stewart, 1991), 263.

3   *Ibid.* at 253.

4   City of Toronto Archives (CTA), RG 9, Reports, box 48, "Annual Report of the Chief Constable of the City of Toronto" (hereafter "ARCC"), 1913.

5   The following statistics are from Helen Boritch and John Hagan, "A Century of Crime in Toronto: Gender, Class, and Patterns of Social Control, 1859-1955," *Criminology* 28, 4 (1990): 567-99, who also document how arrest rates for men decline proportionately.

6   *Ibid.* at 582.

7   *Ibid.*; Carrigan, *supra* note 2.

8   If convicted, a warrant of commitment (typically a pre-printed form) was the legal document that recorded the name of the offender, the charge, the sentence, and the convicting magistrate and that authorized the jails and reformatories to accept the prisoner.

9   "Police Puzzle Over Girl," *(Toronto) Evening Telegram* (12 June 1915), 13 (hereafter *Telegram*); "To Mercer Reformatory," *Telegram* (28 June 1915), 7. These seemingly capricious uses of the vagrancy provisions will be discussed in greater detail in Chapter 4.

10 "A By-Law relating to Public Morals," *Consolidated By-Laws of the City of Toronto*, No. 4305 (1904). This Toronto bylaw did not define what a vagrant was. Section 3 read only: "No person drunk or disorderly, and no vagrant or mendicant shall be, or be found in any street, highway, or public place." The penalty was a fine not exceeding $50, plus costs, or imprisonment for a period not to exceed six months, "unless the said penalty and costs ... are sooner paid" (s. 15).

11 Boritch and Hagan, *supra* note 5 at 581.

12 Michael J. Piva, *The Condition of the Working Class in Toronto, 1900-1921* (Ottawa: University of Ottawa Press, 1979), 11, Table 4.

13 The specific characteristics of, and significance of, repeat offenders will be elaborated in the latter part of this chapter.

14 Nick Larsen, "Canadian Prostitution Control between 1914 and 1970: An Exercise in Chauvinist Reasoning," *Canadian Journal of Law and Society* 7, 2 (1992): 137-56.

15 Although the year 1914 is not part of my overall survey of the jail registers, I did look at the registers for that year, and there are no listings of "prostitution" under trade. In other words, the disappearance of this entry under "occupation" is very abrupt.

16 Peter Oliver, "'To Govern by Kindness': The First Two Decades of the Mercer Reformatory for Women," in Jim Phillips, Tina Loo, and Susan Lewthwaite, eds., *Essays in the History of Canadian Law*, Vol.5, *Crime and Criminal Justice* (Toronto: Osgoode Society for Canadian Legal History/ University of Toronto Press, 1994), 542-43. See, too, Wendy Reumper, "Locking Them Up: Incarcerating Women in Ontario, 1857-1931," in Louis A. Knafla and Susan W.S. Binnie, eds., *Law, Society, and the State: Essays in Modern Legal History* (Toronto: University of Toronto Press, 1995), 351-78. Reumper uses larger time frames but finds a similar pattern. Her data shows that 16 percent of Mercer inmates were listed as prostitutes in the period from 1880 to 1899, while only 2 percent of inmates were officially entered as prostitutes in the period from 1899 to 1917 (p. 364).

17 "Robbed on College Street," *Telegram* (29 September 1920), 19.

18 For excellent studies that deconstruct the racialization of justice, see Constance Backhouse, *Colour-Coded: A Legal History of Racism in Canada, 1900-1950* (Toronto: Osgoode Society for Canadian Legal History/University of Toronto Press, 1999); James W. St. G. Walker, *"Race," Rights and the Law in the Supreme Court of Canada: Historical Case Studies* (Waterloo: Wilfrid Laurier University Press, 1997).

19 Kelly Hannah-Moffat, *Punishment in Disguise: Penal Governance and Federal Imprisonment of Women in Canada* (Toronto: University of Toronto Press, 2001); Joan Sangster, *Regulating Girls and Women: Sexuality, Family, and the Law in Ontario, 1920-1960* (Toronto: Oxford University Press, 2001); Reumper, *supra* note 16; Oliver, *supra* note 16; Carolyn Strange, "'The Criminal and Fallen of Their Sex': The Establishment of Canada's First Women's Prison, 1874-1901," *Canadian Journal of Women and the Law* 1 (1985): 79-92.

20 See, especially, Hannah-Moffat, *supra* note 19; Strange, *ibid.*

21 Ontario, Legislative Assembly, "Annual Report of Prison Inspector," *Sessional Papers*, No. 25, 1913.

22 "Government Farms for Erring Women," *(Toronto) Daily Star* (26 September 1913), 9 (hereafter *Star*).

23 "An Industrial Farm for Women Offenders," *Star* (27 September 1913), 9; see, too, "May Erect Prison Farm for Women," *Star* (21 May 1913), 2.

24 The Concord was ultimately opened as an adjunct to the already-existing Langstaff Men's Municipal Jail Farm, and the superintendent for the men's farm was also responsible for the women's farm. However, the Concord did employ female matrons who supervised the day-to-day operations.

25 Reumper, *supra* note 16 at 370.

26 Loraine Gordon, "A Short Statistical Study of the Industrial Farm for Women at Concord, 1914-1935," (1982) [unpublished, archived at Osgoode Hall Law School Library, York University]; and Loraine Gordon, "A Statistical Survey of the Mercer/Vanier Registers 1880-1972," (1981) [unpublished, archived at Osgoode Hall Law School Library, York University].

27 Kelly Pineault, "'Mentally Weak' or 'Inherently Bad': The Regulation and Reform of Women 'Criminals' at the Concord Industrial Farm for Women, 1915-1935" (Honours History Paper, Trent University, 1997).

28 See, too, *Partial Justice: Women, Prisons and Social Control* (New Brunswick, NJ: Transaction Publishers, 1990), in which Nicole Han Rafter makes a similar observation about federally sentenced women in Progressive-era America. She distinguishes between those women (typically young, white, and deemed reformable) who were sentenced to reformatories and those women (typically black and older) who were sentenced to correctional facilities, where detention, not reclamation, was the goal. Reformatories could not have claimed the success rates they did, Rafter argues, were it not for a selection process that determined their inmates and sent "problem" women elsewhere.

29 Carolyn Strange, *Toronto's Girl Problem: The Perils and Pleasures of the City, 1880-1930* (Toronto: University of Toronto Press, 1995), 134.

30 Reumper, *supra* note 16.

31 Judith Fingard, *The Dark Side of Life in Victorian Halifax* (Porter's Lake, NS: Pottersfield Press, 1989), 191.

32 Mary Anne Poutanen, "The Homeless, the Whore, the Drunkard, and the Disorderly: Contours of Female Vagrancy in the Montreal Courts, 1810-1842," in Kathryn McPherson, Cecilia Morgan, and Nancy M. Forestell, eds., *Gendered Pasts: Historical Essays in Femininity and Masculinity in Canada* (Don Mills: Oxford University Press, 1999), 29-47.

33 *Ibid.* at 30.

34 *Ibid.* at 38.

35 John Pratt, "Dangerousness and Modern Society," in Mark Brown and John Pratt, eds., *Dangerous Offenders: Punishment and Social Order* (New York: Routledge, 2000), 39.

36 Archives of Ontario (AO), RG 20-100-1, series A, Toronto (York) Jail, Jail Registers, 1913 (hereafter "Jail Registers").

37 I did not count women who appeared more than once on the same charge.

38 Hereafter, repeat offenders will be identified by the dates of their first and last recorded appearance. Thus, Lizzie would be identified as Lizzie C. (1922-31).

39　This is not the same as saying that this was Lizzie's first appearance in court. One year later, in 1923, her Mercer Inmate case file included the notation that, although it was her first time serving a sentence at the Mercer, Lizzie already had twenty previous convictions: AO, RG 20-50-1, MS 3060-65, Andrew Mercer Ontario Reformatory for Women, Inmate Case Files (hereafter "Mercer Inmate Case Files"), 1923, no. 5428.

40　*Housekeeper* is distinguishable in this column from *housework* and *housewife,* and more often than not there was a correlation between this occupation and the charge on which women appeared in court. One of Lizzie's arrests was, in fact, for being a keeper of a house of ill fame.

41　It is only possible to see whether the convicted women paid their fine if they were still at the city jail at the time of payment. That is, if the woman was fined under the Toronto bylaw, and had been transferred to the Concord Women's Farm, the option of paying the fine from jail still existed but was not recorded (see note 11). Although I have consulted the Concord's inmate case files, sadly, these are not very useful. They consist mostly of warrants of commitments, which themselves are not kept in strict chronological order. For statistical analyses of commitments to the Concord, see Pineault, *supra* note 27 and Gordon, *supra* note 26.

42　Mercer Inmate Case Files, *supra* note 39, no. 5118.

43　As it pertains to probation, this lack of documentation was not only deliberate but a source of pride. In its first annual report, the Toronto Probation Department wrote that the majority of those on probation were under the age of twenty-five: "In other words, probation is being applied to the young offender rather than the old and hardened criminal": Ontario, Legislative Assembly, "First Annual Report of the Probation Officers of the County of York including City of Toronto, 1923," *Sessional Papers,* No. 53 (1924): 8.

44　Mercer Inmate Case Files, *supra* note 39, no. 6483.

45　I have combined the total numbers for charwomen, cooks, dayworkers, domestics, general servants, housemaids, housework, laundresses, and scullerymaids.

46　Fingard, *supra* note 31 at 36.

47　Bureau of Municipal Research, *What Is "The Ward" Going to Do with Toronto? A Report on Undesirable Living Conditions in One Section of the City of Toronto – "The Ward" – Conditions Which Are Spreading Rapidly to Other Districts* (Toronto: The Bureau, 1918), 5.

48　John C. Weaver, "The Modern City Realized: Toronto Civic Affairs, 1880-1915," in Robert F. Harney, ed., *Gathering Place: Peoples and Neighbourhoods of Toronto 1834-1945* (Toronto: Multicultural Historical Society, 1985), 43.

49　On the residential concentration and cultural and political activities of the ward's Jewish population, see Ruth Frager, *Sweatshop Strife: Class, Ethnicity, and Gender in the Jewish Labour Movement of Toronto, 1900-1939* (Toronto: University of Toronto Press, 1992).

50　Weaver, *supra* note 48 at 43.

51　Bureau of Municipal Research, *supra* note 47 at 5.

52　As Frager observes, however, Anglo-Celtic Torontonians were more likely to "blame the impoverished 'foreigners' themselves for the Ward's harsh, overcrowded conditions," rather than the racial structure of poverty itself: *supra* note 49 at 14.

53　Dr. Charles Hastings, *Report of the Medical Health Officer Dealing with the Recent Investigation of Slum Conditions in Toronto* (Toronto: Department of Health, 1911), 4-5.

54　Bureau of Municipal Research, *supra* note 47 at 24.

55　Weaver, *supra* note 48 at 45.

56　"Landlady Goes to Jail," *Telegram* (3 November 1920), 15.

57　See, for example, Ann-Louise Shapiro, *Breaking the Codes: Female Criminality in Fin-de-Siècle Paris* (Stanford: Stanford University Press, 1996); Tina Loo, "Don Cramner's Potlatch: Law as Coercion, Symbol, and Rhetoric in British Columbia, 1884-1951," *Canadian Historical Review* 73, 2 (1992): 125-65; Sally Engle Merry, *Getting Justice and Getting Even: Legal Consciousness among Working-Class Americans* (Chicago: University of Chicago Press, 1990).

58 "Women Mobbed This Man," *Telegram* (14 September 1920), 19. On popular justice, especially through charivaris for sexually inappropriate behaviour, see Bryan Palmer, "Discordant Music: Charivaris and Whitecapping in Nineteenth-Century North America," *Labour/Le Travail* 3 (1978): 5-62.

59 This interconnection between repeat offenders, especially their movements together from bawdy house to bawdy house, is discussed further in Chapter 5.

60 In April 1928 Lizzie lived at 106 Peter Street, an address listed also by Minnie N. (1913-16) in 1913; in July 1928 she lived at 34 Walton Street, which was also occupied by Teresa H. (1922-34) in the same year; and in December 1928 and again in April 1931, Lizzie lived at 54 Walton Street, an address listed twice (in 1928 and 1934) by Daisy H. (1913-34) and once each by Hilda H. (1931) and Edna D. (1928): AO, RG 20-100-8, series D, Toronto (York) Jail, Description Books, 1913-34 (hereafter "Description Books").

61 Description Books, *ibid.,* 1913.

62 Jail Registers, *supra* note 36, 1913. The typical fine for vagrancy in 1913 was $4.25, or $3.00 and costs.

63 See, too, Poutanen, *supra* note 32 and Fingard, *supra* note 31 for similar findings.

64 Mercer Inmate Case Files, *supra* note 39, no. 5384.

65 *Ibid.,* no. 4671.

66 *Ibid.,* no. 5428 and no. 4756.

67 Mercer inmates were sent to the Toronto General Hospital, including the Burns Unit for labour and delivery, for any medical services beyond the capabilities of the reformatory's infirmary. The Toronto General Hospital would send a bill for the cost of services to the Mercer. If neither the inmate nor her relatives had the money to cover the services, the superintendent would submit the hospital bill to the provincial secretary, who would pay it upon her recommendation. Thus, when Daisy H. received her teeth, Emma O'Sullivan submitted a receipt to the government for Daisy, "who has no money. The cost of the plates will be about nine dollars and fifty cents." The request for the money was approved. *Ibid.,* no. 4756.

68 *Ibid.,* no. 5078.

69 "Would Rather Marry Than Go to Jail," *Star* (5 January 1923), 5.

70 "Policeman Absent, Reconciliation Fails," *Star* (18 June 1925), 2.

71 Mercer Inmate Case Files, *supra* note 39, no. 4465.

72 Poutanen, *supra* note 32 at 45.

73 "Woman's Sentence Brings Big Protest; Inquiry is Ordered," *Globe* (27 August 1931), 11, 12. Despite the headline, no inquiry was held.

Chapter 4: "What chance is there for a girl?"

1 "Girl Who Was Boy Is Defiant in Court," *(Toronto) Daily Star* (3 September 1913), 1 (hereafter *Star*); "Montreal Girl Was Passing as Young Man," *Star* (13 September 1913), 2, "The Little Rebel Was in Court Again To-Day," *Star* (19 September 1913), 2.

2 The concept of unmasking resonates with the insight that early twentieth-century narratives of women cross-dressers drew on metaphors relating to performance, especially stage methaphors associated with male impersonators and the metaphor of the masquerade. See Alison Oran, *Her Husband Was a Woman! Women's Gender-Crossing in Modern British Popular Culture* (London: Routledge, 2007); Marjorie Garber, *Vested Interests: Cross-Dressing and Cultural Anxiety* (New York: Routledge, 1992).

3 "Girl Who Was Boy," *supra* note 1.

4 "The Little Rebel," *supra* note 1.

5 In the end Benedictine would be returned to court, "this time properly attired as a girl," and sent home to Montreal with her mother.

6 Oran, *supra* note 2.

7   "Girl Who Was Boy," *supra* note 1.

8   "Montreal Girl Was Passing as Young Man," *supra* note 1.

9   Oran, *supra* note 2 at 17.

10 *The Criminal Code*, S.C. 1892, c. 29, s. 207(i). One man, arrested for vagrancy, was discharged in police court after it was discovered that the arresting officer had charged him according to the section that "applied only to ladies who are out at night with a reason": "Police Court To-Day," *(Toronto) Evening Telegram* (14 September 1920), 19 (hereafter *Telegram*).

11 *The Criminal Code, ibid.*, s. 207(e)(f).

12 Mary Anne Poutanen, "The Homeless, the Whore, the Drunkard, and the Disorderly: Countours of Female Vagrancy in the Montreal Courts, 1810-1842," in Kathryn McPherson, Cecilia Morgan, and Nancy M. Forestell, eds., *Gendered Pasts: Historical Essays in Femininity and Masculinity in Canada* (Don Mills: Oxford University Press, 1999), 29-47.

13 "Eighth Drunk Charge Sends Woman to Jail," *Star* (12 January 1929), 2. Repeat offenders are identified by the dates of their first and last recorded appearance.

14 "Was Given 90 Days," *Telegram* (8 March 1915), 14.

15 "Police Court News," *Telegram* (13 September 1917), 11.

16 "Girl Found in Taxi Accused of Drinking," *Star* (24 January 1929), 3.

17 *Ibid.*

18 City of Toronto Archives (CTA), RG 9, Reports, box 48, "Annual Report of the Chief Constable of the City of Toronto" (hereafter "ARCC"), 1913.

19 Carolyn Strange, *Toronto's Girl Problem: The Perils and Pleasures of the City, 1880-1930* (Toronto: University of Toronto Press, 1995); Joanne Meyerowitz, *Women Adrift: Independent Wage Earners in Chicago, 1880-1930* (Chicago: University of Chicago Press, 1988); and Kathy Piess, *Cheap Amusements: Working Women and Leisure in Turn-of-the-Century New York* (Philadelphia: Temple University Press, 1986).

20 Carolyn Strange, "From Modern Babylon to a City upon a Hill: The Toronto Social Survey Commission of 1915 and the Search for Sexual Order in the City," in Roger Hall, William Westfall, and Laurel Sefton MacDowell, eds., *Patterns of the Past: Interpreting Ontario's History* (Toronto: Dundurn Pres, 1988), 255-77.

21 AO, RG 4-32, Attorney General of Ontario, Central Registry Files, 1916, no. 2506, Social Survey Commission, *Report of the Social Survey Commission* (Toronto: Carswell, 1915), 13.

22 "Another Bigamy Charge," *Telegram* (8 May 1915), 9.

23 "Police Court To-Day," *Telegram* (23 September 1916), 9.

24 "Police Court To-Day," *Telegram* (20 Nomember 1916), 4.

25 "Six in Women's Court To-Day," *Telegram* (17 February 1913), 17.

26 "Police Court To-Day," *Telegram* (14 September 1917), 22.

27 "Police Court To-Day" *Telegram* (28 June 1915), 13.

28 "Police Court To-Day," *Telegram* (17 November 1916), 24.

29 On Canadian debates about the suppression or toleration of prostitution, see Mariana Valverde, *The Age of Light, Soap, and Water: Moral Reform in English Canada, 1885-1925* (Toronto: McClelland and Stewart, 1991); John McLaren, "The Canadian Magistracy and the Anti-White Slavery Campaign, 1900-1920," in Wesley Pue and Barry Wright, eds., *Canadian Perspectives on Law and Society: Issues in Legal History* (Ottawa: Carleton University Press, 1988), 329-53; James H. Gray, *Red Lights on the Prairie* (Toronto: Macmillan of Canada, 1971).

30 Social Survey Commission, *supra* note 21.

31 Harry S. Wodson, *The Whirlpool: Scenes from Toronto Police Court* (Toronto: n.p., 1917), 156.

32 Cited in Emily Weaver, A.E. Weaver, and E.C. Weaver, eds., *The Canadian Woman's Annual and Social Service Directory* (Toronto: McClelland, Goodchild, and Stewart, 1915), 280.

33 "Great Joy," *Telegram* (21 February 1917), 13.

34 AO, RG 20-50-1, MS 3060-3065, Andrew Mercer Ontario Reformatory for Women, Inmate Case Files (hereafter "Mercer Inmate Case Files"), no. 6840.

35 "Arrested at Docks," *Telegram* (23 February 1915), 15.

36 "Moss Park Spooning Has Court Aftermath," *Star* (19 June 1925), 17.

37 For a fuller discussion, see Joanne Minaker, "Sluts and Slags: The Censuring of the Erring Female," in Gillian Balfour and Elizabeth Comack, eds., *Criminalizing Women* (Halifax: Fernwood, 2006), 79-94; Joan Sangster, *Regulating Girls and Women: Sexuality, Family, and the Law in Ontario, 1920-1960* (Toronto: Oxford University Press, 2001); Strange, *supra* note 19; Mary Odem, *Delinquent Daughters: Protecting and Policing Adolescent Female Sexuality in the United States, 1885-1920* (Chapel Hill: University of North Carolina Press, 1995).

38 Ruth Alexander, *The "Girl Problem": Female Sexual Delinquency in New York, 1900-1930* (Ithaca: Cornell University Press, 1995).

39 Mercer Inmate Case Files, *supra* note 34, no. 5879.

40 *Ibid.*, no. 6842.

41 "Another Bigamy Charge," *supra* note 22.

42 Anxieties about white women working in Chinese restaurants consumed white, middle-class reformers in the 1910s and 1920s. See James W. St. G. Walker, "A Case for Morality: The Quong Wing Files," in Franca Iacovetta and Wendy Mitchinson, eds., *On The Case: Explorations in Social History* (Toronto: University of Toronto Press, 1998), 204-23; Constance Backhouse, "White Women's Labour Laws: Anti-Chinese Racism in Early 20th-Century Canada," *Law and History Review* 14 (1996): 315-68; Madge Pon, "Like a Chinese Puzzle: The Construction of Chinese Masculinity in *Jack Canuck*," in Joy Parr and Mark Rosenfeld, eds., *Gender and History in Canada* (Toronto: Copp Clark, 1996), 88-100.

43 "Honesty Is Rewarded, Jail Term But One Day," *Star* (15 June 1925), 2.

44 "*R. v. Davis* (1930-31)," *Ontario Weekly Notes* 39, 98. A number of other women (sometimes successfully) appealed their convictions, often for vagrancy; unfortunately, very few of these appeals were reported.

45 Vagrancy laws were also supplemented by *An Act Respecting Industrial Refuges for Females*, R.S.O. 1919, c. 84 (the *Female Refuges Act*), which stated that "any female between the ages of fifteen and thirty-five years, sentenced *or liable to be sentenced* to imprisonment in a common jail by a judge may be committed to an Industrial Refuge for an indefinite period not exceeding two years": s. 3(1) (my emphasis). Although there are obvious commonalities and links between vagrancy and the *Female Refuges Act*, I have not included the legislation in my discussion of vagrant women because it was a specific offence. Indeed, few of the detained women in the local jail were there because of a committal under *the Female Refuges Act* (37 in total), although it is likely that many more women were arrested for this offence than are visible in the jail registers. For discussion of this legislation, see Joan Sangster, "Defining Sexual Promiscuity: 'Race,' Gender, and Class in the Operation of Ontario's Female Refuges Act, 1930-1960," in Wendy Chan and Kiran Mirchandani, eds., *Crimes of Colour: Racialization and the Criminal Justice System in Canada* (Toronto: Broadview Press, 2002), 45-63, and Joan Sangster, "Incarcerating 'Bad Girls': The Regulation of Sexuality through the Female Refuges Act in Ontario, 1920-1945," *Journal of the History of Sexuality* 7, 2 (1996): 239-75.

46 "Meeting Social Disease: Not Under Criminal Code," *Telegram* (14 September 1917), 17.

47 "Police Court To-Day," *Telegram* (6 February 1918), 5.

48 Mary-Louise Adams, "In Sickness and in Health: State Formation, Moral Regulation, and Early VD Initiatives in Ontario," *Journal of Canadian Studies* 28, 4 (1993): 117-30.

49 On the relationship between VD and "the race," see Renisa Mawani, "Regulating the 'Respectable' Classes: Venereal Disease, Gender, and Public Health Initiatives in Canada, 1914-35," in John McLaren, Robert Menzies, and Dorothy Chunn, eds., *Regulating Lives: Historical Essays on the State, Society, the Individual, and the Law* (Vancouver: UBC Press, 2002): 170-95.

50 Cited in Adams, *supra* note 48 at 125.

51 *An Act for the Prevention of Venereal Disease*, S.O. 1918, c. 42.

52 Jay Cassels, *The Secret Plague: Venereal Disease in Canada, 1838-1939* (Toronto: University of Toronto Press, 1987). The *VD Act* was similar to the British *Contagious Diseases Act* (the *CD Act*) of 1864, a version of which was passed, but never proclaimed, in Canada. An important difference between the *CD Act* and the *VD Act* is that the latter was gender-neutral, while the former was gender-specific (i.e., to women); also, whereas the *CD Act* in nineteenth-century Britain generated a resistance movement, including a clear feminist challenge, the *VD Act* in twentieth-century Canada received, if anything, enthusiastic support from social reformers, including female reformers. On the British *CD Acts*, see Judith Walkowitz, *Prostitution and Victorian Society: Women, Class, and the State* (Cambridge: Cambridge University Press, 1980).

53 Wodson, *supra* note 31 at 81.

54 See Elsie Gregory MacGill's biography of her mother, Helen, especially Chapter 7, "Her Objectives in Law," for the tensions surrounding MacGill's role as feminist judge and the general legal and public community. Elsie Gregory MacGill, *My Mother the Judge* (Toronto: Peter Martin Associates, 1981). This point is elaborated further in Chapter 6.

55 Helen Gregory MacGill, "Reforming Our Misfits," *Social Welfare* 7 (April 1924): 130.

56 On the (mis)treatment of VD patients at the Mercer Reformatory, especially by Dr. Edna Guest, see Velma Demerson, *Incorrigible* (Waterloo: Wilfrid Laurier University Press, 2004). Demerson suggests that Guest conducted extremely painful and harmful drug trials and other medical experiments on the inmates, not all of whom were actually infected with a venereal disease.

57 Mercer Inmate Case Files, *supra* note 34, no. 5582.

58 *Ibid.*, no. 5664.

59 AO, RG 4-32, *supra* note 21, 1921, no. 1618, "Query re Treatment of Prisoners for VD at Mercer after Release." Given that Patterson did tend to give indeterminate sentences, it is difficult to know why this policy was not followed in Marjory's specific case.

60 "Police Court To-Day," *Telegram* (11 May 1917), 11.

61 "Saved His Wad," *Telegram* (25 September 1920), 32.

62 AO, RG 22-5870, York County Court Judges' Criminal Court, Indictment Case Files, 1913, no. 176-13, and RG 22 5871, York County Court of General Sessions of the Peace, Indictment Case Files (hereafter "CCGS"), 1913, no. 99-13.

63 "Police Court To-Day," *Telegram* (9 February 1918), 8.

64 "Their Night of Adventure," *Telegram* (24 November 1920), 8.

65 Elaine S. Abelson, *When Ladies Go A-Thieving: Middle-Class Shoplifters in the Victorian Department Store* (New York: Oxford University Press, 1989).

66 Margaret Patterson, "The Care of Criminals," in Social Service Congress, *Annual Report of Addresses and Proceedings* (Ottawa: n.p., 1914), 226-30.

67 "Police Court To-Day," *Telegram* (6 July 1915), 10.

68 "Police Court To-Day," *Telegram* (21 February 1917), 13.

69 "Honesty Is Rewarded," *supra* note 36.

70 "Police Court To-Day," *Telegram* (13 November 1920), 23.

71 "Was Given 90 Days," *Telegram* (8 March 1915), 14.

72 "Young Wife and Mother Had Taken $100 Ring," *Telegram* (26 February 1915), 18; "For Child's Sake," *Telegram* (27 February 1915), 15.

73 "Says She Meant to Pay for the Goods Later On," *Star* (10 September 1913), 8.

74 "Matron and Maid Face Jail," *Telegram* (4 February 1918), 7.

75 "Mothers and Girls Caught Shoplifting," *Star* (2 September 1913), 2; CCGS, *supra* note 62, nos. 162-13, 163-13, and 164-13.

76 Helen Boritch and John Hagan find that although female crime rates dropped in the early twentieth century, the incidence of female fraud rates grew disproportionately (to male incidences of

fraud and to female crime rates generally). Helen Boritch and John Hagan, "A Century of Crime in Toronto: Gender, Class, and Patterns of Social Control, 1859-1955," *Criminology* 28, 4: 579.

77 "Cared for Sick Relative," *Telegram* (24 September 1914), 23.

78 "Five Days in Jail for Girl," *Star* (16 April 1914), 5.

79 "Girl Stole to Live," *Telegram* (7 January 1915), 7.

80 Social Survey Commission, *supra* note 21. See, especially, 44-50.

81 Magda Fahrni, "'Ruffled' Mistresses and 'Discontented' Maids: Respectability and the Case of Domestic Service, 1880-1914," *Labour/Le Travail* 39 (Spring 1997): 70.

82 "Wives Stole Food for Idle Husbands," *Star* (9 September 1913), 8.

83 Fahrni, *supra* note 81 at 89.

84 "Police Court To-Day," *Telegram* (12 June 1915), 22.

85 "Police Court To-Day," *Telegram* (21 January 1915), 4

86 "Missed Money from Safe," *Telegram* (16 June 1915), 5; "Police Court To-Day," *Telegram* (22 June 1915), 6; "Hotel Maid Gets 60 Days," *Telegram* (23 June 1915), 13.

87 Wodson, *supra* note 31 at 153-55.

88 Farhni, *supra* note 81 at 81.

89 Helen Boritch, "Gender and Criminal Court Outcomes: A Historical Analysis," in Chris McCormick and Len Green, eds., *Crime and Deviance in Canada: Historical Perspectives* (Toronto: Canadian Scholars Press, 2005), 124-47.

Chapter 5: "Up again, Jenny?"

1 Drunk charges could be laid as federal (via vagrancy provisions), provincial, or municipal (via the bylaw on public morals) offences. Because neither the jail registers nor the collected warrants of commitments relating to drunk charges specifies which law was violated, I have not attempted to distinguish them here.

2 City of Toronto Archives (CTA), RG 9, Reports, box 48, "Annual Report of the Chief Constable of the City of Toronto" (hereafter "ARCC"), 1913.

3 As Harry Wodson described his job, "The Police Court scribes endeavour to do their work without passion or prejudice. Their duty is to record what happens. The only latitude they enjoy is in the manner of telling the truth. The story itself must be an accurate record of what happened in court ... [T]here is, however, more than one way of saying that X was fined ten dollars for drunkenness": *The Whirlpool: Scenes from Toronto Police Court* (Toronto: n.p., 1917), 35.

4 For an analysis of the conceptualization of intemperance as a lack of self-control, see Mariana Valverde, *Diseases of the Will: Alcohol and the Dilemmas of Freedom* (Cambridge: Cambridge University Press, 1998). On men charged with drunkenness in the police court, see Wodson "Seeing through the Bottle," in *ibid.* at 125-33.

5 "'Booze' and 'Dope' Are Four Women's Curse," *(Toronto) Daily Star* (12 February 1913), 2 (hereafter *Star*).

6 "A By-Law relating to Public Morals," *Consolidated By-Laws of the City of Toronto* No. 4305 (1904).

7 "Moss Park Spooning Has Court Aftermath," *Star* (19 June 1925), 17. See, too, Wodson, who offers his readers a stereotypical Irish woman drinker, who similarly engages in witty repartee with the magistrate (*supra* note 2 at 151). Repeat offenders are identified by the dates of their first and last recorded appearance.

8 Mary Ann Poutanen, "The Homeless, the Whore, the Drunkard, and the Disorderly: Contours of Female Vagrancy in the Montreal Courts, 1810-1842," in Kathryn McPherson, Cecilia Morgan, and Nancy M. Forestell, eds., *Gendered Pasts: Historical Essays in Femininity and Masculinity in Canada* (Don Mills: Oxford University Press, 1999), 29-47; M. Elizabeth Langdon, "Female Crime in Calgary, 1914-1941," in Louis Knafla, ed., *Law and Justice in a New Land: Essays in Western Canadian Legal History* (Toronto: Carswell, 1986), 293-312.

9   Poutanen, *ibid.* at 30.

10 See, for example, Constance Backhouse, "Nineteenth-Century Prostitution Law: Reflection of a Discriminatory Society," *Histoire sociale/Social History* 18, 36 (1985): 387-423.

11 Judith Fingard, *The Dark Side of Life in Victorian Halifax* (Porter's Lake, NS: Pottersfield Press, 1989), 191.

12 Most representative of this approach is Peter DeLottinville, "Joe Beef of Montreal: Working-Class Culture and the Tavern, 1869-1889," *Labour/Le Travail* 8/9 (1981/82): 9-40.

13 Cheryl Krasnick Warsh, "'Oh Lord, pour a cordial in her wounded heart': The Drinking Woman in Victorian and Edwardian Canada," in Cheryl K. Warsh, ed., *Drink in Canada: Historical Essays* (Montreal and Kingston: McGill-Queen's University Press, 1993), 70-91.

14 This does not mean that the actual incidence of alcohol consumption was confined to the "non-respectable" classes. Warsh (*ibid.* at 81) uses admission registers to private hospitals to show that wealthy women were just as susceptible to alcohol addiction or abuse as poor women and that "intemperance was a problem for all classes."

15 *Ibid.* at 76.

16 Mariana Valverde, "'Racial Poison': Drink, Male Vice, and Degeneration in First-Wave Feminism," in Ian Christopher Fletcher, Laura E. Nym Mayhall, and Philippa Levine, eds., *Women's Suffrage in the British Empire: Citizenship, Nation, and Race* (London: Routledge), 33-50.

17 Warsh, *supra* note 13 at 89.

18 *Ibid.* at 90.

19 Renisa Mawani, "In Between and Out of Place: Mixed-Race Identity, Liquor, and the Law in British Columbia, 1850-1913," in Sherene Razack, ed., *Race, Space, and the Law: Unmapping a White Settler Society* (Toronto: Between the Lines, 2002), 51. In particular, Mawani points to the ways that drinking laws were used to contain the mobility of racialized populations in colonial British Columbia.

20 Archives of Ontario (AO), RG 20-50-1, MS 3060-3065, Andrew Mercer Ontario Reformatory for Women, Inmate Case Files (hereafter "Mercer Inmate Case Files"), no. 4575.

21 *Ibid.,* no. 5848. The address 313 Adelaide would emerge often in the case files. The following year, in 1928, Etta G., "colored" and also of 313 Adelaide Street, was charged with breaching the *Liquor Control Act* there. Ten years earlier, in 1917 (and reported in typical racist fashion), John and Elizabeth G. (who had the same last name as Etta) were convicted "for keeping a highly colored resort" at that same address: "Police Court To-Day," *(Toronto) Evening Telegram* (10 May 1917), 15 (hereafter *Telegram*). But 313 Adelaide was probably not simply a liquor joint: also arrested in 1917 (as an inmate) was Mabel S. (1913-17), who was convicted four times, at three different addresses, for keeping her own bawdy house. In 1931 Fannie was again charged within being found in a bawdy house at 313 Adelaide Street.

22 Mercer Inmate Case Files, *supra* note 20, no. 4477; AO, RG 20-100-1, series A, Toronto (York) Jail, Jail Registers, 1916 (hereafter "Jail Registers").

23 Mercer Inmate Case Files, *ibid.,* no. 5118.

24 *Ibid.,* no. 4504.

25 *An Act intituled The Ontario Temperance Act,* S.O. 1916, c. 50.

26 See, for example, "Was No Increase of Drunks," *Telegram* (16 September 1916), 13; "Lucky Boozers Chased Off," *Telegram* (18 September 1916), 5; "Mixed Blessing," *Telegram* (10 August 1917), 5; "Temperance Benefits Proven by Figures," *Star* (3 March 1923), 3; "Drinking by Women on the Decline," *Star* (10 March 1925), 3.

27 For discussion, see Gerald Hallowell, *Prohibition in Ontario, 1919-1923* (Ottawa: Ontario Historical Society, 1972). Liquor could continue to be sold for a variety of reasons – including for sacramental, medicinal, and industrial reasons – but only by distillers or brewers outside Ontario or to those with a licence. Native wines were exempted from the legislation.

28 ARCC, *supra* note 2, 1913, 1916, and 1919.

29 Mercer Inmate Case Files, *supra* note 20, no. 4464.

30 See *ibid.*, nos. 4362, 4409, 4477, 4478, 4505, 4546, 4574, and 4575.

31 "Police Court To-Day," *Telegram* (22 September 1916), 15.

32 "Mr. Corley Has Lemonade," *Telegram* (17 May 1917), 13.

33 AO, RG 8-54, Ontario Board of Parole, Correspondence, container 3 (hereafter "OBP correspondence").

34 In 1921 the Ontario Board of License Commissioners complained that "of those who commit offences against the Act there is a disproportionately large number of foreigners, and of these a still more disproportionately large number are Jews from Poland and Western Russia." Cited in Craig Heron, *Booze: A Distilled History* (Toronto: Between the Lines, 2003), 240.

35 Kelly Pineault, "'Mentally Weak' or 'Inherently Bad': The Regulation and Reform of Women 'Criminals' at the Concord Industrial Farm for Women, 1915-1935" (Honours History Paper, Trent University, 1997).

36 For example, in 1913, when women constituted 6 percent of all arrests, they also made up 66 percent of all charges for keeping a bawdy house and 36 percent of all charges for being an inmate of or frequenting a bawdy house (ARCC, *supra* note 2, 1913).

37 The number of men counted is an underestimate. Unless it was explicitly stated in the jail ledgers, it was much more difficult to ascertain the court that detained men were tried in. These numbers, therefore, represent only those men who I am sure were tried in the Women's Court, and they cannot be said to be in any way an accurate statistical overview. See Joan Sangster, *Regulating Girls and Women: Sexuality, Family, and the Law in Ontario,* 1920-1960 (Toronto: Oxford University Press, 2001), 94-95, Table 6, for official police statistics, 1920-50, on men arrested on these charges.

38 Mercer Inmate Case Files, *supra* note 20, no. 5731.

39 *Ibid.*, no. 6957.

40 AO, RG 22-5870, York County Court Judges' Criminal Court, Indictment Case Files, 1924, no. 20-24. Ruby would later be arrested as a keeper of a disorderly house on Harbord Street (Jail Registers, *supra* note 22, 1928).

41 Sangster, *supra* note 37 at 92-93, does the same in her calculations of bawdy house offences.

42 ARCC, *supra* note 2, 1917, 4.

43 Social Survey Commission, *Report of the Social Survey Commission* (Toronto: Carswell, 1915), 22-23.

44 ARCC, *supra* note 2, 1915, 5.

45 See the various *An Act to Amend the Criminal Code,* S.O. 1913, c. 13; 1915, c. 12; 1917, c. 14; 1920, c. 43; R.S.C. 1927, c. 36.

46 Joh McLaren and John Lowman, "Enforcing Canada's Prostitution Laws, 1892-1920: Rhetoric and Practice," in M.L. Friedland, ed., *Securing Compliance* (Toronto: University of Toronto Press, 1990), 39.

47 Keepers and inmates could still, and almost always did, choose summary process.

48 AO, RG 20-100-8, series D, Toronto (York) Jail, Description Books, 1913-34.

49 Mary Ann Poutanen, "Bonds of Friendship, Kinship, and Community: Gender, Homelessness, and Mutual Aid in Early-Nineteenth-Century Montreal," in Bettina Bradbury and Tamara Myers, eds., *Negotiating Identities in Nineteenth- and Twentieth-Century Montreal* (Vancouver: UBC Press, 2005), 26.

50 Mercer Inmate Case Files, *supra* note 20, nos. 4653 and 4654.

51 "Three Girls Appear in Women's Court," *Star* (10 February 1913), 10.

52 Mercer Inmate Case Files, *supra* note 20, no. 4464; "Dog Couldn't Tell," *Telegram* (28 January 1915), 9.

53 See Poutanen, *supra* note 49 on the complex relationship between street women and men in mid-nineteenth-century Montreal for similar findings.

54 "Police Court To-Day," *Telegram* (28 September 1916), 9.

55 Mercer Inmate Case Files, *supra* note 20, no. 4479. Note that in 1915, prior to the enactment of a provincial *Parole Act,* the federal Department of Justice was responsible for all early release programs.

56 AO, RG 4-32, Attorney General of Ontario, Central Registry Files, 1915, no. 1170, "Re: Appeal, R.v. [Y.]."

57 "Police Court To-Day," *Telegram* (29 August 1916), 17.

58 "Must Remove Uniforms," *Telegram* (16 January 1915), 10.

59 "Jail for Wife Beater," *Telegram* (16 September 1914), 8.

60 See, for example, "Police Court To-Day," *Telegram* (2 June 1915), 7; (28 June 1915), 13; and (23 August 1916), 15. Margaret was also regularly arrested for drunkenness: in 1922 she paid her fine in court, and in 1934 she was again arrested for drunkenness (at 313 Adelaide Street!).

61 Mercer Inmate Case Files, *supra* note 20, nos. 4506 and 4468; "Police Court To-Day," *Telegram* (29 May 1915), 12.

62 "No Mystery in Death of Girl Sent to Jail," *Star* (7 March 1913), 11; "More Long Delay in Court System," *Star* (17 March 1913), 10.

63 "Police Court To-Day," *Telegram* (6 July 1915), 10.

64 "Police Court To-Day," *Telegram* (27 January 1915), 17.

65 See, for example, "Three Girls Appear in Women's Court," *Star* (10 February 1913), 1, 3; the sub-headline in this story read "Vulture Gets 60 Days." Media accounts are replete with these value-laden terms, some of which are attributed to reformers (in this example the reformer in question is Margaret Patterson), while others (such as Wodson's *petticoated fiends*) seem to originate with the reporters themselves.

66 Mercer Inmate Case Files, *supra* note 20, no. 5072.

67 *Ibid.*

68 For general discussion, see Mary E. Campbell, "Sentencing and Conditional Release," in Julian Roberts and David Cole, eds., *Making Sense of Sentencing* (Toronto: University of Toronto Press, 1999), 242-58.

69 *An Act to Amend the Prisons and Reformatories Act*, S.C. 1916, c. 39.

70 Haskayne herself was not directly implicated in the financial scandal surrounding Dunlop, but, because she had been Dunlop's secretary prior to her appointment as an assistant parole officer, she was asked to resign to distance Lavell, and the Parole Board, from the mess completely. Dunlop died before the allegations of financial misappropriation came to court, and the case was never resolved. For general information, see "Former Prison Inspector Now Committed for Trial," *Star* (5 June 1925), 1, 3.

71 Mercer Inmate Case Files, *supra* note 20, nos. 4332 and 4577.

72 *Ibid.*, no. 5743.

73 Why Millie was evaluated by Clarke is not explained. For discussion of Clarke and this psychiatric process, see Jennifer Stephen, "The 'Incorrigible,' the 'Bad,' and the 'Immoral': Toronto's 'Factory Girls' and the Work of the Toronto Psychiatric Clinic," in Louis Knafla and Susan W.S. Binnie, eds., *Law, Society, and the State: Essays in Modern Legal History* (Toronto: University of Toronto Press, 1995), 405-39. For discussion of the mix between psychiatry and criminal justice networks and its influence on determining "deviant" women, see Dorothy Chunn and Robert Menzies, "Out of Mind, Out of Law: The Regulation of 'Criminally Insane' Women inside British Columbia's Public Mental Hospitals, 1888-1973," *Canadian Journal of Women and the Law* 10, 2 (1998): 306-37.

74 It is possible that Millie's boyfriend was black. The address he gave Haskayne was 313 Adelaide (see note 22 above).

75 Mercer Inmate Case Files, *supra* note 20, no. 4414.

76 *Ibid.*, no. 5729.

77 AO, RG 8-53, Ontario Board of Parole, Minute Books, 1910-32.

78 Mercer Inmate Case Files, *supra* note 20, no. 4564.

79 Report of Margaret Patterson to Edna Haskayne, *ibid.*, no. 5878 (emphasis in original).

80 *Ibid.*, no. 5732.

81 OBP correspondence, *supra* note 33, container 14, letter from Alfred Lavell, Chief Parole Officer, to Emerson Coatsworth, Senior Police Court Magistrate, 29 March 1927.
82 "'Booze' and 'Dope,'" *supra* note 5 at 2.

Chapter 6: "Can her justice be just?"

1 In *The Justice Shop* (Toronto: The Sovereign Press, 1931), 98.
2 Archives of Ontario (AO), RG 4-32, Attorney General of Ontario, Central Registry Files, 1929, no. 1917, "Re: Establishment of Domestic Relations Court."
3 "Feminine Forces," *(Toronto) Globe* (15 April 1922), 18 (hereafter *Globe*).
4 Anne Anderson Perry, "Our Women Magistrates," *Chatelaine* (July 1929), 11. This point will be discussed in detail in the body of the chapter.
5 Editorial, *Woman's Century: Official Organ of the National Council of Women of Canada* 4, 1 (1916): 10.
6 "Drinking by Women on the Decline," *(Toronto) Daily Star* (10 March 1925), 3 (hereafter *Star*). Note that this statement contrasts sharply with her philosophy of being lenient with first-time offenders. If Patterson acknowledged this contradiction, she made no public effort to explain it.
7 Cited in Ethel M. Chapman, "How 'Bob's Maggie' Grew into Her Job," *Maclean's* (1 February 1922), 52. See Introduction.
8 Cited in Emily Weaver, A.E. Weaver, and E.C. Weaver, eds., *The Canadian Woman's Annual and Social Service Directory* (Toronto: McClelland, Goodchild, and Stewart, 1915), 280.
9 Dorothy Chunn, "Maternal Feminism, Legal Professionalism, and Political Pragmatism: The Rise and Fall of Magistrate Margaret Patterson, 1922-1934," in Wesley Pue and Barry Wright, eds., *Canadian Perspectives on Law and Society: Issues in Legal* History (Ottawa: Carleton University Press, 1988), 96.
10 "Needs Training in Legal Work," *Globe* (16 March 1922), 15.
11 Chunn, *supra* note 9 at 98.
12 Elsie Gregory MacGill, *My Mother the Judge* (Toronto: Peter Martin Associates, 1981), 157.
13 *Ibid.* at 168.
14 Perry, *supra* note 4.
15 *Ibid.*
16 *Ibid.*
17 Anne E. Wilson, "The Problem of the Missing Girl," *Chatelaine* (March 1929), 8.
18 Although the media reports about the new court were extensive, no reporter sought out Patterson's opinion or questioned her about her absence. However, the *Star* did run a tiny column adjacent to its front-page news about the Domestic Relations Court, in which Patterson was asked her opinion of the new fashion among some women to go stockingless in the summer (she did not see it as necessarily leading to looser morals). See "Stockingless Legs Matter for Girls, Says Magistrate," *Star* (19 June 1929), 1.
19 "Magistrate Patterson Deserving of Censure Is Finding in Inquiry," *(Toronto) Evening Telegram* (1 September 1932), 2 (hereafter *Telegram*), "Magistrate M. Patterson Is Given Verbal Lashing, Renfrew Officer Warned," *Telegram* (14 October 1932), 1, 2.
20 Loraine Gordon, "Doctor Margaret Norris Patterson: First Woman Police Magistrate in Eastern Canada – Toronto – January 1922 to November 1934," *Atlantis* 10, 1 (1984): 106.
21 "Magistrate Orders Arrest of Foreigner," *Star* (13 June 1925), 3.
22 "Three Girls Appear in Women's Court," *Star* (10 February 1913), 10. Repeat offenders are identified by the dates of their first and last recorded appearance.
23 "Police Court To-Day," *Telegram* (6 July 1915), 10.
24 "Must Remove Uniforms," *Telegram* (16 January 1915), 10.

25 Joan Sangster, "'Pardon Tales' from Magistrate's Court: Women, Crime, and the Court in Peterborough County, 1920-50," *Canadian Historical Review* 74, 2 (1993): 162.

26 "She Wanted a Thrill So Demanded $50,000," *Star* (11 June 1925), 1.

27 "Her Second Offence," *Telegram* (25 August 1927), 26.

28 "Eighth Drunk Charge Sends Woman to Jail," *Star* (12 January 1929), 2.

29 "Girl Found in Taxi Accused of Drinking," *Star* (24 January 1929), 3.

30 Perry, *supra* note 4.

31 Alice Jamieson, Calgary Juvenile Court, 1914; Emily Murphy, Edmonton Women's and Juvenile courts, 1916; Helen Gregory MacGill, Vancouver Juvenile Court (for Girls), 1917; Jean Ethel MacLachlan, Saskatchewan Juvenile Court (a travelling court, headquartered in Regina), 1917; Margaret Patterson, Toronto Women's Court, 1922; and Edith Louise Paterson, Vancouver Juvenile Court (for Girls), 1929 (Paterson, a trained lawyer, was appointed when MacGill was removed from the position in 1929).

32 This argument was accompanied by the proviso that few male magistrates had formal legal training either, which was true.

33 On Emily Murphy's tenure as magistrate, see John McLaren, "Maternal Feminism in Action – Emily Murphy, Police Magistrate," *Windsor Yearbook of Access to Justice* 8 (1988): 234-51; Jennifer Henderson, *Settler Feminism and Race Making in Canada* (Toronto: University of Toronto Press, 2003), especially, Chapter 3, "Inducted Feminism, Inducing 'Personhood': Emily Murphy and Race Making in the Canadian West." For Murphy's own views on her role as magistrate, see Emily Murphy, "The Woman's Court," *Maclean's* (January 1920), 27, and "A Straight Talk on Courts," *Maclean's* (October 1920), 1.

34 Beverly Blair Cook, "Moral Authority and Gender Difference: Georgie Bullock and the Los Angeles Women's Court," *Judicature* 77, 3 (1993): 145.

35 Estelle Freedman, *Maternal Justice: Mirian Van Waters and the Female Reform Tradition* (Chicago: University of Chicago Press, 1996), 85.

36 *Ibid* at 90.

37 Estelle Freedman, *Their Sisters' Keepers: Women's Prison Reform in America, 1830-1930* (Ann Arbor: University of Michigan Press, 1981), 59.

38 MacGill, *supra* note 12 at 156.

39 "Hopes to Make Women's Court Social Readjustment Bureau," *Star* (5 January 1922), 3.

40 "Feminine Forces," *supra* note 3.

41 *Ibid*.

42 "Did Not Seek Position," *Star* (6 January 1922), 10.

43 Perry, *supra* note 4.

44 Margaret Patterson, "The Care of Criminals," in Social Service Congress, *Annual Report of Addresses and Proceedings* (Ottawa: n.p., 1914), 228-29.

45 "Did Not Seek Position," *supra* note 42.

46 "Hopes to Make," *supra* note 39.

47 Mariana Valverde, *The Age of Light, Soap, and Water: Moral Reform in English Canada, 1885-1925* (Toronto: McClelland and Stewart, 1991), 48.

48 AO, F 805-5, container 4, Toronto Local Council of Women, Annual Reports (hereafter "TLCW annual reports"), Margaret Patterson, "Report of the Committee on Mental Hygiene," 1925.

49 Margaret Patterson, "Some Needs of the Country as Seen in the Court," in "Report of the Women's Institutes," *Ontario Sessional Papers,* No. 41 (1923). The phrase *home and country* was the motto of the Women's Institutes.

50 "Hopes to Make," *supra* note 39.

51 Toronto Public Library, Biographical Scrapbooks, reel 15, item 268, "Some Strange Letters to Dr. Patterson," *Star Weekly* (14 January 1922).

52 Valverde, *supra* note 47 at 48.

53 Chapman, *supra* note 7.

54 See Carlotta Hacker, *The Indomitable Lady Doctors* (Toronto: Clark, Irwin and Co., 1974).

55 "Hopes to Make," *supra* note 39.

56 "Consecrated Common-Sense is Quality New Magistrate Will Bring to Task on Bench," *Globe* (5 January 1922), 1.

57 Cook, *supra* note 34 at 144.

58 "Consecrated Common-Sense," *supra* note 56.

59 "Hopes to Make," *supra* note 39.

60 "She Wanted a Thrill," *supra* note 26.

61 AO, RG 8-54, Ontario Board of Parole, Correspondence, container 11, letter from Mrs. Morris to Alfred Lavell, Chief Parole Officer, 8 July 1925 (hereafter "OBP correspondence").

62 "Was This Not Severe and Unjust?" *Star* (18 June 1925), 32.

63 OBP correspondence, *supra* note 61, container 11, letter from A.E. Lavell to Mr. L.P. Rees, 7 July 1925.

64 *Ibid.*, letter from Mr. L.P. Rees to A.E. Lavell, 8 July 1925.

65 *Ibid.*, letter from A.E. Lavell to Mr. L.P. Rees, 9 July 1925.

66 "*R. v. Davis* (1930-31)," *Ontario Weekly Notes* 39, 98.

67 *Telegram* (25 August 1927), 26.

68 Gordon notes that "one reporter actually present in the court that day" told Patterson, "I would rather be outside than inside, Your Worship": Gordon, *supra* note 20 at 106.

69 *Ibid.*

70 "Her Second Offence," *supra* note 27.

71 "Woman Broke Jail to See Sick Baby," *Star* (7 September 1927), 33; "Jailed on Birthday for Visiting Baby," *Star* (14 September 1927), 33; "Broke Jail to See Baby," *Telegram* (14 September 1927), 17; "Fled 'Good Shepherd's' Fold to See Her Dying Child; 3-Month Term the Penalty," *Telegram* (15 September 1927), 25; "Counsel Will Ask for Clemency, Seeks Home for Occilla Gereau," *Telegram* (16 September 1927), 27; and "Girl's Sentence Seems Severe, Says Atty.-Gen'l," *Telegram* (17 September 1927), 25. The following account of Gereau's case draws upon all these articles.

72 "Jailed on Birthday," *ibid.*

73 "Fled 'Good Shepherd,'" *supra* note 71.

74 For a contemporary description of the Home of the Good Shepherd, see "Good Shepherd Home Inmates Not Paid for Work in Laundry," *Telegram* (16 September 1927), 1, 3.

75 "Woman Broke Jail," *supra* note 71.

76 Although interviewed by the *Telegram,* the nuns did not admit any role in Gereau's eventual recapture. However, given that Gereau had announced her intentions to them (which they corroborated), it seems likely that they were the ones to tell police where to look for her while she was at large.

77 "Fled 'Good Shepherd,'" *supra* note 71.

78 *Ibid.*

79 "Counsel Will Ask for Clemency," *supra* note 71.

80 "Girl's Sentence Seems Severe," *supra* note 71.

81 "Jailed on Birthday," *supra* note 71.

82 *Ibid.*

83 *Ibid.*

84 "Drinking by Women," *supra* note 6.

85 "Fled 'Good Shepherd,'" *supra* note 71.

86 "Counsel Will Ask for Clemency," *supra* note 71.

87 *Ibid.*

88 "Fled 'Good Shepherd,'" *supra* note 71.

89 The substance of the letter strongly suggests that "Help the Weak" was a "reformed" prostitute herself.

90 "Hard Lot Of Stray Girls: They Have No Hope," *Telegram* (24 September 1927), 30. "Help the Weak" made a few factual errors. Cook's first sentence was served for possession of drugs, not for vagrancy; she was also wrong to suggest that Cook was sent to the Home of the Good Shepherd, like Gereau. Cook served her sentence at the Mercer Reformatory.

91 Chunn, *supra* note 9 at 108.

92 *Journal of Comparative Legislation* 18 (1918): 200-9. For a feminist view of early women lawyers, see Mary Jane Mossman, *The First Women Lawyers: A Comparative Study of Gender, Law and the Legal Professions* (Oxford: Hart Publishing, 2006).

93 Margaret Patterson, "Bad Girl," *Chatelaine* (October 1935): 8.

94 For an example of the acknowledgment of the courage of the female magistrates, see Perry (*supra* note 4), who claimed that the women were engaged in a "heroic effort ... to sew up the seamy sides of life."

95 Margaret Patterson, "Report of the Committee on Equal Moral Standard," in National Council of Women of Canada, *Yearbook* (Ottawa: The Council, 1915).

Conclusion

1 Margaret Patterson, "Bad Girl," *Chatelaine* (October 1935), 8.

2 Archives of Ontario (AO), RG 20-50-1, Andrew Mercer Ontario Reformatory for Women, Inmate Case Files, no. 5861 (hereafter "Mercer Inmate Case Files"). Obviously, this letter never made its way to Joe.

3 There is no indication of whether or not this request was approved.

4 Mercer Inmate Case Files, no. 4474.

5 Clara's escape was only partially successful. She managed to elude capture for several weeks and found a job as a domestic in a home in Toronto. She was eventually discovered and returned to the Mercer. The escape changed her behaviour, however, and she was a model prisoner thereafter. She was released on parole five months after her recapture. She was paroled as a domestic servant to the very home in which she had worked during her time at large.

6 "Honesty Is Rewarded, Jail Term But One Day," *Star* (15 June 1925), 2.

7 Elaine S. Abelson, *When Ladies Go A-Thieving: Middle-Class Shoplifters in the Victorian Department Store* (New York: Oxford University Press, 1989), 169.

8 Mary Ann Poutanen's work stands out as an important exception: "Bonds of Friendship, Kinship, and Community: Gender, Homelessness, and Mutual Aid in Early-Nineteenth-Century Montreal," in Bettina Bradbury and Tamara Myers, eds., *Negotiating Identities in Nineteenth- and Twentieth-Century Montreal* (Vancouver: UBC Press, 2005), 25-48.

9 Franca Iacovetta and Wendy Mitchinson, "Introduction: Social History and Case Files Research," in Franca Iacovetta and Wendy Mitchinson, eds., *On the Case: Explorations in Social History* (Toronto: University of Toronto Press, 1998), 11.

10 Laura Lee Downs, "If 'Woman' Is Just an Empty Category, Then Why Am I Afraid To Walk Alone at Night? Identity Politics Meets the Postmodern Subject," *Comparative Studies in Society and History* 35, 2 (1993): 416.

11 Ethel M. Chapman, "How 'Bob's Maggie' Grew into Her Job," *Maclean's* (1 February 1922), 52.

Bibliography

Archival Sources

Archives of Ontario (AO)
Andrew Mercer Ontario Reformatory for Women, Inmate Case Files, 1910-35, RG 20-50-1, MS 3060-3065.
Attorney General of Ontario, Central Registry Files, RG 4-32.
Board of Health, Correspondence, RG 62, A-1.
Concord Industrial Farm for Women, Inmate Case Files, 1915-35, RG 20-165-2, MS 3080-82.
Criminal Assize Clerk Indictment Reports, York, RG 22-391.
General Sessions, Case Files, RG 22 5871.
Ontario Board of Parole, Correspondence, 1915-31, RG 8-54.
Ontario Board of Parole, Minute Books, 1910-32, RG 8-53.
Provincial Council of Women, Minute Books, 1920-43, F 798-1, MU 2342.
Toronto Local Council of Women, Annual Reports, 1926-66, F 805-5, container 4.
Toronto Local Council of Women, Minutes, 1903-38, F 805-1, container 1.
Toronto (York) Jail, Description Books, 1911-35, RG 20-100-8, series D.
Toronto (York) Jail, Jail Registers, 1910-35, RG 20-100-1, series A.
York County Court of General Sessions of the Peace, Indictment Case Files, RG 22-5871.
York County Court Judges' Criminal Court, Indictment Case Files, RG 22-5870.

City of Toronto Archives (CTA)
"A By-Law relating to Public Morals," *Consolidated By-Laws of the City of Toronto*, No. 4305 (1904).
Annual Reports, Chief Constable, City of Toronto, 1913-34, RG 9, Reports, box 48.

Library and Archives Canada (LAC)
Denison Papers, MG 29, E 29.

Toronto Public Library (TPL)
Margaret Patterson, biographical scrapbooks.

Newspapers
Jack Canuck
(Toronto) Globe
(Toronto) Daily News
(Toronto) Daily Star
(Toronto) Evening Telegram

Government Publications

Ontario Sessional Papers
Legislative Assembly. "Annual Report of Prison Inspector," *Sessional Papers*, 1910-35.
Legislative Assembly. "First Annual Report of the Probation Officers of the County of York including City of Toronto, 1923," *Sessional Papers*, No. 53 (1924).

Statutes of Canada

An Act to Amend the Criminal Code, R.S.C. 1927, c. 36.

An Act to Amend the Criminal Code, S.C. 1913, c. 13.

An Act to Amend the Criminal Code, S.C. 1915, c. 12.

An Act to Amend the Criminal Code, S.C. 1917, c. 14.

An Act to Amend the Criminal Code, S.C. 1920, c. 43.

An Act to Amend the Prisons and Reformatories Act, S.C. 1916, c. 39.

The Criminal Code, R.S.C. 1906, c. 146.

The Criminal Code, S.C. 1892, c. 29.

Statutes of Ontario

An Act intituled The Ontario Temperance Act, S.O. 1916, c. 50.

An Act for the Prevention of Venereal Disease, S.O. 1918, c. 42.

An Act to Provide for the Appointment of Probation Officers, S.O. 1922, c. 103.

An Act Respecting the Andrew Mercer Ontario Reformatory for Females, S.O. 1913, c. 78.

An Act Respecting Industrial Refuges for Females, R.S.O. 1919, c. 84.

An Act Respecting the Reformatory for Ontario, S.O. 1913, c. 77.

The Police Magistrates' Amendment Act, S.O. 1921, c. 4.

Published Books and Articles, 1910-35

"A Long Stride toward Adjustment," editorial, *Woman's Century: Official Organ of the National Council of Women of Canada* 4, 1 (June 1916): 10.

Becker, Elizabeth. "What Ontario Women Want: The Double Standard Shown in the Criminal Code," *Woman's Century: Official Organ of the National Council of Women of Canada* 6 (June 1918): 34.

Black, Robson. "A Dollar and Costs," *Canada Monthly* 14, 4 (1913): 8.

Bureau of Municipal Research. *What Is "The Ward" Going to Do with Toronto? A Report on Undesirable Living Conditions in One Section of the City of Toronto – "The Ward" – Conditions Which Are Rapidly Spreading to Other Districts* (Toronto: The Bureau, 1918).

Chapman, Ethel M. "How 'Bob's Maggie' Grew into Her Job," *Maclean's* (1 February 1922), 52-53.

Coatsworth, Emerson. *Report on the Administration of Criminal Justice Treatment of Prisoners in New York, Chicago, Detroit and Toronto* (Toronto: King's Printer, 1920).

"Courts of Domestic Relations," *Social Welfare* 5 (February 1923): 106-7.

"Courts of Domestic Relations – A Step in the Evolution of Justice," *Social Welfare* 1 (October 1929): 19.

Covington, May, ed. *Toronto Women's Directory* (Toronto: n.p., 1919).

Denison, George Taylor. *Recollections of a Police Magistrate* (Toronto: Musson Book Co., 1921).

"Equal Moral Standard," editorial, *Woman's Century: Official Organ of the National Council of Women of Canada* 6 (July 1918): 5.

Gemmill, William N. "Chicago Court of Domestic Relations," *Annals of the American Academy of Political and Social Sciences* 52 (1914): 115-23.

Harkness, D.B., Judge. *Courts of Domestic Relations: Duties, Methods and Services of Such Courts – Are They Needed in Canada?* (Ottawa: Canadian Council on Child Welfare, 1924).

Hastings, Charles, Dr. *Report of the Medical Health Officer Dealing with the Recent Investigation of Slum Conditions in Toronto* (Toronto: Department of Health, 1911).

Lang, Edith. "The Canadian Criminal Code," *Woman's Century: Official Organ of the National Council of Women of Canada* 6 (Special edition, 1918): 185.

MacGill, Helen Gregory. "Reforming Our Misfits," *Social Welfare* 7 (April 1924): 130.

Murphy, Emily. "A Straight Talk on Courts," *Maclean's* (October 1920), 1.

–. "The Woman's Court," *Maclean's* (January 1920), 27.

National Council of Women of Canada. *Yearbooks* (Ottawa: The Council, 1910-35).

Paddon, Mary. "The Inferior Criminal Courts of New York City," *Journal of Criminal Law and Criminology* 11, 1 (1920): 8-20.

Patterson, Margaret. "Bad Girl," *Chatelaine* (October 1935), 8.

–. "The Care of Criminals," in Social Service Congress, *Annual Report of Addresses and Proceedings* (Ottawa: n.p., 1914): 226-30.

–. "Some Needs of the Country as Seen in the Court," in "Report of the Women's Institutes," *Ontario Sessional Papers,* No. 41 (1923).

–. "The Women's Court of Toronto," *Social Welfare* 10 (July 1925): 188.

Perry, Anne Anderson. "Is Women's Suffrage a Fizzle?" *Maclean's* (1 February 1928): 6.

–. "Our Women Magistrates," *Chatelaine* (July 1929), 11.

Pigeon, Helen D. "Policewomen in the United States," *Journal of Criminal Law and Criminology* 18 (1927): 372-77.

Popple, A.E. "Police Court Systems," *Canadian Law Times* 41 (1921): 523.

"*R. v. Davis* (1930-31)," *Ontario Weekly Notes* 39, 98.

Riddell, William Renwick. "Women as Practitioners of Law," *Journal of Comparative Legislation* 18 (1918): 200-9.

Social Survey Commission. *Report of the Social Survey Commission* (Toronto: Carswell, 1915).

Weaver, Emily, A.E. Weaver, and E.C. Weaver, eds. *The Canadian Woman's Annual and Social Service Directory* (Toronto: McClelland, Goodchild, and Stewart, 1915).

Whitin, Frederick H. "The Women's Night Court in New York City," *Annals of the American Academy of Political and Social Sciences* 52 (1914): 181-87.

Wilson, Anne Elizabeth. "The Problem of the Missing Girl," *Chatelaine* (March 1929), 8.

Wodson, Harry S. *The Justice Shop* (Toronto: Sovereign Press, 1931).

–. *The Whirlpool: Scenes from Toronto Police Court* (Toronto: n.p., 1917).

Secondary Sources

Abelson, Elaine S. *When Ladies Go A-Thieving: Middle-Class Shoplifters in the Victorian Department Store* (New York: Oxford University Press, 1989).

Adams, Mary-Louise. "In Sickness and in Health: State Formation, Moral Regulation, and Early VD Initiatives in Ontario," *Journal of Canadian Studies* 28, 4 (1993): 117-30.

Alexander, Ruth. *The "Girl Problem": Female Sexual Delinquency in New York, 1900-1930* (Ithaca: Cornell University Press, 1995).

Ambrose, Linda. *For Home and Country: The Centennial History of the Women's Institutes in Ontario* (Erin, ON: Boston Mills Press, 1996).

Appier, Janis. "Preventive Justice: The Campaign for Women Police, 1910-1940," *Women and Criminal Justice* 4, 1 (1992): 3-36.

Backhouse, Constance. *Colour-Coded: A Legal History of Racism in Canada, 1900-1950* (Toronto: Osgoode Society for Canadian Legal History/University of Toronto Press, 1999).

–. "Nineteenth-Century Prostitution Law: Reflection of a Discriminatory Society," *Histoire sociale/Social History* 18, 36 (1985): 387-423.

–. *Petticoats and Prejudice: Women and Law in Nineteenth-Century Canada* (Toronto: Osgoode Society for Canadian Legal History/Women's Press, 1991).

–. "White Women's Labour Laws: Anti-Chinese Racism in Early 20th-Century Canada," *Law and History Review* 14 (1996): 315-68.

Badgley, Kerry. *Ringing in the Common Love of Good: The United Farmers of Ontario, 1914-125* (Montreal and Kingston: McGill-Queen's University Press, 2000).

Banks, Margaret. "The Evolution of the Ontario Courts, 1788-1981," in David Flaherty, ed., *Essays in the History of Canadian Law, Vol. 2* (Toronto: Osgoode Society for Canadian Legal History, University of Toronto Press, 1983), 492-572.

Bannerman, Jean. *Leading Ladies, Canada* (Belleville, ON: Mika Publishing, 1977).

Best, Joel. "Looking Evil in the Face: Being an Examination of Vice and Respectability in St. Paul as Seen in the City Press, 1865-83," *Minnesota History* 50, 6 (1987): 241-51.

Bland, Lucy. *Banishing the Beast: Sexuality and the Early Feminists* (New York: New Press, 1995).

–. "In the Name of Protection: The Policing of Women in the First World War," in Carol Smart and Julia Brophy, eds., *Women-in-Law: Explorations in Law, Family, and Sexuality* (London: Routledge and Kegan Paul, 1985), 23-45.

–. "Purity, Motherhood, Pleasure or Threat? Definitions of Female Sexuality 1900-1970's," in Sue Cartledge and Joanne Ryan, eds., *Sex and Love: New Thoughts on Old Contradictions* (London: Women's Press, 1983), 8-29.

Boritch, Helen, "Gender and Criminal Court Outcomes: A Historical Analysis," in Chris McCormick and Len Green, eds., *Crime and Deviance in Canada: Historical Perspectives* (Toronto: Canadian Scholars Press, 2005), 124-47.

Boritch, Helen, and John Hagan. "A Century of Crime in Toronto: Gender, Class, and Patterns of Social Control, 1859-1955," *Criminology* 28, 4 (1990): 567-99.

Burr, Chris. "'Roping in the Wretched, the Reckless, and the Wronged': Narratives of the Late Nineteenth-Century Toronto Police Court," *Left History* 3, 1 (1995): 83-108.

Campbell, Mary E. "Sentencing and Conditional Release," in Julian Roberts and David Cole, eds., *Making Sense of Sentencing* (Toronto: University of Toronto Press, 1999), 242-58.

Canning, Kathleen. "Feminist History after the Linguistic Turn: Historicizing Discourse and Experience," *Signs* 19, 2 (1994): 368-404.

Carrigan, D. Owen. *Crime and Punishment in Canada: A History* (Toronto: McClelland and Stewart, 1991).

–. *Juvenile Delinquency in Canada: A History* (Concord, ON: Irwin Publishing, 1998).

Carty, Linda. "The Discourse of Empire and the Social Construction of Gender," in Enakshi Dua and Angela Robertson, eds., *Scratching the Surface: Canadian Anti-Racist Feminist Thought* (Toronto: Women's Press, 1999), 35-47.

Cassels, Jay. *The Secret Plague: Venereal Disease in Canada, 1838-1939* (Toronto: University of Toronto Press, 1987).

Chunn, Dorothy. *From Punishment to Doing Good: Family Courts and Socialized Justice in Ontario* (Toronto: University of Toronto Press, 1992).

–. "Maternal Feminism, Legal Professionalism, and Political Pragmatism: The Rise and Fall of Magistrate Margaret Patterson, 1922-1934," in Wesley Pue and Barry Wright, eds., *Canadian Perspectives on Law and Society: Issues in Legal History* (Ottawa: Carleton University Press, 1988), 91-117.

–. "Regulating the Poor in Ontario: From Police Courts to Family Courts," *Canadian Journal of Family Law* 6 (1987): 85-102.

Chunn, Dorothy, and Shelley Gavigan. "Welfare Law, Welfare Fraud, and the Moral Regulation of the 'Never Deserving' Poor," *Social and Legal Studies* 13, 2 (2004): 219-43.

Chunn, Dorothy, and Robert Menzies. "Out of Mind, Out of Law: The Regulation of 'Criminally Insane' Women inside British Columbia's Public Mental Hospitals, 1888-1973," *Canadian Journal of Women and the Law* 10, 2 (1998): 306-37.

Clapp, Elizabeth. *Mothers of All Children: Women Reformers and the Rise of Juvenile Courts in Progressive Era America* (University Park: Pennsylvania State University Press, 1998).

Cook, Beverly Blair. "Moral Authority and Gender Difference: Georgia Bullock and the Los Angeles Women's Court," *Judicature* 77, 3 (1993): 144-55.

Craven, Paul. "Law and Ideology: The Toronto Police Court, 1850-80," in David Flaherty, ed., *Essays in the History of Canadian Law, Vol. 2* (Toronto: Osgoode Society for Canadian Legal History/University of Toronto Press, 1983): 248-307.

DeLottinville, Peter. "Joe Beef of Montreal: Working-Class Culture and the Tavern, 1869-1889," *Labour/Le Travail* 8/9 (1981/82): 9-40.

Demerson, Velma. *Incorrigible* (Waterloo: Wilfrid Laurier University Press, 2004).

Deutsch, Sarah. *Women and the City: Gender, Power and Space in Boston, 1870-1940* (New York: Oxford University Press, 2000).

Downs, Laura Lee. "If 'Woman' Is Just an Empty Category, Then Why Am I Afraid to Walk Alone at Night? Identity Politics Meets the Postmodern Subject," *Comparative Studies in Society and History* 35, 2 (1993): 414-24.

Dua, Enakshi. "Beyond Diversity: Exploring the Ways in Which the Discourse of Race Has Shaped the Institution of the Family," in Enakshi Dua and Angela Robertson, eds., *Scratching the Surface: Canadian Anti-Racist Feminist Thought* (Toronto: Women's Press, 1999): 237-59.

Dubinsky, Karen. *Improper Advances: Rape and Heterosexual Conflict in Ontario, 1880-1929* (Chicago: University of Chicago Press, 1993).

Dubinsky, Karen, and Franca Iacovetta. "Murder, Womanly Virtue, and Motherhood: The Case of Angelina Napolitano, 1911-1922," *Canadian Historical Review* 72, 4 (1991): 505-31.

Fahrni, Magda. "'Ruffled' Mistresses and 'Discontented' Maids: Respectability and the Case of Domestic Service, 1880-1914," *Labour/Le Travail* 39 (Spring 1997): 69-97.

Fingard, Judith. *The Dark Side of Life in Victorian Halifax* (Porter's Lake, NS: Pottersfield Press, 1989).

Foucault, Michel. *The History of Sexuality, Volume 1: An Introduction,* trans. Robert Hurley (New York: Vintage Books, 1980).

Frager, Ruth. *Sweatshop Strife: Class, Ethnicity, and Gender in the Jewish Labour Movement of Toronto, 1900-1939* (Toronto: University of Toronto Press, 1992).

Freedman, Estelle. *Maternal Justice: Miriam Van Waters and the Female Reform Tradition* (Chicago: University of Chicago Press, 1996).

–. *Their Sisters' Keepers: Women's Prison Reform in America, 1830-1930* (Ann Arbor: University of Michigan Press, 1981).

Garber, Marjorie. *Vested Interests: Cross-Dressing and Cultural Anxiety* (New York: Routledge, 1992).

Garland, David. *Punishment and Welfare: A History of Penal Strategies* (London: Gower, 1985).

Glasbeek, Amanda. "Maternalism Meets the Criminal Law: The Case of the Toronto Women's Court," *Canadian Journal of Women and the Law* 10, 2 (1998): 480-502.

–, ed. *Moral Regulation and Governance in Canada: History, Context, and Critical Issues* (Toronto: Canadian Scholars Press, 2006).

Gordon, Linda. *Heroes of Their Own Lives: The Politics and History of Family Violence* (New York: Viking Penguin Books, 1988).

–. *Pitied But Not Entitled: Single Mothers and the History of Welfare, 1890-1935* (Cambridge, MA: Harvard University Press, 1994).

Gordon, Loraine. "Doctor Margaret Norris Patterson: First Woman Police Magistrate in Eastern Canada – Toronto – January 1922 to November 1934," *Atlantis* 10, 1 (1984): 95-109.

–. "A Short Statistical Study of the Industrial Farm for Women at Concord, 1914-1935" (1982) [unpublished, archived at Osgoode Hall Law School Library, York University].

–. "A Statistical Survey of the Mercer/Vanier Registers, 1880-1972" (1981) [unpublished, archived at Osgoode Hall Law School Library, York University].

Gorham, Deborah. "The 'Maiden Tribute of Modern Babylon' Re-examined: Child Prostitution and the Idea of Childhood in Late-Victorian England," *Victorian Studies* 21 (1978): 353-79.

Gray, James H. *Red Lights on the Prairie* (Toronto: Macmillan of Canada, 1971).

Hacker, Carlotta. *The Indomitable Lady Doctors* (Toronto: Clark, Irwin and Co., 1974).

Hallowell, Gerald. *Prohibition in Ontario, 1919-1923* (Ottawa: Ontario Historical Society, 1972).

Hannah-Moffat, Kelly. *Punishment in Disguise: Penal Governance and Federal Imprisonment of Women in Canada* (Toronto: University of Toronto Press, 2001).

Hay, Douglas. "Time, Inequality and Law's Violence," in Austin Sarat and Thomas R. Kearns, eds., *Law's Violence* (Ann Arbor: University of Michigan Press, 1992), 141-73.

Henderson, Jennifer. *Settler Feminism and Race Making in Canada* (Toronto: University of Toronto Press, 2003).

Heron, Craig. *Booze: A Distilled History* (Toronto: Between the Lines, 2003).

Hobson, Barbara Meil. *Uneasy Virtue: The Politics of Prostitution and the American Reform Tradition* (New York: Basic Books, 1987).

Hoff, Joan. "Gender as a Postmodern Category of Paralysis," *Women's History Review* 3, 2 (1994): 149-68.

Homel, Gene. "Denison's Law: Criminal Justice and the Police Court in Toronto, 1877-1921," *Ontario History* 73, 3 (1981): 171-86.

Hunt, Alan. "Foucault's Expulsion of Law: Toward a Retrieval," *Law and Social Inquiry* 17, 1 (1992): 1-48.

–. *Governing Morals: A Social History of Moral Regulation* (Cambridge: Cambridge University Press, 1999).

Hunt, Alan, and Gary Wickham. *Foucault and Law: Towards a Sociology of Law as Governance* (London: Pluto Press, 1994).

Iacovetta, Franca, and Wendy Mitchinson. "Introduction: Social History and Case Files Research," in Franca Iacovetta and Wendy Mitchinson, eds., *On the Case: Explorations in Social History* (Toronto: University of Toronto Press, 1998), 3-21.

Jeffreys, Sheila. *The Spinster and Her Enemies: Feminism and Sexuality, 1880-1930* (London: Pandora Press, 1985).

Kechnie, Margaret. "Rural Women's Role in the 'Great National Work of Home-Building': The Women's Institutes in Early Twentieth-Century Ontario," *Canadian Woman Studies* 20, 2 (2000): 118-24.

Klein, Alice, and Wayne Roberts. "Besieged Innocence: The 'Problem' and Problems of Working Women – Toronto, 1896-1914," in Janice Acton, ed., *Women at Work in Ontario, 1850-1930* (Toronto: Canadian Women's Educational Press, 1974), 211-60.

Ladd-Taylor, Molly. *Mother-Work: Women, Child Welfare and the State, 1890-1930* (Chicago: University of Illinois Press, 1993).

Langdon, M. Elizabeth. "Female Crime in Calgary, 1914-1941," in Louis Knafla, ed., *Law and Justice in a New Land: Essays in Western Canadian Legal History* (Toronto: Carswell, 1986), 293-312.

Larsen, Nick. "Canadian Prostitution Control between 1914 and 1970: An Exercise in Chauvinistic Reasoning," *Canadian Journal of Law and Society* 7, 2 (1992): 137-56.

Lentz, Susan A. "Without Peers: A History of Women and Trial by Jury Part One – From the Women's Sphere to Suffrage," *Women and Criminal Justice* 11, 3 (2000): 83-106.

–. "Without Peers: A History of Women and Trial by Jury Part Two – The Law of Jury Service in the Twentieth Century," *Women and Criminal Justice* 11, 4 (2000): 81-101.

Levine, Philippa. *Prostitution, Race and Politics: Policing Venereal Disease in the British Empire* (London: Routledge, 2003).

–. "Women and Prostitution: Metaphor, Reality, History," *Canadian Journal of History/Annales canadiennes d'histoire* 28 (1993): 480-94.

Loo, Tina. "Don Cramner's Potlatch: Law as Coercion, Symbol, and Rhetoric in British Columbia, 1884-1951," *Canadian Historical Review* 73, 2 (1992): 125-65.

MacGill, Elsie Gregory. *My Mother the Judge* (Toronto: Peter Martin Associates, 1981).

Mackintosh, Phillip Gordon. "Scrutiny in the Modern City: The Domestic Public and the Toronto Local Council of Women at the Turn of the Twentieth Century," *Gender, Place and Culture* 12, 1 (2005): 29-48.

Maltby, Richard. "The Social Evil, the Moral Order and the Melodramatic Imagination, 1890-1915," in Jacky Bratton, Jim Cook, and Christine Gledhill, eds., *Melodrama: Stage Picture Screen* (London: British Film Institute, 1994).

Martin, Jane Roland. "Methodological Essentialism, False Differences, and Other Dangerous Traps," *Signs* 19, 3 (1994): 630-57.

Mawani, Renisa. "In Between and Out of Place: Mixed-Race Identity, Liquor, and the Law in British Columbia, 1850-1913," in Sherene Razack, ed., *Race, Space, and the Law: Unmapping a White Settler Society* (Toronto: Between the Lines, 2002), 47-69.

–. "Regulating the 'Respectable' Classes: Venereal Disease, Gender, and Public Health Initiatives in Canada, 1914-35," in John McLaren, Robert Menzies, and Dorothy Chunn, eds., *Regulating Lives: Historical Essays on the State, Society, the Individual, and the Law* (Vancouver: UBC Press, 2002), 170-95.

Maynard, Steven. "On the Case of the Case: The Emergence of the Homosexual as a Case History in Early Twentieth-Century Ontario," in Franca Iacovetta and Wendy Mitchinson, eds., *On the Case: Explorations in Social History* (Toronto: University of Toronto Press, 1998), 65-87.

–. "Sex, Court Records, and Labour History," *Labour/Le Travail* 33 (Spring 1994): 187-93.

McLaren, Angus. *Our Own Master Race: Eugenics in Canada, 1885-1945* (Toronto: McClelland and Stewart, 1990).

McLaren, John. "The Canadian Magistracy and the Anti-White Slavery Campaign, 1900-1920," in Wesley Pue and Barry Wright, eds., *Canadian Perspectives on Law and Society: Issues in Legal History* (Ottawa: Carleton University Press, 1988), 329-53.

–. "Maternal Feminism in Action: Emily Murphy, Police Magistrate," *Windsor Yearbook of Access to Justice* 8 (1988): 234-51.

McLaren, John, and John Lowman. "Enforcing Canada's Prostitution Laws, 1892-1920: Rhetoric and Practice," in M.L. Friedland, ed., *Securing Compliance* (Toronto: University of Toronto Press, 1990), 21-87.

Merry, Sally Engle. *Getting Justice and Getting Even: Legal Consciousness among Working-Class Americans* (Chicago: University of Chicago Press, 1990).

Meyerowitz, Joanne. *Women Adrift: Independent Wage Earners in Chicago, 1880-1930* (Chicago: University of Chicago Press, 1988).

Minaker, Joanne. "Sluts and Slags: The Censuring of the Erring Female," in Gillian Balfour and Elizabeth Comack, eds., *Criminalizing Women* (Halifax: Fernwood, 2006), 79-94.

Mossman, Mary Jane. *The First Women Lawyers: A Comparative Study of Gender, Law and the Legal Professions* (Oxford: Hart Publishing, 2006).

Myers, Tamara. *Caught: Montreal's Modern Girls and the Law, 1869-1945* (Toronto: University of Toronto Press, 2006).

–. "Women Policing Women: A Patrol Woman in Montreal in the 1910s," *Journal of the Canadian Historical Association* 4 (1993): 229-45.

Odem, Mary. *Delinquent Daughters: Protecting and Policing Adolescent Female Sexuality in the United States, 1885-1920* (Chapel Hill: University of North Carolina Press, 1995).

–. "Single Mothers, Delinquent Daughters, and the Juvenile Courts in Early Twentieth Century Los Angeles," *Journal of Social History* 25, 1 (1991): 27-43.

Oliver, Peter. "'To Govern by Kindness': The First Two Decades of the Mercer Reformatory for Women," in Jim Phillips, Tina Loo, and Susan Lewthwaite, eds., *Essays in the History of Canadian Law*, Vol. 5, *Crime and Criminal Justice* (Toronto: Osgoode Society for Canadian Legal History/University of Toronto Press, 1994), 516-71.

Oliver, Peter, and Michael D. Whittingham. "Elitism, Localism, and the Emergence of Adult Probation Services in Ontario, 1893-1972," *Canadian Historical Review* 68, 2 (1987): 225-58.

Oran, Alison. *Her Husband Was a Woman! Women's Gender-Crossing in Modern British Popular Culture* (London: Routledge, 2007).

Palmer, Bryan. "Discordant Music: Charivaris and Whitecapping in Nineteenth-Century North America," *Labour/Le Travail* 3 (1978): 5-62.

Pederson, Diana. "Keeping Our Good Girls Good: The YWCA and the 'Girl Problem,' 1870-1930," *Canadian Woman Studies* 7, 4 (1986): 20-24.

Pierson, Ruth Roach. "Experience, Difference, Dominance, and Voice in the Writing of Canadian Women's History," in Karen Offen, Ruth Roach Pierson, and Jane Rendall, eds., *Writing Women's History: International Perspectives* (Bloomington: Indiana University Press, 1991), 79-106.

Piess, Kathy. *Cheap Amusements: Working Women and Leisure in Turn-of-the-Century New York* (Philadelphia: Temple University Press, 1986).

Pineault, Kelly. "'Mentally Weak' or 'Inherently Bad': The Regulation and Reform of Women 'Criminals' at the Concord Industrial Farm for Women, 1915-1935" (Honours History Paper, Trent University, 1997).

Piva, Michael J. *The Condition of the Working Class in Toronto, 1900-1921* (Ottawa: University of Ottawa Press, 1979).

Pon, Madge. "Like a Chinese Puzzle: The Construction of Chinese Masculinity in *Jack Canuck*," in Joy Parr and Mark Rosenfeld, eds., *Gender and History in Canada* (Toronto: Copp Clark, 1996), 88-100.

Poutanen, Mary Anne. "Bonds of Friendship, Kinship, and Community: Gender, Homelessness, and Mutual Aid in Early-Nineteenth-Century Montreal," in Bettina Bradbury and Tamara Myers, eds., *Negotiating Identities in Nineteenth- and Twentieth-Century Montreal* (Vancouver: UBC Press, 2005), 25-48.

–. "The Homeless, the Whore, the Drunkard, and the Disorderly: Contours of Female Vagrancy in the Montreal Courts, 1810-1842," in Kathryn McPherson, Cecilia Morgan, and Nancy M. Forestell, eds., *Gendered Pasts: Historical Essays in Femininity and Masculinity in Canada* (Don Mills: Oxford University Press, 1999), 29-47.

Pratt, John. "Dangerousness and Modern Society," in Mark Brown and John Pratt, eds., *Dangerous Offenders: Punishment and Social Order* (New York: Routledge, 2000), 35-47.

Rafter, Nicole Hahn. *Partial Justice: Women, Prisons and Social Control* (New Brunswick, NJ: Transaction Publishers, 1990).

Reumper, Wendy. "Locking Them Up: Incarcerating Women in Ontario, 1857-1931," in Louis A. Knafla and Susan W.S. Binnie, eds., *Law, Society, and the State: Essays in Modern Legal History* (Toronto: University of Toronto Press, 1995), 351-78.

Rosen, Ruth. *The Lost Sisterhood: Prostitution in America, 1900-1918* (Baltimore: Johns Hopkins University Press, 1982).

Rutherford, Paul. *The Making of the Canadian Media* (Toronto: McGraw-Hill Ryerson, 1978).

Sangster, Joan. "Defining Sexual Promiscuity: 'Race', Gender, and Class in the Operation of Ontario's Female Refuges Act, 1930-1960," in Wendy Chan and Kiran Mirchandani, eds., *Crimes of Colour: Racialization and the Criminal Justice System in Canada* (Toronto: Broadview Press, 2002), 45-63.

–. *Girl Trouble: Female Delinquency in English Canada* (Toronto: Between the Lines, 2002).

–. "Incarcerating 'Bad Girls': The Regulation of Sexuality through the Female Refuges Act in Ontario, 1920-1945," *Journal of the History of Sexuality* 7, 2 (1996): 239-75.

–. "'Pardon Tales' from Magistrate's Court: Women, Crime, and the Court in Peterborough County, 1920-50," *Canadian Historical Review* 74, 2 (1993): 161-97.

–. *Regulating Girls and Women: Sexuality, Family, and the Law in Ontario, 1920-1960* (Toronto: Oxford University Press, 2001).

Schlossman, Steven, and Stephanie Wallach. "The Crime of Precocious Sexuality: Female Juvenile Delinquency in the Progressive Era," *Harvard Educational Review* 48 (1978): 65-95.

Scott, Joan. "The Evidence of Experience," *Critical Inquiry* 17, 4 (1991): 773-97.

Shapiro, Ann-Louise. *Breaking the Codes: Female Criminality in Fin-de-Siècle Paris* (Stanford: Stanford University Press, 1996).

Smart, Carol. *Feminism and the Power of Law* (London: Routledge, 1989).

Snell, James G. "Courts of Domestic Relations: A Study of Early Twentieth-Century Judicial Reform in Canada," *Windsor Yearbook of Access to Justice* 6 (1986): 36-60.

Solomon, Freda. "Progressive Era Justice: The New York City Women's Court" (Paper presented to the Seventh Berkshire Conference on the History of Women, Wellesley, Massachusetts, 19-21 June 1987).

Stansell, Christine. *City of Women: Sex and Class in New York, 1789-1860* (Chicago: University of Illinois Press, 1987).

Stephen, Jennifer. "The 'Incorrigible,' the 'Bad,' and the 'Immoral': Toronto's 'Factory Girls' and the Work of the Toronto Psychiatric Clinic," in Louis A. Knafla and Susan W.S. Binnie, eds., *Law, Society, and the State: Essays in Modern Legal History* (Toronto: University of Toronto Press, 1995), 405-39.

Strange, Carolyn. "'The Criminal and Fallen of Their Sex': The Establishment of Canada's First Women's Prison, 1874-1901," *Canadian Journal of Women and the Law* 1 (1985): 79-92.

–. "From Modern Babylon to a City upon a Hill: The Toronto Social Survey Commission of 1915 and the Search for Sexual Order in the City," in Roger Hall, William Westfall, and Laurel Sefton Mac-Dowell, eds., *Patterns of the Past: Interpreting Ontario's History* (Toronto: Dundurn Press, 1988), 255-77.

–. "Stories of Their Lives: The Historian and the Capital Case File," in Franca Iacovetta and Wendy Mitchinson, eds., *On the Case: Explorations in Social History* (Toronto: University of Toronto Press, 1998), 25-48.

–. *Toronto's Girl Problem: The Perils and Pleasures of the City, 1880-1930* (Toronto: University of Toronto Press, 1995).

–. "Wounded Womanhood and Dead Men: Chivalry and the Trials of Clara Ford and Carries Davies," in Franca Iacovetta and Mariana Valverde, eds., *Gender Conflicts: New Essays in Women's History* (Toronto: University of Toronto Press, 1992), 149-88.

Strange, Carolyn, and Tina Loo. *Making Good: Law and Moral Regulation in Canada, 1867-1939* (Toronto: University of Toronto Press, 1997).

–. "The Moral of the Story: Gender and Murder in Canadian True Crime Magazines of the 1940s," in Margaret Thornton, ed., *Romancing the Tomes: Popular Culture, Law and Feminism* (London: Cavendish Publishing, 2002), 221-40.

Toronto Local Council of Women. *Nothing New Under the Sun: A History of the Toronto Council of Women, 1893-1978* (Scarborough: Reg Willson Printing Co., 1978).

Valverde, Mariana. *The Age of Light, Soap, and Water: Moral Reform in English Canada, 1885-1925* (Toronto: University of Toronto Press, 1991).

– *Diseases of the Will: Alcohol and the Dilemmas of Freedom* (Cambridge: Cambridge University Press, 1998).

–. "'Racial Poison': Drink, Male Vice, and Degeneration in First-Wave Feminism," in Ian Christopher Fletcher, Laura E. Nym Mayhall, and Philippa Levine, eds., *Women's Suffrage in the British Empire: Citizenship, Nation, and Race* (London: Routledge, 2000), 33-50.

–. "'When the Mother of the Race Is Free': Race, Reproduction, and Sexuality in First-Wave Feminism," in Franca Iacovetta and Mariana Valverde, eds., *Gender Conflicts: New Essays in Women's History* (Toronto: University of Toronto Press, 1992), 3-26.

Valverde, Mariana, and Lorna Weir. "The Struggles of the Immoral: Preliminary Remarks on Moral Regulation," *Resources for Feminist Research* 17, 3 (1988): 31-34.

Walker, James W. St. G. "A Case for Morality: The Quong Wing Files," in Franca Iacovetta and Wendy Mitchinson, eds., *On the Case: Explorations in Social History* (Toronto: University of Toronto Press, 1998), 204-23.

–. "Race," Rights and the Law in the Supreme Court of Canada: Historical Case Studies (Waterloo: Wilfrid Laurier University Press, 1997).

Walkowitz, Judith. *City of Dreadful Delight: Narratives of Sexual Danger in Late-Victorian London* (Chicago: University of Chicago Press, 1992).

–. *Prostitution and Victorian Society: Women, Class, and the State* (Cambridge: Cambridge University Press, 1980).

Warsh, Cheryl Krasnick. "'Oh Lord, Pour a Cordial in Her Wounded Heart': The Drinking Woman in Victorian and Edwardian Canada," in Cheryl K. Warsh, ed., *Drink in Canada: Historical Essays* (Montreal and Kingston: McGill-Queen's University Press, 1993), 70-91.

Washburn, Josie. *The Underworld Sewer: A Prostitute Reflects on Life in the Trade, 1871-1909* (Lincoln: University of Nebraska Press, 1997 [1909]).

Weaver, John C. "The Modern City Realized: Toronto Civic Affairs, 1880-1915," in Robert F. Harney, ed., *Gathering Place: Peoples and Neighbourhoods of Toronto, 1834-1945* (Toronto: Multicultural Historical Society, 1985), 39-72.

Willrich, Michael. *City of Courts: Socializing Justice in Progressive Era Chicago* (Cambridge: Cambridge University Press, 2003).

Index

male defendants, 148, 149; on marital equity, 42; and National Council of Women, 56, 58; on offenders, 8-9; and Ontario Women's Institute, 190n88; philosophy, 153-56; on police courts, 1, 2; power, 18; public critique, 159-60, 162, 165-66; qualifications, 36-40; removal, 45, 191n100; report on Women's Court, 59; rhetoric, 206n65; salary, 189n46; scope of powers, 139; sentences, 43-44, 138, 202n59; sentencing, 82, 88, 90; sexist treatment of, 207n18; and socialized justice, 42; "tour" of Women's Court, 65-67; v. Cecile Gereau, 161-67; v. Myrtle Cook, 157-61; on vagrant woman, 99-100; vision of feminized justice, 44; on Women's Court, 11, 33, 193n42

Paul, Rose, 158

Pecalis, Betty, 157-58

Pederson, Diana, 15

Pednoit, Carrie, 158

penalties, 193n38; for bawdy house offences, 131-32; BOTA offences, 125; men v. women, 49; for morals offences, 53

Perry, Anne Anderson, 151, 153, 156, 160, 210n94

Pierson, Ruth Roach, 186n86

Pineault, Kelly, 79-80

Police Magistrates Act, 35

police officers, 12, 73, 95-96; female, 60-61, 192n26, 194n50; male, 60

politicization: of criminal justice system, 49-50, 52-53, 59; of male prerogatives, 60, 191n8; of masculine hegemony, 51; of sentencing, 63; of sexuality, 72

politics: of coercion, 13-14; of feminized justice, 32-33, 69; of the girl adrift, 106; of maternal care, 12; of maternal justice, 16; of moral standards, 50-52, 53, 64, 66-68, 152; of motherhood, 15; and practical reform, 180-81; of prostitution, 52; of reform, 47; of sexuality, 68, 193n34; of Toronto reformers, 4-5, 183n33; of urban uplift, 97

Poutanen, Mary-Ann, 80, 89, 96, 122

poverty, 67, 82, 85-86, 87-90, 198n52

power: of the court, 5; disciplinary, 14, 144-45; and knowledge, 54; of magistrates, 6; maternal, 17-18; relations, 101; of the state, 96; of TLCW, 19

press corps, 8, 183n22, 186nn87-89, 203n3

press reports, 22; on bawdy house keepers, 134; on Code amendments, 53; on crime, 1-2, 62,

67, 161-62; on cross-dressers, 92-93; discrepancies, 183n41; on moral respectability, 115; on policewomen, 60; and race, 76; racist, 204n21; and reformers, 178; sensationalized, 148-49, 161-63, 164-65; on shoplifters, 111-12; on street theft, 109-10; on vagrancy cases, 104-5; on Women's Court, 3

Price (attorney general), 43, 148, 164

Prisons and Reformatories Act, 137

privilege: bestowed, 143, 144, 145, 150, 157, 158; of legal authority, 179

probation, 198n43

prohibition, 126, 204n27

property crimes, 71, 176; v. disorderly behaviours, 109

prostitutes / prostitution: attitudes toward, 75, 99; double standard and, 50-51, 52-53; Mercer inmates, 196n16; as metaphor, 51-52; moral cartography, 128-29, 132-34, 204n21; occasional, 97-98; as occupation, 196nn15-16; professional, 99, 128-29; and sexual slavery, 58; street, 98-99, 100. See also cases, prostitution

protection: from exposure, 62, 89-90; of girls, 105; institutional, 123, 154, 166; legal, 32, 42; maternal, 16; moralized justice, 121; and punishment, 8, 26, 146, 156; from seduction, 48-49; v. punishment, 94

Provincial Council of Women (Ontario), 40, 45-46

public order offences, 71-72, 74

punishment: coercive, 175; physical, 174, 210n3; power and, 5, 18; and protection, 146; protection and, 8, 26; reclamation and, 11; and treatment, 156; v. character building, 151-52; v. reform, 63, 195n74; as weapon, 165; women's, 12, 53

racism, 76, 103-4, 109, 121, 123, 139-40, 157-60, 198n52, 204n19

Rafter, Nicole Han, 197n28

Ratcliffe, Lucy, 89-90, 166-67, 179, 186n93, 198n73

recidivism / recidivists, 80-90, 197n38, 198nn39-40, 200n13, 203n7; and crime statistics, 79-80, 80-81; demographics, 85-86, 120-21; and drunkenness, 24-25, 96, 119-22, 124-25, 129-30, 150, 177, 205n40, 206n60; and justice system, 120-21, 179; liquor law offences, 122-28; offences of, 75, 109, 128-35; Roman Catholic, 74; sentencing and, 63, 65-66

Valverde, Mariana, 15, 54, 123, 154, 193n39
Van Waters, Miriam, 16, 152
Vancouver, 106, 147, 184n51
VD Act. See An Act for the Prevention of Venereal Disease (1918)
venereal disease: and immorality, 104-5; search for sufferers, 105-6; and sentences, 106-7
violent crime, 71

Ward, the, 198n52; during prohibition, 127; slum conditions, 85-86
warrant of commitment, 23, 72, 83, 196n8
Warsh, Cheryl, 122
White Slave Committee. *See* Toronto Local Council of Women (TLCW), Committee for an Equal Moral Standard
white slave narratives, 193n34
white slavery panic, 58-59, 166
Whitton, Charlotte, 36
William, William Rednick, 167
Wiseman, Benedictine/Jimmy, 92-94, 199n5
Wodson, Harry S., 22, 71, 99, 183n20, 186n90, 196n1, 203n3, 203n7; on Patterson, 143; rhetoric, 206n65
womanhood: and gendered behaviour, 92-93; idealized, 169; prescribed boundaries, 102
women: black, 76; cross-dressers, 92-93, 199n2; economic vulnerability, 75-76; First Nations, 76; humiliation of, 2, 62; interracial relationships, 123, 139; as lawyers, 167; legal discrimination, 44; parole officers, 186n92; partnerships with men, 133-34; police officers, 60; probation officers, 195n68; reformers *v.* criminalized, 186n93; regulation of bodies, 32; relation to criminal justice system, 80-90; relations among, 67, 86, 144-45, 149; relations with criminal justice system, 5; relations with criminal law, 31; relationships among, 19, 25-26, 121-22, 175; right of jury duty, 61-62; subordination, 14, 68; victimization, 166; young, 173
women reformers: activism, 12-13, 16, 49-50; influence, 13-14, 78-80; *v.* criminalized women, 186n93; view of male officers, 60. *See also* lobbying
Woman's Century, 48, 49, 51, 146
women's courts, 13
women's crime, 71, 74-80, 177; causes, 171-72; identified, 146
women's criminality: moral categories of, 173
Women's Institutes, 39
Women's Police Court (Toronto): contradictions, 18; dual nature, 2-4, 9-10, 11, 26; experiences of, 175-76; failure, 46-47; familial model, 31; feminist intervention, 69-70; as feminist reform project, 178; foundational values, 113, 169-70; functions, 175-76; fundamental role, 94; great achievement, 69; history, 28; legitimacy, 98, 99, 112, 158; male chivalry and, 29-34; material context, 21; maternal feminists, 116; men, 205n37; middle-class white politics, 13-14; multifaceted, 169; and one-time offenders, 117-18; opening day, 31, 187n12; opening day cases, 7-11; Patterson's magistracy and, 143-44; purpose, 9, 11; records, 178; rhetoric, 150; site of redress, 40-41; TLCW achievement, 12-18; unique, 47; *v.* morals courts, 32-33; visiting roster, 59; and womanhood, 92-93
women's social reform movements, 16, 123. *See also* Toronto Local Council of Women (TLCW)
Wood, J.N., 59, 193n42

C.L. Ostberg and Matthew E. Wetstein
*Attitudinal Decision Making in the Supreme
Court of Canada* (2007)

Chris Clarkson
*Domestic Reforms: Political Visions and
Family Regulation in British Columbia,
1862-1940* (2007)

Jean McKenzie Leiper
Bar Codes: Women in the Legal Profession
(2006)

Gerald Baier
*Courts and Federalism: Judicial Doctrine
in the United States, Australia, and Canada*
(2006)

Avigail Eisenberg (ed.)
*Diversity and Equality: The Changing
Framework of Freedom in Canada* (2006)

Randy K. Lippert
*Sanctuary, Sovereignty, Sacrifice: Canadian
Sanctuary Incidents, Power, and Law* (2005)

James B. Kelly
*Governing with the Charter: Legislative and
Judicial Activism and Framers' Intent* (2005)

Dianne Pothier and Richard Devlin (eds.)
*Critical Disability Theory: Essays in
Philosophy, Politics, Policy, and Law* (2005)

Susan G. Drummond
*Mapping Marriage Law in Spanish Gitano
Communities* (2005)

Louis A. Knafla and Jonathan Swainger (eds.)
*Laws and Societies in the Canadian Prairie
West, 1670-1940* (2005)

Ikechi Mgbeoji
*Global Biopiracy: Patents, Plants, and
Indigenous Knowledge* (2005)

Gerald Kernerman
*Multicultural Nationalism: Civilizing
Difference, Constituting Community* (2005)

Florian Sauvageau, David Schneiderman,
and David Taras, with Ruth Klinkhammer and
Pierre Trudel
*The Last Word: Media Coverage of the
Supreme Court of Canada* (2005)

Pamela A. Jordan
*Defending Rights in Russia: Lawyers, the
State, and Legal Reform in the Post-Soviet
Era* (2005)

Anna Pratt
*Securing Borders: Detention and
Deportation in Canada* (2005)

Kirsten Johnson Kramar
*Unwilling Mothers, Unwanted Babies:
Infanticide in Canada* (2005)

W.A. Bogart
*Good Government? Good Citizens? Courts,
Politics, and Markets in a Changing Canada*
(2005)

Catherine Dauvergne
*Humanitarianism, Identity, and Nation:
Migration Laws in Canada and Australia*
(2005)

Michael Lee Ross
*First Nations Sacred Sites in Canada's
Courts* (2005)

Andrew Woolford
*Between Justice and Certainty: Treaty
Making in British Columbia* (2005)

John McLaren, Andrew Buck, and Nancy
Wright (eds.)
*Despotic Dominion: Property Rights in
British Settler Societies* (2004)

Georges Campeau
*From UI to EI: Waging War on the Welfare
State* (2004)

Alvin J. Esau
*The Courts and the Colonies: The Litigation
of Hutterite Church Disputes* (2004)

Christopher N. Kendall
Gay Male Pornography: An Issue of Sex Discrimination (2004)

Roy B. Flemming
Tournament of Appeals: Granting Judicial Review in Canada (2004)

Constance Backhouse and Nancy L. Backhouse
The Heiress vs the Establishment: Mrs. Campbell's Campaign for Legal Justice (2004)

Christopher P. Manfredi
Feminist Activism in the Supreme Court: Legal Mobilization and the Women's Legal Education and Action Fund (2004)

Annalise Acorn
Compulsory Compassion: A Critique of Restorative Justice (2004)

Jonathan Swainger and Constance Backhouse (eds.)
People and Place: Historical Influences on Legal Culture (2003)

Jim Phillips and Rosemary Gartner
Murdering Holiness: The Trials of Franz Creffield and George Mitchell (2003)

David R. Boyd
Unnatural Law: Rethinking Canadian Environmental Law and Policy (2003)

Ikechi Mgbeoji
Collective Insecurity: The Liberian Crisis, Unilateralism, and Global Order (2003)

Rebecca Johnson
Taxing Choices: The Intersection of Class, Gender, Parenthood, and the Law (2002)

John McLaren, Robert Menzies, and Dorothy E. Chunn (eds.)
Regulating Lives: Historical Essays on the State, Society, the Individual, and the Law (2002)

Joan Brockman
Gender in the Legal Profession: Fitting or Breaking the Mould (2001)